Praise for *The Power of Story*

"This is an entertaining, accessible, and valuable addition to the world of self-help books."

Library Journal

"Jim Loehr's principles have helped unleash the creativity, capability, and potential of top-performing people throughout P&G. This book can do the same for knowledge workers everywhere."

A. G. Lafley
Chairman of the Board & CEO
Procter & Gamble

"Jim has brought to print many of the key insights that he has so successfully used to help athletes, business executives, and other leaders confront and change their own personal stories. I know his coaching works because I have seen it change the lives of many of PepsiCo's leaders."

Steve Reinemund
Former CEO
PepsiCo

"Being fully engaged as a Navy SEAL demands skillful management of all four sources of energy—physical, emotional, mental, and spiritual. This passionate and convincing book can change one's life through the process of facing your own personal truth, determining those aspects of your life you hold most important, and crafting an action plan to complete your life's mission. The young men who successfully complete SEAL training have, in their own way, done just that! Jim's wisdom can be anyone's wisdom, and his energy and passion can be shared among us all."

Rear Admiral Ray Smith
Former Commander of the Navy SEALs
U.S. Navy (retired)

"Dr. Jim Loehr's concept of Old Story/New Story is so transformational that I introduced it to my entire senior leadership team. Today our New Stories, supported by daily rituals, are enabling Panda Express restaurants to continue our rapid growth toward two billion dollars in revenue."

Tom Davin
Chief Executive Officer
Panda Restaurant Group, Inc

"You might think you've heard ⟨...⟩ his. Jim Loehr's remarkable combinatio⟨...⟩enticity provides a unique and powerful⟨...⟩th your life. The information and tools ⟨...⟩reciated

elements of our leadership development work and have made a real difference in many people's lives."

Jon Anastasio
Vice President, Learning & Development
Nordstrom, Inc.

"Jim's principles, one of which is changing your story, are without a doubt the most powerful tools available for individuals and companies in order to thrive in today's fast-changing global business climate. By applying the gems of wisdom within this text, you can literally transform your future. The true testimony is in the life of the author. I have witnessed Jim walk this talk for over a decade."

Phebe Farrow Port
VP Global Management Strategies
The Estée Lauder Companies

"Jim Loehr's *The Power of Full Engagement* has had a powerful effect on my life and career over the last few years. *The Power of Story* provides new perspectives and a compelling recipe to recharge the spirit and plan for an exciting and fulfilling rest of your life."

Kerry Clark
CEO
Cardinal Health

"Jim Loehr's latest book is 'mission critical' for anyone looking to expand their capacity in their personal or professional lives. *The Power of Story* offers wonderful insights into how we can all increase and manage our energy and, more importantly, focus it on the things that matter most to each of us."

Peter K. Scaturro
Former CEO
U.S. Trust

"Jim Loehr's practice-based work on story is consistent with a recent wave of academic research on self-narratives in psychology. The upshot: What we say to ourselves creates our reality and guides our actions. Jim's work teaches us that through the stories we tell ourselves and others about what is possible and impossible, we limit ourselves or unleash unimagined potential."

Susan J. Ashford
Associate Dean for Leadership Programming & the Executive MBA Program
University of Michigan

"Just recently, we announced a plan to bring a condensed version of the program to *all* of our 2,300 employees. Jim's new book, *The Power of Story,* brilliantly captures the essence of how and why the program works."

Paul N. Leone
President
The Breakers

"Jim Loehr has done it again! *The Power of Story* is an amazing book that will powerfully impact your life by helping you change the stories you tell yourself and tell to others. The book is filled with profound insight and wisdom and yet is extremely pragmatic and useful. Many books say they can change your life; this is one of the few that actually can."

Stephen M. R. Covey
Author
The Speed of Trust: The One Thing That Changes Everything

"The health care industry is focused only on cost and not on the whole story. Changing peoples' stories is the solution to our health care crisis. *The Power of Story* is a model of success for addressing our nation's health care crisis."

Steve Altmiller
President/CEO
San Juan Regional Medical Center

"*The Power of Story* provides great insight into the importance of understanding the stories that shape us and how to create new stories. After reading the book, I felt reconnected with my purpose in life and have even more clarity on my training mission. As always, it is a joy to read anything written by Jim Loehr. He is a great coach and inspiration to us all!"

Anne Whitaker
Vice President & Business Unit Head, Acute Care Specialty Division
GlaxoSmithKline

The Power of Story

Change Your Story,
Change Your Destiny
in Business and in Life

JIM LOEHR

Free Press
New York London Toronto Sydney

FREE PRESS
A Division of Simon & Schuster, Inc.
1230 Avenue of the Americas
New York, NY 10020

First Free Press trade paperback edition October 2008

FREE PRESS and colophon are trademarks of Simon & Schuster, Inc.

For information about special discounts for bulk purchases,
please contact Simon & Schuster Special Sales at
1-800-456-6798 or business@simonandschuster.com

Note to Readers
The names and identifying details concerning some individuals have been changed.

Manufactured in the United States of America

9   10

The Library of Congress has cataloged the hardcover edition as follows:

Loehr, James E.
The power of story : rewrite your destiny in business and in life / Jim Loehr.
p.   cm.
1. Change (Psychology).   2. Success.   3. Self-perception.
4. Storytelling—Psychological aspects.   I. Title.
BF637.C4L64   2007
650.1—dc22   2007028654

ISBN-13: 978-0-7432-9452-2
ISBN-10:   0-7432-9452-1
ISBN-13: 978-0-7432-9468-3 (pbk)
ISBN-10:   0-7432-9468-8 (pbk)

To my mother, Mary,
for her relentless efforts in helping me get my
story straight,

and to my three sons, Mike, Pat, and Jeff,
who have been and always will be the epicenter of
my life story.

The life of every man is a diary in which he means to write one story, and writes another; and his humblest hour is when he compares the volume as it is with what he vowed to make it.

—JAMES M. BARRIE

Contents

Part Two

New Stories 151

I drink too much, exercise too little, am 35 pounds overweight, have high cholesterol, have already had heart surgery. My father died relatively young from a heart attack. I have four young children.

I don't feel I'm doing a good job anywhere—home, work, family, self. I'm overwhelmed.

I accomplish all these things, I have 2,200 people under me, but I lost God, the most important thing in my life. I lost my spirituality.

I spend too little time playing with my kids. They look forward to the babysitter coming because she plays with them more than I do.

I feel unappreciated and taken for granted—my spouse does not understand the magnitude of my workload. Work consumes all my energy.

The career I have chosen and love threatens the most sacred part of my life, my relationship with my three sons.

I've lost my passion for what I'm doing, both in my career and in my personal life.

—Seven representative fragments, from a database of tens of thousands, of high-achieving, "successful" businesspeople, who were asked to describe the themes and tone of their life stories. One of them is mine.

INTRODUCTION

It sounded like a good story, once upon a time. I'd finally taken the bold step of resigning from the satisfying, commanding position I'd had for years—head of a progressive community mental health center in rural Colorado—to pursue my long-held professional dream: combining my loves of psychology and sports by establishing a business that specialized in helping athletes to achieve optimum performance, redefining how they ate, practiced, rested and recovered and, most important, perceived themselves. The leap was both exciting and scary to me. This was the early 80s and I knew of no one doing anything quite like it. But after weathering my initial anxieties—financial uncertainty; scrambling to establish credibility and get clients; moving to Denver, where there was more activity—my dream began to morph into reality. I came into contact with world-class athletes, especially tennis players, eager to have me aid them in fulfilling *their* professional dreams—of becoming their best possible competitive selves. The idea of helping to pioneer a new area in psychology was intoxicating. From the indications, I was making a difference in the lives of my clients. The work ignited levels of passion and commitment in me I'd never known.

With my new career, though, came travel, lots and lots of it. Tokyo this week, London the next, then on to New York; no sport involves more globe-trotting than professional tennis. And because of my increasingly high-profile success with tennis players (among them Monica Seles, Jim Courier, Aranxta Sanchez-Vicario, and the Gullikson brothers), I began to attract clients from other sports, too—golfers (like Mark O'Meara), hockey players (Mike Richter, Eric Lindros), Olympians (speed skater Dan Jansen), basketball players (Grant Hill), football and baseball players, collegiate stars and All-Pros. Sure, my career frequently took me away from my children, the most important thing in the world to me, but this was the time of life—this, right now, I thought—to devote my best energy to my career, so that I might achieve maximum success and thus be the best person and role model I could for them.

Anyway, that's the story I told myself as a father.

The reality was different. Every time I returned home, I felt like a stranger. Increasingly, my three sons didn't know very much about who I was or what I was doing. So accustomed did they become to my not being there that when I *was* home I felt like a fringe character. Most frightening of all, I didn't know who *they* were becoming.

Gain professional success but lose something far more precious in the process—what kind of story was that? I had long thought of myself as a father who would do anything for his kids, yet increasingly I wasn't seeing or knowing them. Was that a story I would ever want to share with others? Was it a story *I* could live with? Couldn't I just ignore it and deal with it later? Like, in a year or two (or three), when I would really, truly be established professionally?

More and more, the way I was letting my life play out haunted me. My greatest failure would be to fail my boys. Yet the way I was going, I was fast-tracked for it. I felt guilty, desperate to come up with a better way—either that or return to my career as staff psychologist, where I had no travel demands but also minimal professional fulfillment. To maintain my current career, I needed to correct *something* or watch as my story as father fossilized into tragedy.

When I could, I brought my sons with me to sporting events, especially over the summer; the U.S. (tennis) Open, right before school started up again, was a particular treat. But as much as we enjoyed being together, these were special occasions—a bit unreal, hyperkinetic, not on home turf.

The true turning point was a simple promise I made one day to my boys. "Any night I'm not home," I told them, "I'll call without fail at eight PM. You don't even have to answer the phone. Just know when it rings at eight that it's me. And I'm thinking about you. And missing you. And wanting to connect with you."

I vowed to myself that it wouldn't matter if I was in the Far East or Florida, at dinner with a client or out on the court banging forehands at the reigning Wimbledon junior champion. From that day on, somewhere between 7:55 and 7:59 PM, I would excuse myself to make my call.

So I started to call, every night I was out of town. And an amazing thing happened. The boys, I was told, didn't just answer the phone; they *dove* for it. For that special interlude, we were apart but we weren't. I could keep up with what they had done in school, what sports they had played, what was exciting them. The incidental stuff, the mortar of their day. If they had a conflict or got a bad grade, we talked it through. My energy and focus were fixed completely on them. The nightly call was confirmation for them that I was thinking about them every single day, no matter in what corner of the earth I found myself, and that every single day they were a part of my life. And they could hear what I'd been up to.

It was one little ritual between my sons and me but it made a huge difference. It only helped me to rewrite my story as a father.

Stories that don't work happen to everyone, not just to the weak or incapable. In fact, they may happen *more* often to the "successful" among us. I see it every day, at the Human Performance Institute, in Orlando, Florida, where we moved our business in 1995. After my two oldest boys had gone off to college, I left Colorado in search of the place where the most world-class athletes trained and lived. That place turned out to be southern Florida. Although I had begun my new calling by working with athletes, our clientele soon expanded to include high achievers in the medical profession; in law enforcement, including Navy SEALs, the Army Special Forces, and the FBI's elite anti-terrorist force; and businesspeople, who now make up the bulk of our work. Their companies—Procter & Gamble, PepsiCo, Citigroup, Glaxo-SmithKline and KPMG, to name a few, as well as mid-sized and smaller companies, too, across a wide range of sectors—began sending us their CEOs, CFOs, other senior leaders, and entire departments or business units (sales, HR, operations), in the hopes of improving the three P's: performance, productivity, profitability. The only way for my team and me to help the thousands of individuals we see each year to improve in these areas—short of dynamiting and rethinking the many tired, entrenched practices and beliefs of corporate culture (that's for another book)—is to help those who come through the program to commit genuinely to improving themselves. And the only way to do *that*, we have learned, is to get participants to confront the truth about their current flawed stories.

What do I mean by "story"? I *don't* intend to offer tips on how to fine-tune the mechanics of telling stories to enhance the desired effect on listeners. And though this book very much concerns itself with the American businessperson (among others), by "story" I do not mean the boilerplate, holier-than-thou pronouncement often found in the Mission Statement area of corporate websites, or the Here's-why-we'll-absolutely-meet-our-fourth-quarter-numbers!-narrative-yarn-turned-pep-rally that team leaders often like to spin to rally the troops.

No, I wish to examine the most compelling story about storytelling—namely, how we tell stories *about* ourselves *to* ourselves. Indeed, the idea of "one's own story" is so powerful, so native, that I hardly consider it a metaphor, as if it's some new lens through which to look at life. Your life *is* your story. Your story *is* your life. When stories we read or watch or listen to are triumphant, they are so because they fundamentally remind us of what is most true or possible in life—even when it's an escapist romantic comedy or sci-fi fantasy or fairy tale. If you are human, then you tell yourself stories—positive ones and negative, consciously and, far more than not, subconsciously. Stories that span a single episode, or a year, or a semester, or a weekend, or a relationship, or a season, or an entire tenure on this planet. Telling ourselves stories helps us navigate our way through life because they provide structure and direction. "Just seeing my life as a story," said one of my clients, head of HR for a national hotel chain, "allowed me to establish a sort of road map, so when I have to make decisions about what I need to do, [the map] makes it easier, takes away a lot of stress." Indeed, we are actually *wired* to tell stories: The human brain, according to a recent *New York Times* article about scientists investigating *why* we think the way we do, has evolved into a narrative-creating machine that takes "whatever it encounters, no matter how apparently random" and imposes on it "chronology and cause-and-effect logic." Writes Justin Barrett, psychologist at Oxford University, "We automatically, and often unconsciously, look for an explanation of why things happen to us, and 'stuff just happens' is no explanation" (which feeds one possible theory for why we need, or even create, God or gods). Stories impose meaning on the chaos; they organize and give context to our sensory experiences, which otherwise might seem like no more than a fairly colorless sequence of facts. Facts are meaningless until you create a story around them. For example, losing your wallet or being in a car accident is what factually happened but the meaning or significance you give to the lost wallet or the car accident is the theme of your story—for example, "I'm a careless person" or "Bad things happen to me" or "I often get into trouble but always escape without major damage." A story is our creation of a reality; indeed, our story matters *more* than what actually happens. Is there really any difference, as someone famously asked, between the life of a king who sleeps twelve hours a day dreaming he's a pauper, and that of a pauper who sleeps twelve hours a day dreaming he's a king?

By "story," then, I mean those tales we create and tell ourselves and others, and which *form the only reality we will ever know in this life.* Our stories may or may not conform to the real world. They may or may not inspire us to take hope-filled action to better our lives. They may or may not take us where we ultimately want to go. But since *our destiny follows our stories*, it's imperative that we do everything in our power to get our stories right.

For most of us, that means some serious editing.

To edit a dysfunctional story, you must first identify it. To do *that*, you must answer the question: *In which important areas of my life is it clear that I cannot achieve my goals with the story I've got?* Only after confronting and satisfactorily answering this question can you expect to build new reality-based stories that *will* take you where you want to go.

Is this all starting to sound a little New Agey? I'm not surprised. But hold on. I understand you may be thinking: *Life as story?* The whole concept strikes you, perhaps, as a tad . . . soft. *I don't look at my life in terms of story*, you say.

I disagree. Your life is the most important story you will ever tell, and you're telling it right now, whether you know it or not. From very early on you're spinning and telling multiple stories about your life, publicly and privately, stories that have a theme, a tone, a premise—*whether you know it or not*. Some are for better, some for worse. No one lacks material. Everyone's got a story.

And thank goodness. Because our capacity to tell stories is, I believe, just about our profoundest gift. Perhaps the true power of the story metaphor is best captured by this seeming contradiction: We employ the word "story" to suggest both the wildest of dreams ("It's just a story . . .") and an unvarnished depiction of reality ("Okay, what's the story?"). How's that for range?

The problem? Most of us aren't writers. "I'm not a professional novelist," one client said to me, when finally the time came for him to put pen to paper. "If this is the story of my life, you're damn right I'm intimidated. Can you just give me a little help in how to get this out?"

That's what I intend to do in this book. First, help you to identify how pervasive story is in life, *your* life, and, second, to rewrite it.

Every life has elements to it that every story has—beginning, middle, and end; theme; subplots; trajectory; tone. Earl Woods, Tiger's father and coach, early on taught his son that during each professional round of golf that Tiger would someday play, there would be at least one troublesome shot—in deep rough, behind a tree, buried in a bunker, wherever—that he would hit so brilliantly it would never be forgotten in the annals of golf. Sure enough, years later, on Tiger's toughest shots and in his most competitive situations, the trajectory of his story (not to mention the flight of the ball) has always soared: To him, such moments aren't obstacles but opportunities. In fact, what Tiger is perhaps most fondly known and admired for—more even than his gorgeous swing, his clutch ability, his consistency, his game face and fist-pump—is his astonishing capacity to make a great shot out of what, just seconds before, had appeared to be an impossible lie. Some of that comes from talent, of course. But more of it comes from a sureness that is the product of a compelling, enduring story embedded deep in his psyche.

Story is everywhere in life. Perhaps your story is that you're responsible for the happiness and livelihoods of dozens of people around you, and you're the unappreciated hero. If you see things in more general terms, maybe your story is that the world is full of traps and misfortune—at least for you—and you're the perpetual victim. (*I'm always so unlucky . . . I always end up getting the short end of the stick . . . People can't be trusted and will take advantage of me if I give them the chance.*) If you're focused on one subplot—work, say—then maybe your story is that you sincerely want to execute the major initiatives with which your company has entrusted you, yet you're imprisoned by technology (e-mail, cell phone, BlackBerry) and thus can never get far enough from the forest to see the trees. Maybe your story is that you must keep chasing even though you already seem to have a lot (even too much), because the point is to get more and more of it—money, prestige, power, control, attention. Maybe your story is that you and your children just can't connect, as once was true of me and mine. Or your story might be essentially a *rejection* of another story—for instance, you may denounce your restrictive religious upbringing, and everything you do is filtered through that rejection.

Story is everywhere. Your body tells a story. The smile or frown on your face, your shoulders thrust back in confidence or slumped roundly in despair, the liveliness or fatigue in your gait, the sparkle of hope and joy in your eyes or the blank stare, your fitness, the size of your gut, the tone and strength of your physical being, your overall presentation—those are all part of your story, one that's especially apparent to everyone else. We judge books by their covers not simply because we're wired to judge quickly but because the cover so often provides astonishingly accurate clues to what's going on inside. What's your story about your physical self? Does it truly work for you? Can it take you where you want to go in the short term? How about ten years from now? What about thirty?

You have a story around your company, though your version may depart wildly from your colleague's or your boss's or your direct report's or your customer's. You have a story about your family. Your country. Anything that consumes our energy can be a story, even if we don't always call it a story. There's the story of you and your faith. The story of your marriage. The story of you and public service. The story of you and alcohol, or you and food, or you and anger, or you and impossible expectations. The story of you, the friend. The story of you, your father's son or your mother's daughter. The story of you and TV-watching. Some of these stories work and some of them fail. According to my professional experience, an astounding number of these stories, once they're identified, are deemed failures—not by me, mind you (though given the descriptions I hear, I'd agree), but by the people living them.

Like it or not, there will be a story around your death. What will it be? Will you die a senseless death? Perhaps you drank too much and failed to buckle your seat belt and were thrown from your car, or you died from colon cancer because you refused to undergo an embarrassing colonoscopy years before when the disease was treatable, or after years of bad nutrition, no exercise, and abuse of your body you suffered a fatal heart attack at age forty-nine. "Senseless death" means that it didn't have to happen when it happened; it means your story didn't have to end the way it ended. Think about the effect the story of your senseless death might have on your family, on those you care about who you're leaving behind. How would that story impact *their* life stories? Ask yourself, *Am I okay dying a senseless death*? Your immediate reaction is almost certainly, "No! Of course not!" Yet so many of the people I see, every one of whom responds exactly that way, are following stories that will lead them to that senseless death as assuredly as a gun glimpsed in Act I, as Chekhov told us, *must* go off in Act II.

I'm not trying to be morbid. Story—which dies if deprived of energy—is not about death but life. Yet if you continue to tell a bad story, if you continue to give energy to a bad story, then you will almost assuredly beget another bad one, or ten. Why is abuse so commonly passed from one generation to the next? How much is the recurrence of obesity, diabetes, and certain other diseases across families a genetic predisposition, and how much the repetition of a dangerous story about food and physical exertion? Harry Chapin's poignant ballad "Cat's in the Cradle"—in which a busy father continually promises to "get together" soon with his son, who dreams of growing up to be just like dad—breaks your heart not merely because it chronicles the tragedy of their non-relationship but because, in the final, devastating verse, the father, an old man now, finally *does* have time to get together with his son . . . only now it's his son, a grown man, who has no time for his dad, proof that the terrible story has looped, and may loop again.

Unhealthy storytelling is characterized by a diet of faulty thinking and, ultimately, long-term negative consequences. This undetectable yet inexorable progression is not unlike what happens to coronary arteries from a high-fat, high-cholesterol diet. In the body, the consequence of such a diet is hardening of the arteries (among other maladies); in the mind, the consequence of bad storytelling is hardening of the categories, narrowing of the possibilities, calcification of perception. Both roads lead to tragedy, often quietly. The buildup of plaque in the arteries caused by a poor diet is impossible to recognize at the time: We eat unhealthily but are unable to detect any immediate negative consequences, certainly not from one given meal, no matter how unhealthy. It's almost as if we got away with it ("I don't feel anything bad!"). It's Boiling Frog Syndrome: The frog in the pot doesn't sense the gradual rise in temperature, can't detect the danger he's in—until it's too late and he's cooked. The same holds true for faulty storytelling. While we do it, we can't sense the full negative impact it's having. "It's not all that bad," we conclude. Our marriage is "okay." Our job is "not terrible." Yet whether we sense it or not, the energy we repeatedly give to bad stories actually reconfigures our neural architecture. The cumulative effect of our damaging stories will have tragic consequences on our health, happiness, engagement, and performance. Because we can't confirm the damage our defective storytelling is wreaking, we disregard it, or veto our gut reactions to make a change. Then one day we awaken to the reality that we've become cynical, negative, angry. That's now who we are. Though we never quite saw it coming, that's now our true story.

It's not just individuals who tell stories about themselves; groups do it, too. Nations and religions and universities and sports teams and political parties and labor unions each tell stories about themselves to capture the imagination of their constituencies. Companies tell their stories to engage their customers and, increasingly, their workforce, stories which must be internally consistent and powerful if they're to succeed over time. The Starbucks story: Our home is your home away from home, a place where strangers are transformed into members of a community; to give our story integrity and durability, we aim to treat all our people, from customers to employees to independent coffee-growers around the world, with equal dignity and respect. AARP's story: Retirees and the elderly need and deserve to feel that, as we age, life gets better, full of health, happiness, and balance; to be credible, those in our organization must model this life, too. I've worked with companies that desire to enhance both their bottom lines and the lives of their stakeholders. How do they accomplish that at a fundamental level? By editing their story. Intel has done it, as has Estée Lauder, as has Takeda Pharmaceuticals. The same with smaller companies like San Juan (New Mexico) Regional Medical Center, which is now "telling a story" that has changed the very way they do medicine and interact with the community they serve. Throughout the book I will detail how such organizations and their employees have reworked their story to the great advantage of both their business and their culture.

For twenty-five years, my business partner, Jack Groppel, and I and now our team at the Human Performance Institute (HPI) have studied human behavior and performance, and we've been privileged to witness many success stories of positive behavioral change: better relationships at home and at work, better job performance, weight loss and all-around improved health and lowering of health risks; love, excitement, joy, and the discovery of talents heretofore buried. My experience has led me to see that these changes may be brought about by a unique integration of all the human sciences, most important among them performance psychology, exercise physiology, and nutrition. My scientific training has led me to a belief in hard data.

We've gathered a wide range of meaningful information from more than 100,000 individual clients, from several hundred companies and affiliations, across a wide demographic of geography, background, and market segments; 70% of our clientele come from the corporate world, 85% of that from the Fortune 500. Our clients are in their 40s (46%), 50–56 (22%), 34–39 (26%), with some younger or older. We measure physical data such as the participant's blood chemistry, body fat, and dietary, exercise, and sleep habits; personality data such as 360 evaluations (assessments from the key people in one's professional circle—colleagues, direct reports, superiors—along with one's family), as well as extensive self-analysis (multiple choice and fill in). Increasingly in the last five years we've included a "storytelling" inventory, in which the participant is asked to describe, candidly and often for the first time, the message, or story, that his or her choices convey to the world.

As a psychologist by training, I believe in the usefulness of data as a guide; as a businessman, one who deals frequently with businesspeople, I know that we succeed or fail by results. That's nothing new: When coaching athletes, I've always worked on retainer fees too small even to cover my expenses; the big payday happened only if I made something extraordinary and tangible happen. So, say, if a player ranked 100 in the world came to me, we might draw up a contract that stipulated that I got paid only when (if) he or she cracked the top 10, or made the final of a Grand Slam, or achieved some other indisputable signpost of competitive success. The burden was always on me to deliver.

The same is true now. We expect success and usually achieve it. Early on in the executive workshop we run fifty to seventy-five times a year, I ask, "How many of you, when you really make up your mind to do something, almost always do it?" It's the rare occasion when even one person in the room doesn't raise his or her hand. By the second day, it's not atypical for a C-level executive or the like to look as if he or she had been hit by a lightning bolt of recognition that will change his or her life for the better, and presumably forever. Of those who come through our Orlando headquarters, our data show that 30% are "profoundly" moved (their preferred word), while another 50% make smaller but inarguably significant changes. Kirk Perry, VP at Procter & Gamble, a company that has sent hundreds of employees through our program, said that a six-month follow-up found "80% [of those who'd been through our workshop] had some specific, measurable improvement in their lives."

Of course, some people who pass through our doors are utterly unaffected by what we do and what they're exposed to. Why? Some feel their "story" needs no major reworking (and perhaps they're absolutely right). Some fail to buy in to what we do because they're just moving too fast. For some, the timing isn't right (though, as I intend to show, there can only ever be one time to make changes: *now*). Whatever the reason, for virtually every group we encounter, 20%—the percentage is like clockwork—are simply not interested in what we have to say.

I respect that. Our program was not designed to push an agenda or a political view. While I passionately believe that the story metaphor is universal and, with awareness, can be extraordinarily beneficial, it "works" only when the individual is willing to look hard at the major problem areas in his or her life, explore why they're problems (up to a point; this is *not* psychotherapy), then meaningfully change the problem elements, be they structure or content, which are causing a profound lack of productivity, fulfillment, engagement, and sense of purpose. We work *with* people. We don't stand over them and make them do something they don't want.

Unlike many practitioners in the field of performance improvement, I do not believe you can have it all. It's an absurd proposition. I don't believe that every day will be a great day, that you can eliminate regret and despair and worry, that you will always be moving forward, that you will always succeed, that you won't veer off track again. I *do* believe that you can have what is most important to you. And that this is achievable if you're willing to follow the steps of the process advocated within these pages.

Who are the people who come to HPI with dysfunctional life stories that need serious editing? They are, simply put, among the smartest, most talented, most ambitious, most creative people in their communities and professional circles. Some participants even bring, or return with, spouses, friends, or parents. They tend to have lots of responsibility, they're accountable for a great deal that goes on in their companies, they often make lots and lots of money . . . yet, perhaps ironically, for all their accomplishments they can't seem to get their stories right. On the questionnaire we ask clients to fill out before they come down to Florida for our two-and-a-half-day sessions (or to the one- and two-day off-sites we conduct around the country and the world), they are asked, among other things, to write down some of the most important parts of their life story. "My father died young of emphysema," wrote the CEO of his family's company. Later on the questionnaire, he wrote, "I smoke two packs a day." Still later, describing one of his goals for the now fifty-year-old company, he wrote, "On the evening celebrating our company's seventy-fifth anniversary, I want to be able to look back on yet another quarter-century of quality, growth, and profitability."

How can these three sentences possibly follow from each other without their author acknowledging that, taken together, they add up to utter nonsense? Especially when the author is superbly gifted in so many other areas?

"The most important thing in my life is my family," wrote one senior VP, "and if things continue in the direction they're going, I'm almost certainly heading for divorce and complete estrangement from my children."

I'll give him this much: At least he sees the car crash coming.

In *The Power of Full Engagement*, a book I co-authored with Tony Schwartz in 2003, I argued that one of our biggest problems is rooted in our flawed belief that simply investing time in the things we care about will generate a positive return. That belief and the story that flows from it are simply not true. We can spend time with our families, be present at dinnertime, have lunches with our direct reports, remember to call home when traveling, put in forty-five minutes on the treadmill five days a week—we can do all of it but if we're too exhausted, too distracted, too frustrated and angry when "doing" these things, the positive return we hoped for will simply not materialize. Without investing high-quality, focused energy in the activity before you, whatever it may be, setting time aside simply takes us from absenteeism to *presenteeism*—a condition increasingly plaguing American business, a vague malady defined as impaired job performance because one is medically or otherwise physically or psychologically compromised. Is a worker who's too fatigued or mentally not there for eight hours really better than no worker? How about a parent? A spouse? Time has value *only* in its intersection with energy; therefore, it becomes priceless in its intersection with extraordinary energy—something I call *full engagement*.

In what areas are you *disengaged* right now? Whatever the answer, you're likely to lay a good deal of the blame for this disengagement on external facts—overwork, the time and psychic demands of dealing with aging parents, frequent travel, an unsupportive spouse, a high-maintenance team at work, not enough hours in the day, debt, a slipped disk, not my fault, out of my hands, too much to do, always on call—but such excuse-making is neither helpful nor accountable. (Funny: We enjoy the privilege of being the final author of the story we write with our life, yet we possess a marvelous capacity to give ourselves only a supporting role in the "writing" process, while ascribing the premier, dominant, true authorial role to our parents, our spouse, our kids, our boss, fate, chance, genetics, bad weather, or lousy interest rates. Anyone or anything but us appears to have more influence in moving the metaphorical pen across the paper.) Getting our stories right in life does not happen without our understanding that *the most precious resource that we human beings possess is our energy*. The energy principle still holds, and is crucial to ideas in this book, too; I maintain that it is at the heart of any solution not only to our individual problems but also to our collective, national ones—our health care problem, our obesity problem, our stress problem, our multi-tasking problem.

In recent years, though, I've come to see that, amazingly, the key to almost all of our problems, more fundamental even than poor energy management, is *faulty storytelling*, because it's storytelling that *drives* the way we gather and spend our energy. I believe that stories—again, not the ones people tell us but the ones we tell ourselves—determine nothing less than our personal and professional destinies. And the most important story you will ever tell about yourself is the story you tell *to* yourself. (Mind if I repeat that? *The most important story you will ever tell about yourself is the story you tell to yourself.*) So, you'd better examine your story, *especially* this one that's supposedly the most familiar of all. "The most erroneous stories are those we think we know best—and therefore never scrutinize or question," said paleontologist Stephen Jay Gould. Participate in your story rather than observing it from afar; make sure it's a story that compels you. Tell yourself the right story— the rightness of which only *you* can really determine, only *you* can really feel—and the dynamics of your energy change. If you're finally living the story you want, then it needn't—it shouldn't and won't—be an ordinary one. It can and will be extraordinary. After all, you're not just the author of your story but also its main character, the hero. Heroes are never ordinary.

In the end, your story is not a tragedy. Nor is it a comedy or a romance or a thriller or a drama. It's something else. What label would you give the story of your life, the most important story you will ever tell? To me, that sounds like an epic.

End of story.

Part One

Old Stories

If an idiot were to tell you the same story every day for a year, you would end by believing it.

—Horace Mann

One

THAT'S YOUR STORY?

S low death.

An uglier two-word phrase it's hard to find. But if you're at all like the people I see in our workshops, then I'm afraid you understand the phrase all too well.

How did it come to this?

What am I doing?

Where am I going?

What do I want?

Is my life working on any meaningful level? Why doesn't it work better?

Am I right now dying, slowly, for something I'm not willing to die for?

WHY AM I WORKING SO HARD, MOVING SO FAST, FEELING SO LOUSY?

One man I heard about was quite literally going through slow death. A senior executive at a big firm, he was home the last few weeks of his life, in the final stage of cancer, in and out of lucidity, medicated so heavily that his tongue loosened and he regularly spewed his unfiltered, apparently truest thoughts. He cursed at his wife as never before, using vile, demeaning language—all while she was caring for him day and night, knowing these were his last days on earth, the final days of their long marriage. He did the same to his kids when they visited, making an already difficult situation for them nearly intolerable, and certainly bringing them nothing remotely like peaceful closure. Mostly, though, the man's most shocking, blistering commentary was reserved, in absentia, for his boss: vicious, intermittently coherent paroxysms of resentment and contempt for the president of his firm who, it was painfully obvious now, the dying executive blamed for most of the anger, frustration, and general rottenness he'd felt the past two decades.

Slow death. It comes in different forms. Two years ago a heart surgeon came to our institute. The first morning he had his blood work done and took a turn in the BodPod (a chamber inside which one's lean body mass can be measured with exceptional accuracy, through the displacement of air rather than water). His results were borderline alarming—extremely elevated levels of cholesterol, glucose, blood lipids, triglycerides, C-reactive protein. He was given a copy of the results.

When his turn came to discuss the meaning of the numbers and how to approach them, the surgeon said, "I don't want to talk about it."

"You know what these numbers mean," said Raquel Malo, our director of nutrition and executive training.

"Of course I do," he snapped. "I'm a doctor!"

"What if I was your patient and I got these numbers?"

"I'd be all over you."

"Yet you're telling me—"

"I said I don't want to talk about it."

"But—"

"Change the subject or I'm on the next plane home," he said. "Don't bring it up again while I'm here."

Two days later the doctor left, having done nothing to address his perilous health, or even to acknowledge there was anything to address. He returned to his thriving medical practice, where he would continue to caution patients to reduce their risk of cardiovascular disease. (Of all the demographics we see, health care providers as a group hover near the bottom in fitness and physical well-being.)

Slow death: what a harsh phrase. Is that really what's happening to all those people, the ones who start out contented by what is good and pure in life—a simple cup of coffee, a few seemingly reasonable life goals (a nice salary, say, and one's own home)—and who, once they've achieved those goals, can't even be satisfied because they've already moved on to life's next-sized latte (six-figure salary, second home, three cars), only to move on to something double-extra grande when that's achieved, a continual supersizing that guarantees one can't ever be fulfilled?

Okay. Not everyone I see or hear about is dying slowly. But to judge from the responses we get, workshop after workshop, year after year—and each year it gets worse—whatever it is they're doing sure doesn't sound fun. It doesn't even sound like getting by. I read the frustration and disappointment in their self-evaluations and hear it in their own voices, if and when they're comfortable enough to read aloud from their current dysfunctional story, the autobiographical narrative they attempt to write the first day at HPI, but usually don't finish until the night before our last day together.

"Life is hard and getting harder," read one senior VP, with a very big house, a very big salary, and dozens of direct reports. "My current life story is stagnant . . . On a scale of 1 [worst] to 5 [best], I'd give my health and family each a 2 . . . My biggest feeling about myself is complete disappointment . . . I have virtually no energy . . . I'm completely addicted to cell phones and PDAs."

"The tone of my story is cynical, sarcastic, and ironic," read a forty-three-year-old woman who runs a successful telecom business in the Southwest. "I'm driven to achieve solely for the purpose of being able to point to the accomplishment, and the recognition I receive . . . I need a more positive view of my future . . . I do NOT embrace the idea that the story I tell about what happens is more important than what actually happens . . . My current life story is sad and depressing . . . My health is a 2, work a 3, happiness and friendship each a 2 . . ."

"I'm deeply disappointed in myself and always extremely self-critical," wrote a managing director in a financial services firm. "My happiness is a 1; I'm as unhappy as can be. I'm getting divorced after thirty-three years of marriage . . . My greatest weakness is that I don't trust anyone anymore. The dominant theme in my life is distrust."

I hardly think it's overstating to call these tragic stories.

As the workshop progresses and people's defenses start to melt away, we hear more and more of these stories. By almost any reasonable standard, these stories exemplify failure; in many cases, disaster. There is no joy to be found in them, and even precious little forward movement. In every workshop, nearly everyone has a dysfunctional story that is not working in at least one important part of his or her life: stories about how they do not interact often or well with their families; about how unfulfilling the other significant relationships in their lives are; about how—despite all that extracurricular failure—they're not even performing particularly well at work (!), or, if they are, about how little pleasure they gain from it; about how they don't feel very good physically and their energy is depleted.

On top of all that (isn't that enough?), they feel guilty about their predicaments. They know, on some almost buried level, that their life is in crisis and that the crisis will not simply go away. Their company is not going to make it go away. The government is not going to make it go away. God is not going to make it go away.

And so they wake up one morning to the realization that the bad story they for so long only feared has become finally their life, *their* story. Not that this development is their fault. No. Nor is there a heck of a lot to be done about it.

It's a competitive, cutthroat world out there.

God knows, I want to change but I simply can't. I'll get eaten up and beaten by someone who's willing to sacrifice everything.

The world moves faster today than it did a generation ago.

Hey, at least I see my family some weekends. At least we've got a roof over our heads. At least I exercise twice a week.

What am I supposed to do—quit my job?

These are the facts of my life. There's nothing I can do about them.

My life is a known quantity, so why mess with it even if it's killing me?

Let me repeat that one: . . . *even if it's killing me.*

As corporate consultant Annette Simmons says in her book, *The Story Factor*, "People don't need new facts—they need a new story."

Recently I conducted a seminar with thirty-two engineers from a profitable company who'd been sent to us not of their own desire—if it was up to them, it soon enough became obvious, they'd have preferred to undergo a colonoscopy and root canal simultaneously—but because the head of their division, a recent and enthusiastic attendee of the program, felt it would be useful for them and thus for the company. I could tell that the brainpower in the room, judged on sheer intellectual payload, was staggering. Each engineer had a position of considerable authority, each had several direct reports, each was veteran enough at the company to feel part of the fabric that made it what it was. Early in the session, I asked what might be done to improve their situations at work. Not a single hand went up. When I asked what they thought about their latest job evaluations, the few who spoke expressed the same general idea: They were doing about as well as they expected; there wasn't much that would make things worse or better. It was what it was.

Over the next half hour, though, I was able to start eliciting some details. Many of them said they couldn't pay much attention to their health because, well, there was obviously no time to exercise before or after work, and to exercise in the middle of the afternoon would feel, as one said, "almost like you're irresponsible."

"Is there an actual rule against it?" I asked.

"It's unwritten," he said. "Everyone can feel it."

So there it was. The corporate culture was at fault. Nothing to be done about it. It was what it was.

I asked for a new show of hands: How many *did* get regular exercise? Four engineers out of thirty-two responded.

"They're single," said one of the others. Everyone laughed.

"Really?" I said. I turned to the Exercising Four. "How many of you have spouses and children?"

Three of the four raised their hands.

"You're married with kids, yet you work out," I said to them. "How is this possible?" I asked the three if they thought that the time they spent exercising was jeopardizing their careers, in the long term, or making it more difficult to get work done, in the short.

No, said each. "It makes me *more* productive," said one.

I then asked the whole group of thirty-two how many had dinner with their family at least three nights a week. Only five did . . . and—what do we have here?—three of the five were the Exercisers Married with Children.

Some people just figure it out. Why them and not others?

As we continued to talk, it became apparent gradually (engineers and scientists are tough nuts) that almost everyone in this room full of high-achievers and leaders felt as if they were caught in a brutal culture, one which allowed them no breathing room, which compromised their health. Many of them said outright it was the company's fault. But among the three who exercised and ate dinner regularly with their families, the prevailing attitude was, in the words of one, "If you have to blame the damn institution, then get out." Another said, "Don't be a victim. Your boss is not going to change."

Finally, I asked a question I thought might get a robust response. "How many of you think there's a lot of brilliance in this room?"

Every arm shot up.

"Suppose," I said, "that your boss walked in here and said, 'Okay, I want to use all the intelligence in this room to reverse-engineer a culture that would allow our people to take better care of themselves, to actually feel great enthusiasm and initiative about work, and to spend meaningful time with their family.'" I looked around the room. "What's the chance you could come up with that?"

Again, every arm went up.

"But wait," I said. "This new culture you're all going to create, this one that helps you feel healthier and more connected—remember: It must continue to drive the bottom line. Is that really possible?"

"Absolutely," said one excitedly, and I saw heads nod in agreement all around the room. "I'm certain we can do it. But no one's ever made that proposition."

IS YOUR COMPANY EVEN TRYING TO TELL A STORY?

We've examined the corporate story the worker hears. Let's see what story the company is typically telling.

First: They need you and you need them. (Ideally, they also *want* you and you also *want* them, but that may not be part of your company's story.) The typical company, circa early twenty-first century, is saying that the fast-paced business world being what it is—what with globalization and outsourcing and downsizing and automation and synergies and streamlining and broadband and maybe Wall Street breathing down its neck, etc.—it *must* make increasing demands on your life. Keep swimming or die. Which means longer hours for you, ergo less time for your family and yourself. It means holding meetings during lunch or before or after the workday proper, which essentially kills your chance to exercise and stay in shape. (And let's just order in any food that's fast during meetings to maximize efficiency.) Oh, right: And while all this is going on, the company—continually stressing its imperative to move forward if it is to survive at all—also demands that you frequently change directions, reinvent the very way you operate, completely alter how you conduct business.

Everyone who likes that story, raise your hand.

Older workers, in particular—those who've "seen it all before"—are likely to undermine the story for such a company. So, too, anyone else who fears that he or she may be relatively easy to eliminate, or may have a diminished role in the transformed company. To these employees, the story their company is telling may be exciting in the abstract, or exciting to Wall Street, but it's potentially humiliating for them. Among these workers, suspicion, cynicism, and distrust run rampant. While the defiant worker publicly may appear vested in the change process, privately he tells himself: *New thinking be damned.* He works subversively to undermine the new directive. He knows that, for the new initiatives to take, everyone must embrace them. Not him. He will go through the motions but he is *not* going to make any real course corrections.

And so, like a dinosaur, he moves closer and closer to extinction.

The employee loses and the company loses as well. Entire organizations have been undermined by storytelling that excludes a significant portion of their workforce. Failure to align the evolving corporate story with the aspirations of the individual employees, up and down the workforce—the very ones who have been enjoined to help write that new, improved story—has systemic implications. Athletes routinely give up on playing hard for coaches they deem excessively punitive or inconsistent; the bond of their mutually aligned stories—to win a championship—is undermined because the coach's story does not seem to allow for the inevitable particularities of any individual athlete's story. Mutiny is not just what happens when ship captains indefensibly change or robotically stick to the rules but also when kings, CEOs, and schoolteachers do it. Organizations have been undermined by refusing to alter their story when it clearly wasn't working. In the mid-1980s, IBM, despite growing evidence to the contrary, thought major course corrections were unnecessary. For a time, they seemed to forget that customers were part of the story, too. When there is no story alignment among the company, its workers, and whatever other forces need to be considered for the company to be profitable, the company eventually fails; its story has failed. Revenues and market share had to dwindle sufficiently before IBM finally had the painful evidence that its story was an unrealistic one. Eventually it recovered, and recovered well, but only after a long overhaul.

If alignment of stories, yours and your company's, is to be achieved—and I believe it's neither as lofty nor as complicated a task as it may sound—then it's ideally generated both from top down (the company side) and bottom up (the worker's side). But let's not get carried away. For our purposes, we'll presume zero input from the company.* It is, after all, corporate culture.

That means the burden to change stories is on you.

PRESENTEEISM

There is a story that business leaders have perpetuated for generations, a story still largely being told today, a story that is, frankly, insane. This story says that the worker's physical body is not business-relevant.

When it comes to physical health and well-being, our clients are for the most part broken. Top-level managers, mid-level, everyone. Regardless of what they may say, most companies don't consider it significant that their workers are physical wrecks, or that this might impact their profitability. Amazingly, only one business school I know of—the University of Michigan's Ross School of Business, which has done physical/health assessments of every one of its MBA candidates (blood work, lean body mass measurements, etc.) and designed research projects to evaluate the influence of physical condition on performance—is bothering to test this proposition.

Yet if we go by the bottom line, then the biggest single crisis facing American business today is inarguably related to health care; more pointedly, it's stress-related—or, as I prefer to call it, *disengagement-related*. According to a *USA Today* survey, one in six U.S. employees is so overworked that his or her annual vacation time doesn't get used up despite the fact that Americans already get the most meager vacation

---

* Fortunately, many chief executives and other senior leaders who've come through our program, while understanding that it's up to each individual participant to face the truth to improve his or her life, have realized that their companies or divisions must *also* do so. We've witnessed dozens of institutions make large-scale organizational change, enabling their story to be more easily aligned with the individual worker's.

time in the industrialized world—half as much as Sweden, and considerably less even than Japan and Korea. Thirty-four percent of workers reported that their jobs were so pressing they had zero downtime at work; 32% ate lunch while working; 32% never left the building once they arrived; 14% felt company management promoted only those who regularly worked late; 19% felt pressure to work when sick or injured; 17% said it was hard to leave work or take time off in an emergency; 8% thought they would be fired or demoted if they became seriously ill. In another survey, work-related stress is cited for inspiring these behaviors: yelling at co-workers (29%), sleep problems (34%), being driven to alcohol (11%), to smoke excessively (16%), and to eat chocolate (26%). Many workers said they were "a physical wreck"; 62% complained of work-related neck or back pain, 44% said they suffered from stressed-out eyes, 38% complained of hand pain. One study implicated stress in 60% to 90% of all work-related medical problems. Another said that 75% of employees believe on-the-job stress is greater now than a generation ago. Another established a link between stress and heart disease. Another concluded that "workplace health and productivity are inextricably linked." Another found a relationship between physical inactivity and cognitive decline "across every group." Obesity is everywhere, as is hypertension, diabetes, alcoholism, divorce. One senior manager confessed to me that he smoked pot in his office just to get through the day. In the last decade the number of workers who call in sick due to stress has tripled, accounting now for one-in-five last-minute no-shows. According to the Bureau of Labor Statistics, employees who take time off from work because of stress, anxiety, or a related disorder are out an average of twenty business days. It is estimated that 20% to 40% of American workers quit their jobs because of stress.

Then there's the vast numbers of workers who show up for work—are present rather than absent—but do so in a fog. In fact, "presenteeism"—impaired performance on the job because of a medical or psychological condition—appears to be a much costlier problem than its productivity-reducing counterpart, absenteeism, and potentially more lethal to the organization because it's not as obvious.

How much does all this cost?

Dow Chemical, which employs 43,000 people, estimates its annual employee health-related costs at $635 million, more than half of which can be attributed to the indirect costs associated with presenteeism.

The Harvard Business Review estimates that presenteeism can cut individual productivity by one-third or more; "many companies' greatest health-related expense," they say, "is the almost invisible decline in productivity resulting from employee health problems, including common ailments such as allergies and headaches." Some employers have estimated that performance loss leads to costs three, five, or ten times more than the direct cost of health treatment. In 2000, the estimated cost to corporate America due to illness related to poor nutrition and obesity was $47 billion. Kent Peterson, past president of the American College of Occupational Medicine, put the annual cost that American business pays because of poor health at *$1 trillion,* which includes the direct cost of medical benefits as well as ill health's impact on productivity. Other studies have shown that stress adds to the cost of doing business not just because of absenteeism and halfhearted work but also because of increased workers compensation claims, litigation (the company ignores stress-related problems at its peril), grievances, higher turnover rate, on-the-job accidents, poor time management, resistance to change, errors in judgment and action, conflict and interpersonal problems, and an increase in customer complaints. (Stressed-out employees virtually guarantee a profitability crisis: According to a study by Reichheld and Sasser of over one hundred companies, a 5% reduction in customer defection translates into anywhere from 30% to 85% increase in profitability.)

How's that for a bottom line?

Some companies, of course, understand perfectly the profound cost of health care and have dealt with it by . . . taking their businesses offshore, where their responsibility to contribute to employee well-being is far less than what it is in this country. Yet there's no real running away from the problem, which is, at its core, cultural.

For years, with relatively few exceptions across many industries, business considered the physical health and well-being of its employees a personal, private issue. At work, employees are generally reluctant to take care of themselves; to do so is largely counterculture. Even on-site wellness centers and corporate fitness initiatives often go massively underused because workers fear that to avail themselves of the facilities suggests a lack of commitment to the company; from the company side, the wellness center is, cynically, viewed not as an investment (in its people and thus in itself) but an expense. Even a write-off.

And the individual can exercise after work, right? Well, not really. To do so suggests you're a bad family man or woman. And if you take a break midmorning or midafternoon, when everyone's circadian rhythms make them less productive anyway? Slacker. And if—heaven forbid—you leave early on Wednesdays to see your child's soccer game? Irresponsible.

Yet if extraordinary physical energy—which directly influences emotional, mental, and even spiritual energy—is the very thing needed for extraordinary productivity, then how can business ignore the demands that the human body makes every day? If you asked a hundred CEOs, "Are happier, healthier employees more productive employees?" I doubt you'd find one to disagree. "Absolutely," they'd say. "A no-brainer." Yet as Michael O'Donnell, editor-in-chief of the *American Journal of Health Promotion*, says, "most companies spend more on carpet than they do on [employee health and well-being]."

I've worked for years in a field where the participant's physical well-being is *never* underemphasized: world-class athletics. When dealing with top athletes, it would be unthinkable, of course, to remove the body from the overall equation. Every athlete develops a reverence for his or her body because it is perceived to be indispensable to achieving success (telling a successful story). It would be absurd for me to say to one of my clients from the NBA or the PGA or the WTA, "Hey, ninety percent of success is mental anyway, so let's skip the physical conditioning." Or if we said to one of the FBI anti-terrorist teams or physicians or air-traffic controllers we've worked with, "It's not important how much you sleep or what you eat or if you ever take recovery breaks. Just focus, assess, and react with maximum precision. And thanks for fighting the war on terror / saving lives / helping to land jets."

It makes no sense, right? Then does it really make sense to expect people in other fields to perform at their best if the body is largely ignored, even abused?

The cost of this "story" I've just outlined is profound and widespread and shouldered by both the company and its individuals; for the individual, the cost is often tragic. The problem is not simply going to go away. Organizations thrive when their people are energized, engaged, nimble, and responsive, yet few organizations, sad to say, can possibly thrive when the energy reserves of their workforce become chronically depleted. When workers are focused on basic physical survival, then excellence, innovation, speed, and productivity become secondary concerns.

Since I've been kicking the corporate world in the teeth for several pages now, it's time to turn our attention to ourselves. If you're one of those workers with just enough energy to claw to survive, perhaps it's time to look at the story you've created and the direction it's taking you in the only life you have.

OLD STORIES

With relatively few variations, people tell stories about basically five major subjects.

1. Work
2. Family
3. Health
4. Happiness
5. Friendships*

By asking yourself basic questions about how you feel about what you do and how you conduct yourself—and by trying honestly to answer them, of course—you begin to identify the dynamics of your story.

Your Story Around Work

Work is not a choice for most of us, yet while we may have little to say about having to work we often have lots to say about its meaning. And because more than half our waking life is consumed by work, how we frame this story is critical to our chance for overall fulfillment and happiness.

How do you characterize your relationship to work? Is it a burden or a joy? Clock-in/clock-out, deep fulfillment, or addiction? What

---

* A longer list, compiled over years of gathering data from clients and including obvious subsets of these five categories:

(1) Work/Job/Boss; (2) Family; (3) Health; (4) Happiness; (5) Friendships; (6) Money; (7) Self-Indulgence; (8) Fame/Power; (9) Death; (10) Sex/Intimacy; (11) Trust/Integrity; (12) Parents; (13) Religion; (14) Spirituality; (15) Love; (16) Food/Diet; (17) Exercise; (18) Children; (19) Spouse/Partner; (20) Other.

compels you to get up every day and go to work? The money? Is the driving force increased prestige, power, social status? A sense of intrinsic fulfillment? The contribution you're making? Is it an end in itself or a means to something else? Do you feel *forced* to work or *called* to work? Are you completely engaged at work? How much of your talent and skill are fully ignited? What's the dominant tone—inspired? challenged? disappointed? trapped? overwhelmed? Does the story you currently tell about work take you where you want to go in life? If your story about work isn't working, what story *do* you tell yourself to justify it, especially given the tens of thousands of hours it consumes?

Suppose you didn't need the money: Would you continue to go to work every day? In the space below (or on a pad or one of the blank pages at the back of this book), write down five things about your job that, if money were no issue, you would like to continue (the camaraderie, specific responsibilities/tasks, your relationship to a colleague or mentor, having a corner office, etc.):

1. _____

2. _____

3. _____

4. _____

5. _____

Your Story Around Family

What's your story about your family life? In the grand scheme, how important is family to you? To hear my clients tell it and to read their responses on our questionnaires, family is, far and away, the most oft-cited number one element in the average person's life. *It's why I work so hard . . . Nothing is more important to me . . . Everything I do, I do for them.* Most readers will recognize these sentiments, I suspect.

So . . . is your current story about family working? Is the relationship with your husband, wife, or significant other where you want it to be? Is it even close to where you want it to be? Or is there an unbridgeable gap between the level of intimacy, connection, and intensity you feel with him or her and the level you'd like to experience?

Is your story with your children working? How about your parents? Your siblings? Other family members?

If you continue on your same path, what is the relationship you're likely to have, years from now, with each of your family members? If your story isn't working with one or more key individuals, then what's the story you tell yourself to allow this pattern to persist? To what extent do you blame your job for keeping you from fully engaging with your family? (*Really?* Your *job* is the reason you're disengaged from the most important thing in your life, the people who matter most to you? How does that happen?) According to your current story, is it even possible to be fully engaged at work and also with your family?

Your Story Around Health

What's your story about your health? What kind of job have you done taking care of yourself? What value do you place on your health, and why? If you continue on your same path, then what will be the likely health consequences? If you're not fully engaged with your health, then what's the story you tell yourself and others—particularly your spouse, your kids, your doctor, your colleagues, and anyone who might look up to you—that allows you to persist in this way? If suddenly you awoke to the reality that your health was gone, what would be the consequences for you and all those you care about? How would you feel if the end of your story was dominated by one fact—that you had needlessly died young?

Do you consider your health just one of several important stories about yourself but hardly toward the top? Does it crack the top three? How about the top five? If you have been overweight, or consistently putting on weight the last several years; if you smoke; if you eat poorly; if you rest infrequently and never deeply; if you rarely, if ever, exercise; if you regularly take loads of medication or other types of drugs; if you have a family medical condition whose occurrence or severity might reasonably be diminished, perhaps even avoided altogether, by taking better care of yourself . . . what is the story you tell yourself that explains how you deal, or don't deal, with these issues? Is it a story with any rhyme or reason? Do you believe that spending time exercising or otherwise taking care of yourself, particularly during the workday, sets a negative example for others (it's selfish, lazy, unprofessional, shows misaligned priorities)? Do you hope your children will emulate the story you're telling about health?

Given your physical being and the way you present yourself, do you think the story you're telling is the same one that others are hearing? Could it be vastly different, when seen through their eyes?

Think to a time when you were very ill, so sapped of energy that you didn't even feel like reading a book in bed. Do you remember any promises you made to yourself while lying in bed? As in, "I don't ever want to feel this way again. If and when I regain my health, I'm going to . . ."? Write down three promises you made:

1. _____

2. _____

3. _____

Your Story Around Happiness

What's your story about your happiness? How would you rate your happiness over the last six months? Is your answer acceptable to you? According to your story, how important is happiness and how do you go about achieving it? Are you clear about where or how happiness might be realized for you? If there is something out there—some activity, some person—that dependably brings you happiness, how long has it been since you encountered it or her or him? What do you think is the connection, if any, between engagement and happiness? If your level of happiness is not where you want it to be, then what's the story you tell yourself that explains why it's not happening at this point in your life? If you continue on the same trajectory, then what kind of happiness do you expect is likely in your future, short-term and long?

Do you consider your own happiness an afterthought? An indulgence? A form of selfishness? Have you removed joy—joy, as opposed to contentment—from the spectrum of emotions you expect and wish to experience during the remainder of your life?

Jot down ten moments/occasions during the last thirty days where you experienced joy.

1. _____ 2. _____

3. _____ 4. _____

5. _____ 6. _____

7. _____ 8. _____

9. _____ 10. _____

Your Story Around Friends

What's your story about friendship? According to your story, how important are friends? How fully engaged are you with them? (That is, don't calculate in your mind simply how often you see them but what you do and how you are when you're together.) If close friendships are important to you, yet they are clearly not happening in your life, what is the story you tell yourself that obstructs this from happening?

In what way, if any, might friendships be connected to health and happiness for you? To what extent are friendships important to your realizing what you need and want from life? If you have few or no friends, why is that? Is this a relatively recent development—that is, something that's happened since you got married, for example, or had a family, or got more consumed by work, or got promoted, or got divorced, or experienced a significant loss, or moved away from your hometown?

When you think of your closest friendships over the last five years, can you say any of them has grown and deepened? According to a Gallup poll, people who have a best friend at work are seven times more likely to be engaged in their job, get more done in less time, have fewer accidents and are more likely to innovate and share new ideas. An employee's satisfaction jumps by almost 50% when he or she has a close relationship at the workplace. (And if your best friend has a healthy diet, you are *five times more likely* to eat healthy yourself.)

Suppose you had no friends—what would that be like? This may seem like a morbid exercise but write down three ways in which being completely friendless might make your life poorer (no one to turn to in times of crisis and celebration, no one to mourn your passing, etc.).

1. _____

2. _____

3. _____

WRITE YOUR CURRENT STORY
(OR TRY TO)

The following are the first steps in a process we've devised and refined over the years, from feedback our clients have provided. It starts with you writing your current story—a first draft. Eventually, after some hard and honest work—and several drafts—you'll have produced a story that accurately reflects the way things have been going in your life. Then you'll discard this current story, recasting it now as your "old story," and replace it with your new, forward-moving story.

But that's getting ahead of ourselves—especially considering that the majority of those I've worked with have not quite "gotten" their current story on the first attempt.

STEP 1: Identify the important areas of your life where the stories you tell yourself or others are clearly not working. They simply do not take you where you ultimately want to go—for example, with personal relationships, work, financial health, physical health; with your boss, your daughter, your morning routine. Ask yourself: *In what areas is it clear I can't get to where I want to go with the story I've got?*

1. _____

2. _____

3. _____

4. _____

5. _____

Keep going, if you have more.

STEP 2: Articulate as clearly as possible the story you currently have that isn't working. Put it down on paper. Eventually we'll refer to this as your Old Story.

Here are five examples from clients. I don't think it's an exaggeration to say that all five have experienced enormous professional success.

Greg: *I have an overwhelming, all-consuming drive for results, holding myself totally accountable for my company's performance, especially poor performance. And this is how it's supposed to be for a leader. It comes with the territory. I am ultimately doing all that I do to provide the best for my family, which they don't understand. They don't understand, especially my wife (!), that I need the time at home to work through the issues I have in my job. At work, when we are having tough results, I need to jump into the business to understand the issues and direct our course of action to turn things around. I will be the one that ultimately gets asked what we are doing to fix the situation. I need to have the answers, which means I don't have time to let the team find their way.*

Janine: *My life—the way that it is—does not allow me any time for me, and I'm okay with that. Exercise time is time I need to spend with my family or get work done. I don't have the luxury of time to focus on something so selfish. Also, eating right is too difficult—so why even bother? The main thing is that I eat something, anything. The right food is not readily accessible anyway. I have a pretty high metabolism, so it's not a big deal when I don't eat right—and sometimes it just feels good to eat a lot of unhealthy things—it's a huge stress reliever for me.*

Paul: *I am an impostor sneaking by under the radar. I've gotten to where I am out of pure luck. I don't know what I'm doing and am petrified that people will discover the truth. I work hard and fear leaving the office because I am certain, if found out, I will be fired. I have considered personal executive coaching but deep inside don't believe it will help. I've also broken my pact with my wife to share in childcare responsibilities, so I've failed there as well. I blame all my misery and feelings of* *failure on my job rather than creating the opportunities that I really want in my life.*

Tricia: *My "great" job has changed drastically. The company has created an organization that makes no sense and is operationally set up for failure. I have huge increases in responsibility, including businesses and people over which I have no authority. The company looks to me for answers when, in fact, they should be solving these issues at a structural or strategic level. My job has significantly increased in demand and volume and I simply don't have sufficient staff to cover what is expected. I'm frustrated, I'm angry, I'm resentful.*

Ken: *I'm a 35-year-old African-American, senior executive for one of the biggest, most challenging companies in the world. I rose very quickly and now the pressure is on me. No one can understand or appreciate what I face on a daily basis. I have so many expectations to live up to, both at work and at home. My family should try to understand how hard I work and how much I do for them. They don't know how this terrifying fear of failure burdens me every single day. My voice inside keeps saying, "You cannot fail, you cannot let people down." But my voice also says, "I don't have time for me, I don't feel in control and someday soon, my flaws will be discovered." My work expectations are beyond my level of competence. My world at home has a similar theme. I love my wife but I know she's going to attack me for something I have not done right and she's probably right. Eventually, I just shut down, mentally and emotionally. I have no time for friends or community. Inside I'm a complete wreck and I have no clue what to do about it.*

Before you begin writing your own Old Story:

Really bring it to life. Express your logic, your rationale, your thinking process about why you've been living the way you have. By getting it down on paper, you can see it, study it, break it down, judge how it flows (or stumbles) as a story. Write in the voice you typically use privately with yourself. Don't hold back. If it's a rationalizing, scapegoating voice, then use that. If it's bitter or prideful, use it. This story—initially, anyway—is for your eyes, no one else's, so don't write your story scared; no need to be diplomatic or politically correct. At some point you may wish to share it with others, as many people do in our workshops.

Some tricks to a more authentic story:

- Exaggerating your voice often makes it easier to recognize how destructive and illogical the story you've been telling yourself actually is. For example, if you feel used and taken for granted, listen to the voice and capture both the message and the emotion in your writing. Instead of writing the more muted, slightly dishonest, "When I get home I can't give my kids the time they want because I still have work calls to make"—as one client wrote in the first draft of his Old Story—get down and dirty, as he did when he nailed his whiniest, most immature, but honest inner voice by his final draft: "My kids don't appreciate what I do, it's insensitive of them to keep hounding me, and I'm actually angry at them because they want me to play Monopoly with them the instant I walk through the door." If that's the way you think—no matter how ugly it sounds—capture it.
- Just as novelists and screenwriters go through dozens of drafts before they get it right, prepare to go through *several rewrites* before you can effectively capture the voice, content, and essence of your faulty Old Story. Clients tell me they go through three, eight, fifteen drafts. When it's right, you'll know it.
- Just as writers emphasize detail, you, too, should *get as specific and concrete* as you can with your Old Story. Capture the nuances of how you talk to yourself and the logic of your thinking. The elements of a story that make it persuasive or not—theme, tone, major characters, pace—provide color and texture to life, so try to capture them on paper.

Okay. Now take a stab at your Old Story.

Old Story

_____

_____

_____

_____

_____

_____

_____

_____

_____

_____

_____

_____

_____

Note your feelings as you're reading and writing your old story. Clients often experience shock, embarrassment, even self-loathing when they write and read their Old Stories as they genuinely face their rationale for the first time. "This story is making me sick as I write it," one client wrote as part of his story.

You can only really write your New Story—eventually—if you've isolated what it is about your Old Story that's faulty. (If there's nothing faulty in it, then there's no reason to write a new one, right?) How do you do that?

STEP 3: Identify the faulty elements of your old story by asking yourself three questions, about both the total story and each of the individual points it makes:

1. Will this story take me where I want to go in life (while at the same time remaining true to my deepest values and beliefs)?
2. Does the story reflect the truth as much as possible?
3. Does this story stimulate me to take action?

These three questions are the foundations for the three rules of good storytelling, which we will cover in detail. Your Old Story usually flouts one or more of these rules, often all three. I refer to them short-handedly as Purpose, Truth, and Hope-Filled Action. It's the lack of one or more of these criteria that makes your Old Story flawed and ultimately unworkable. In your New Story, on the other hand, all three rules will be addressed and conformed to. *You simply cannot tell a good story without satisfying each and every one of these three elements.*

So: Does your Old Story work for you?

The answer will be found by holding it up, first, against your purpose in life. Is this story you wrote above, the one you're right now living and have been for some time, moving you toward fulfilling and remaining true to that great purpose?

Two

THE PREMISE OF YOUR STORY, THE PURPOSE OF YOUR LIFE

There are two towers in downtown Orlando, each 175 feet high and separated by a distance of 36 feet. To anyone who walks across a plank that spans the roofs, my institute will award a certified check for $5 million. We'll pay the taxes on it. The chance of success: 80%. This is no joke. Interested?

Whenever I make this offer in our workshops—typically fifteen to thirty individuals in the room, mostly Type A's—maybe one hand goes up, rarely more than three, often none. (I tell them the offer is hypothetical only after the exercise is over.)

I then add, in the interest of full disclosure, that it's preferable to make the crossing in the morning, after the fog clears. And that there may be some wind issues, though the gusts are rarely severe. Anyone?

Maybe the one or two hands stay up, maybe not.

Did I give the plank's dimensions? Twelve inches wide, 1¼ inch thick, a little give. No way should that frighten you; were the plank laid on the floor, you could absolutely walk across it without teetering off, no problem. (And *no*, you can't win the money by crawling across on your stomach; someone always asks that.). So: Five mil, 80% chance of success. Hello?

The same one or two hands.

Obviously the offer is not compelling enough. All right, then: To anyone who crosses from one roof to another—*a measly twelve yards! on a strong plank easily wide enough for you to walk across!*—the institute will pay *$50 million*, tax free.

A whopping four or five hands go up this time (five million bucks ain't what it used to be). Obviously, the offer *still* lacks universal appeal. Let's see . . .

Okay, how about this: You're standing on the roof of Tower A. Thirty-six feet away, on the roof of Tower B, stands your family. To save their lives, you must cross the plank. Who's up for it?

I'll let you guess how many hands go up.

He who has a why to live, said Nietzsche, can bear with almost any how.

You guessed right: Every single hand goes up, every single time. (In his insightful and powerful book, *What Matters Most*, Hyrum Smith employed a similar analogy to illustrate how our actions are thoroughly dependent on the stakes involved.) I have yet to meet a person who, given the proposition laid out above—risk your life or the lives of your family members—has said that he or she would *not* walk that narrow plank, 175 feet above the concrete, battling occasional gusts and a one-in-five chance of dying. (By the way, I chose "80% chance of success" arbitrarily, since no one has ever actually made the crossing.)

I present the wood plank example not to show clients that saving their family from harm is their ultimate purpose in life—it's *a* purpose, a vital one, but not *the* purpose, not the reason you are on this earth—but to show just how dramatically our story, and our willingness to spend energy and take risk, change when there is a great purpose. In short, when the stakes are a large sum of money—almost never a transcendent purpose—no one walks across that plank. When the stakes are love and life and that which has incalculable value, everyone goes.

Purpose is the epicenter of everyone's life story. *Purpose is one of the three foundations of good storytelling.*

Without purpose, no character in a book or a movie would do anything interesting, meaningful, memorable, worthwhile. Without purpose, our life story has no meaning. It has no coherence, no direction, no inexorable momentum. Without purpose, our life still "moves" along—whatever that means—but it lacks an organizing principle. A mother of four quoted in Dan McAdams's book, *The Redemptive Self: Stories Americans Live By*, may have captured it most eloquently and bittersweetly when she said, "I know what to do when I get up every day, but do I really know where I'm going?" Without purpose, it is all but impossible to be fully engaged. To be extraordinary.

With purpose, on the other hand, people do amazing things: good, smart, productive things, often heroic things, unprecedented things. For example, a sizable number of women smokers who've never had luck quitting do so the instant they find out they're pregnant. Suddenly there's a purpose, a higher calling that pulls at them more strongly than even the most irresistible addiction. For the next nine months, these women are amazing, not even touching a cigarette, or barely. It's an impressive feat. This new purpose—protecting growing life—succeeds to move her to action where the lesser purpose—not harming her own health—failed repeatedly to move her, despite pleas by concerned partners, parents, friends. Perhaps those pleas to not smoke failed because their purpose seemed not so much lesser as theoretical: Lung cancer, emphysema, and other health complications may occur but then again they may not, and even if they do, they will likely descend in the fog of the future, maybe a very distant future. In contrast, there's nothing theoretical about life growing inside one's belly. The baby squirms inside you. So these women make this profound change, motivated by a noble purpose.

And then, guess what? Within months of delivering new life into the world, most of them pick up a cigarette again and resume smoking.

I am not here to slam new mothers who smoke. It goes without saying that there's no shortage of individuals, you and me included, who do things counterproductive to our own self-interest and the interest of those we care about most. I've already shared with you some of their stories, tales that spill over with contradiction. "My son Noah is the most important part of my life," wrote an executive in his questionnaire. Yet on our "If you continue on the path you're on, where will you end up?" scale, where 1 = "in trouble" and 5 = "where I want to be," he rated his family a 1, and admitted that almost everything that might have a profound impact on his son's well-being and development was disastrously off: the executive's relationship with his wife, the amount of time he spent (or did not spend) with his son, the quality of time he *did* spend with him (completely disengaged). In this case, as in so many others, it's not that the individual lacked a purpose. Indeed, he seemed to have one—at least claimed to have one—but then *he went about living his life and telling a story that supported that purpose hardly at all.* And if that's so, then what does it mean, really, to have a purpose? Or do you just say you have a purpose to cover yourself? Or do you not understand the meaning of the word "purpose"?

Purpose is the thing in your life you will fight for. It is the ground you will defend at any cost. Purpose is not the same as "incentive," but rather the motor *behind* it, the end that drives why you have energy for some things and not for others. So while the executive cited above and ten thousand others I've seen may actually articulate their purpose to themselves and to others, articulation is not nearly enough; in fact, it is really not even worthy of a pat on the back, so long as one continues to live one's life in a way that does very little, if anything, to support that purpose. Indeed, to say you have a purpose and then to do nothing about it is, first, a sham and, last, a tragedy.

Most people who have been living in this way, when pushed to be thoughtful, will quickly identify what they claim to be their true purpose in life. In the workshops we ask our clients to think about this very question, and then think about it again, because eventually they will need to write it down, so they can look at it and decide if that really feels like their true purpose, something to live and die for.

To find one's true purpose sometimes takes work. Fortunately, the skill it requires is one that every person is blessed with.

For a few people, naming one's purpose comes with remarkable ease. The individual feels it in the deepest part of his or her soul; the purpose has always been there, even if it got lost for a very long while, remaining unexpressed to oneself and to those who are the objects of one's purpose. (Deep, enduring purpose is virtually always motivated by a desire for the well-being of others.) The simultaneously elusive, yet blindingly obvious nature of purpose recalls the legendary pronouncement by U.S. Supreme Court Justice Potter Stewart, when explaining what constituted pornography: While acknowledging the difficulty in defining it, he said, "I know it when I see it."

You know purpose when you see it. The purpose of Erik Weihenmayer, who became blind as a teenager, was to demonstrate that all things are possible, for him and anyone—so he became a mountain climber who scaled all seven of the world's great summits, including Mount Everest. The purpose of Daniel M., a CEO who attended our workshop with his management team, was to not die without connecting with his daughter—so he made a dinner date week after week after week with the teenager he'd virtually ignored since she was born, enduring her justified contempt every Wednesday night for months until finally she turned her chair, slightly, so that her back was no longer to him; until finally she directed some monosyllables his way; until finally she engaged him in a conversation; until finally, after three years of his persistently and consistently pursuing his purpose, she let him be the loving father to her that they both wanted him to be.

To author a workable, fulfilling new story, you will need to ask yourself many questions and then answer them, none more important than those that concern purpose. Purpose is the sail on the boat, the yeast in the bread. Once you know your purpose—that is, *what matters*—then everything else can fall into place. Getting your purpose clear is your defining truth. What is the purpose of your life? To make your parents proud? To keep your children out of harm's way? To be the most successful earner in your circle? To leave the world a better place than when you entered it? To honor God? To live to a hundred? To seek out adventure and risk? Whatever it is, it had better be something for which you will cross a narrow plank 175 feet above the ground, gusts of wind or no gusts, seven days a week, no questions asked.

Once you find your purpose, you have a chance to live a story that moves you and those around you.

THE WORDS ON YOUR TOMBSTONE

Remember when your mother asked you, "Are you telling me a story or is that really true?" The assumption being: A story is what you concoct to keep yourself out of trouble. But your mother's error was the same one many of us make when we think of stories. We fail to recognize that *everything we say is a story*—nothing more, nothing less. It would have been more accurate for Mom to have said, "I know you're telling me a story, but I need to know if your story truly reflects the facts or if you're intentionally making things up to get out of trouble or to get what you want." On the other hand, no mother—thank God—talks like that.

With every story, it is vital that one understand the purpose behind what is being said. The critical first step to getting our stories right is ensuring that the story we are telling at the moment is aligned with our *ultimate mission in life*, a phrase I use largely interchangeably with "purpose"—as in *the* purpose, not just *a* purpose. Your Ultimate Mission is the thing that continually renews your spirit, the thing that *gets* you to stop and smell the roses. It is the indomitable force that moves you to action when nothing else can, yet it can ground you with a single whisper in your quietest moment; it is at once the bedrock of your soul and (as the phrase goes) the wind beneath your wings. It spells out the most overarching goals you want and need to achieve in your time here, and the manner in which you feel you must do it (that is, you pursue these goals in accordance with your values and beliefs).

Our ultimate mission must be clearly defined. If you find this difficult to do, ask yourself: "If I was standing at the rear of the chapel listening to people eulogize me at my own funeral, like Tom Sawyer and Huck Finn get to do, what would it gladden me to hear? What might someone say up there, or around my burial plot, that would make me think, 'Hey, I guess I really *did* lead a worthwhile life'?" By envisioning the end of your life, by coming to terms with the question, *How do I want to be remembered?* or *What is the legacy I most want to leave?* you provide yourself with your single most important navigational coordinate: *fundamental purpose, which henceforth will drive everything you do.* By envisioning the end of your life, you are, in simplest terms, pausing to define what could reasonably be called a purposeful life, as lived by you.

After you finish reading this paragraph, close your eyes. Visualize a tombstone: yours. It's got your name engraved in it, the year of your birth and (imagined) year of death. Can you see it? What does it say underneath? Is it simply the word "beloved" and numerous familial relationships? Is that okay? Does it work for you? Does it say more? Does it need to?

Now I know that tombstones almost never state the deceased's ultimate purpose. (Every now and then you'll see one that says something like "He lived to help others," though it's hard to know whether that was really their purpose or the purpose the survivors wanted etched for perpetuity.) Still, it doesn't hurt to imagine your own tombstone, if for no reason other than to think about where you're headed.

It's the ultimate game; the ultimate endgame. You must answer this seemingly simple, maddeningly simple query in a way that fully satisfies you. If you don't, then you'll find it pretty nearly impossible to make the necessary course corrections your life almost certainly requires.

YOUR ULTIMATE MISSION, OUT LOUD

When I work to get clients to define and refine their Ultimate Mission, I almost always have to get tough with them. I put them through a vigorous interrogation to make sure that when they've reached their "answer," they haven't done so by fooling or mischaracterizing themselves. Amazingly, almost no one gets his or her ultimate mission on the first attempt. Often, an individual will come up with a purpose that sounds deep and good—*My ultimate mission is to give my family the financial security I never had, by becoming a managing director of my firm*—but which, upon scrutiny, is flimsy or undercooked, not yet at the most fundamental level of purpose—e.g., *My ultimate mission is to be an extraordinary father, husband, and leader in my community, and a role model for generations to come.*

Given its influence over you—its often invisible influence—your ultimate mission merits being written down as early in life as possible, and modified and deepened with every passing year until death.

Yet most people never write down their purpose. Or say it out loud. Or even think about what it might be in its purest form. Often the first time an individual's purpose is articulated is at his or her funeral, and then only if he or she is lucky enough to have a eulogizer who saw his or her purpose for what it was. During our two-and-a-half-day workshops in Orlando, we encourage—okay, "require" is more like it—clients to actually write their Ultimate Mission, just as they must write their Old Story and New Story, just as they will write their Training Missions and Rituals (more on those later). Committing your Ultimate Mission to writing, year after year, keeps the most important navigational tool we human beings possess always within our reach.

Because your Ultimate Mission is concerned with the biggest-ticket stuff, not small-scale goals, the language employed when writing it is often grand, perhaps even grandiose. While we of course encourage participants to come up with their own words to express themselves, the word "extraordinary" recurs by far the most often. (At least, that is, with our American clients: To those raised in the United States, the word connotes "special," "the pinnacle," even "heroic"; ambitious as it sounds, "extraordinary" seems more attainable than "perfect," less vague and value laden than "great" or "excellent." To many of our non-

American clients, however, particularly our European participants, the word "extraordinary" borders on arrogance. "Being the best father I can be and a good leader" or "To be a decent mother" is more their style of phrasing.)

Here are examples of Ultimate Missions from clients. I won't say which ones I believe may not be quite there yet; I can't say which solid-sounding ones won't, in the end, be heeded:

To be an extraordinary daughter to my parents, extraordinary sister to Bob, and the most positive and peaceful force in my field within the next ten years.

To be a fully connected man whose devotion to his family is an inspiration to others.

To be a role model for working moms, and an extraordinary volunteer.

My mission is to pursue a life of happiness and success at work, aiming toward a future marriage with a future potential family. I, no one else, hold the key to this happiness.

To live in such a way that I create hope in others.

To know, to feel, and to be flourishing so that my actions and words might inspire and benefit my family, my students, and all sentient beings.

My focus is not on the destination but on the trip that takes me there.

To passionately love and be loved by my wife and three sons. To have strong and caring relationships with my brothers, sisters, and friends. To lead with strength and concern. To leave a positive and lasting legacy for the people I have known and loved.

I want to bestow strong values.

To be recognized as a high performer. To have a strong positive impact.

Make a bigger impact in the next 50 years than I did in the first.

To raise two daughters to become happy and fulfilled adults. To instill in them values of hard work and caring about people. To have them be friends and stay close with each other all their lives. To continue to challenge myself and grow.

To serve God by serving other individuals, my family, my co-workers, and under-served people/groups.

To make a meaningful change that otherwise would not have happened. In doing so, to create the means for a better future for my family.

My mission is to be all I can be.

Be there for my girlfriend and family, friends and colleagues, and always have them know I'm the person they can count on.

My mission in life is to be happy.

My ultimate mission is to always remain in awe of the universe and everything in it.

To be remembered as someone who pulled off an Agassi in the second half of his life. *

To explore and experience the world.

To prove that I can have it all: a close connection to God, a passionate love with my husband, loving guidance of my children, a rewarding career, intellectual pursuits and a healthy (hot) body.

---

* Andre Agassi, the fantastically talented and inspiring tennis player, had a brilliant early career; then seemed to lose some desire and focus and faltered to the point of career oblivion; then, after rededicating himself physically and mentally (and emotionally, and spiritually), returned for another brilliant run that lasted for several years. On the eve of his retirement, he said, "This is a close of a certain chapter of my life."

What's your Ultimate Mission? Before you write it down—using whatever words that speak to you and move you; you're writing this, after all, for yourself, no one else—ask yourself these questions:

- How do you want to be remembered?
- What is the legacy you most want to leave for others?
- How would you most like to hear people eulogize you at your funeral?
- What is worth dying for?
- What makes your life really worth living?
- In what areas of your life must you truly be extraordinary to fulfill your destiny?

My Ultimate Mission is_____

_____

_____

_____

As clients try to get at their Ultimate Mission, one of my responsibilities is to do all I can to ensure that he or she doesn't (continue to) spend the rest of his or her life chasing a *fraudulent purpose*.

OUTING FALSE PURPOSE

Of all the groups we work with, top-class athletes are one of the two demographics that consistently tower above the rest in their native comprehension of the life-as-story concept, and in their embrace of the notion that true success is realizable when one consciously crafts an ambitious, achievable story and then sticks to it. (Law enforcement is the other.) And yet, as you'll see, even athletes struggle mightily to hit the story's bull's-eye—that is, to nail the precise, deep purpose that drives every one of their life choices.

Who'd have thought jocks could teach us about story? And yet they can. There are several reasons for this, I think. One, the athlete's career is relatively short, and its arc, like the arc of a story, can be more easily imagined—far more easily, say, than the arc of an entire life, or a career that lasts forty or fifty years. Two, the competition itself—be it a match, tournament, or season—is easily characterized in story terms, with a beginning, middle, and unmistakable end, and a tone that's similarly non-negotiable (e.g., victory and/or statistically measurable improvement = happy ending). Three, the athlete's life from early youth on is so structured, on a daily and seasonal basis, as well as a physical basis—the training, the meets, the maintenance of fitness, the ebbs and flows of intensity, the very geometry of the workplace, the frequent potential for discernible turning points—and thus structure, one of the pillar elements of story, soon enough becomes innate to the athlete. Four, in the prime of an athlete's competitive years, when his or her daily life is so radically different from that of most of us, he or she requires extra structure to maintain sanity and success, and story is nothing if not structuring.

I think there's one more reason, too. When you enter the topmost tier of athletic competition, where everyone has a rocket serve, or drives the ball 320 yards, or has immaculate technique—just like you—the difference between being number one in the world and number 427 is almost always something other than physical. Having a better story than your opponent may be the difference, and *you can't have a great story unless you get your purpose right.*

One of the top tennis players in the world—I'll call her Barbara—contacted me in the hope of righting her game. Since rising as high as number 5 two years before coming to me, her ranking had fallen considerably and she was now losing in the first and second rounds of tournaments to far less talented players. Even more bothersome to Barbara and those around her, competing and practicing were no longer sources of pleasure to her. She had a natural effervescence and an easy smile the first time she visited me, but tennis, she stated flatly, was no longer fun. It had become a chore. She wanted to fix things.

"What's your story?" I asked her when she sat down in my office. "Why do you play?"

I could see that wasn't what she expected.

To her credit, she entertained my question. After a couple of moments, she said, "I guess . . . ," then paused to think some more. "I want to be a success."

"What does that mean?" I asked.

"To be number one in the world," she said, rather unconvincingly.

"Okay. So you become number one in the world. When it's all over, your tombstone reads, 'She Was Number One In The World.' You'd be good with that?"

She looked terribly unsatisfied. She shook her head.

I asked her again, "Why do you play?"

She took a breath and thought some more. "I'd like to have a nice place to live. I like nice cars. I love cars. Oh, God. It sounds so terrible. I don't want that on my tombstone, either. You're just confusing me."

We went through this exercise a few more times, and each time she abandoned her answer as quickly as she offered it.

"Here's your assignment tonight," I told her. "I want you to really think about what your ultimate mission is. What you're all about. What keeps you playing. It has to come from you, no one else. Not your coach, not your mother, not your agent, not your sponsors. Don't come into the office unless you can tell me that. Okay?"

She left. She was not smiling.

The next day, Barbara walked into my office. Actually, that's not accurate: She *bounced* into my office. She was bubbly. On fire. She couldn't stop smiling.

"I got it, I got it," she said as soon as she sat down. "I thought about it all night long and then I finally got it. But I'm afraid to tell you."

"Why?"

"You're going to think it's stupid. Maybe you'll think it's not challenging me."

"Try me."

"Okay," she said, and took a big breath. "I want to be sunshine. I want to be sunshine to every person I care about and everyone who watches me play."

I nodded. "And on your tombstone, if it says, 'She brought sunshine to people everywhere,' would that be okay?"

"Yes," she said, nodding and smiling broadly.

"Will you be afraid to lose when you're out there?"

"Not if I'm sunshine." She paused. "What do you think?"

"I think you're going to win more than your share," I said. "And now I think we can get to work."

Now that she'd identified her Ultimate Mission—her story's premise—we could begin constructing her story in more detail, with all roads leading to satisfying that purpose, a purpose I found ambitious, noble; a purpose I found, frankly, beautiful. Barbara would win matches and lose them, she would thrive and she would struggle, she would endure long road trips and irritating questions by the press after straight-set wipeouts . . . but for her to achieve success in life, all she needed was to stay true to her goal of radiating sunshine and gratitude, positive energy and joy, on the tennis court and off. If she did that, then there could be joy even in losing. So long as she respected what she did and gave her best and fullest energy to it, and those around her could sense the sincerity of her effort, then, yes: Even as she was losing a match she would be writing a glorious life story. Now we had to come up with rituals to help her craft a story around her family, around her health, money, friends, and every key aspect of her life, so that they were all consistent with her values and her sunshine-filled purpose.

Three days later, her coach called me. "What the hell did you do to her?" he asked. "She loves practicing again. She can't wait to get on the court. She's excited. She's no longer obnoxious and angry to be around."

Barbara started winning again. Over the next few months, she routinely beat all the players her ranking said she should have beaten. And she finally started beating players ranked above her. In an early round of her next Grand Slam event, her first Slam since rediscovering *why* she played tennis, she faced one of the top players in the world, a multiple Grand Slam champion. In their five previous meetings, Barbara had yet to take even a set off the champ.

Barbara won. In straight sets. "I was not fighting myself at all as I used to," she was quoted as saying after the match. "I had so many matches like this where I was really close to beating the top players and finally I did it today."

I'm not suggesting that she would experience unblemished competitive success from there on in—she didn't, and there was more than a little backsliding on her return to the highest ranks. But she played like sunshine the whole way. And in discovering (or rediscovering) her true purpose, one that transcended being defined by a particular seeding or trophy or yearly winnings, each day she couldn't help being far more *engaged* in her life, in the process of training, in the pleasure of playing, and in virtually every important aspect off the court, too.

I've worked with enough athletes to know a false ultimate mission when I hear one. *To be number one in the world. To break a world record. To make the cover of* Sports Illustrated. *To win a national championship.* In each of these cases, when I've pushed my athlete-clients to examine— really examine—whether that goal will hold up as the ultimate crite-rion for success in their lives, their explanations, like Barbara's, quickly melt away. *I made the cover of* Sports Illustrated, *therefore my life was a suc-cess* . . . Really, now: How stupid is that? Is it not safe to say that anyone can detect the insubstantiality, the lack of a rallying point, in that equation? It's as absurd as its negative: *I never made the cover of* Sports Illustrated, *therefore my life was a failure.*

Don't get me wrong: Goals like these—some of them, anyway— have value. Yet all the aspirations above, and similar ones that athletes repeat to themselves with hypnotic, mantra-like regularity, fail to cap-ture *the fundamental purpose* that defines value and meaning in the athlete's life. They, like everyone, need to find *a purpose that satisfies their needs, not just their wants.* When one lives one's life in pursuit of a false purpose, it will eventually come apart. Sooner or later—hopefully sooner—the false purpose will come to seem like a fiction in a world that demands nonfiction. *A flawed purpose always results in a flawed end-ing.* Another tennis player with whom I worked several years ago had as her goal to break into the world top 10. Her story was that, once she achieved such a ranking, she would finally feel happy and truly suc-cessful as a person. In spite of my arguments to the contrary, she per-sisted in her belief. When we began working together, her world ranking was in the 30s. After considerable hard work and dedication, impressive displays of industry driven primarily by her deep belief that it was numerical ranking that would rescue her from feelings of empti-ness and unhappiness, she did it. She broke into the top 10 of women's tennis.

Within twelve months of achieving her fantastic single-digit world ranking, shocked and dismayed that it had had no appreciable effect on her feelings of success and self-worth, she quit the sport.

For executives, their faulty Ultimate Mission may be to become CEO, to own their own business, to become partner, to become finan-cially independent, to retire early. When I press them to scrutinize whether these aspirations can really serve to define ultimate success in their lives, they quickly retreat, just like the athletes, from their initial answers, but often they must come to that painful conclusion very much alone. At the closing session of one workshop, an extremely successful supply-chain manager told the room that the previous night he was able to articulate what his Ultimate Mission had always been. "To devote all my energy and creativity to my business, and do it while still reasonably young, and not worry about my kids unless there's a real crisis," he said. Then he said, as an aside, "I knew that my wife, who's tremendous, would take care of them, and that I would get back to all of them when I was finally financially secure." He paused. "I'm fifty-two and it's never going to end. I missed the opportunity to know my kids." Whenever someone makes such an admission, of course, it's deeply uncomfortable—but not so much because of what the confessor just said but because so many others in the room, often hard-driving executives, are coming to grips with the fact that they've been following similarly faulty purposes. They must acknowledge that they no longer know what they need; that the bigger home they just bought mostly means a continuing escalation to their life; that they, too, will just continue to work harder and longer, no matter what they tell themselves. And that's the reason they're alive? Men, in particular, often think they can't be good parents unless they are great financial providers; then one day they wake up to the reality that the day-to-day needs of their children counted for something, too. And they're fifty-two. Or sixty-three.

Several years ago, I listened as Lance, who worked for a headhunter firm and took home a decent salary, described to me his own faulty Ultimate Mission. He was convinced his life would be so much better and happier if he didn't have to struggle to make ends meet financially. He was sure that his financial condition was inseparably connected to his happiness. He longed for a time when he would be free from the stress of day-to-day bills.

Then he won one of the largest single lotteries in his state's history: over $200 million. (That's *two hundred million*.)

You can guess what happened next, which is what happens with so many lottery winners. He very quickly had to jettison his belief that money brought happiness. Soon, he was overwhelmed by the day-to-day stress of managing his money and trying to establish a meaningful life purpose. When I next talked to him, he admitted that his feeling about himself and his overall happiness were considerably better before his financial windfall. If he had known then what he knew now, he said, he would never have purchased the ticket. His story's premise—that money corresponds to happiness—was completely faulty.

So long as we rely on false purposes to navigate through life, we can be certain that our life story will never bring true fulfillment. We may well catch what we've been chasing, but what we've been chasing will turn out to be a prize not really worth having, at least not at these prices (given the volume of time and energy expended on the chase). If you're unconnected to your true purpose, if you're chasing after the wrong thing, you miss the most exciting part of living.

To find that simple and true purpose can be, as I have said, deceptively hard. It often takes half our life or more to come back to it. It's rare that someone can identify a purpose for himself or herself at a very young age and have it stand up to scrutiny. Michelle Wie, the golf phenom, is one of the rarities, as I found out the first time we met and I asked her—you guessed it—why she played.

"I'm not playing for myself," said Michelle, fourteen at the time. "I'm playing to make a statement, to do some good in the world. I want to be a statement to women that most of the barriers we face are self-imposed. I want girls to think, 'If she can hit the ball 308 yards, on average, what can *I* do?' "

I'm sure my jaw was hanging. *Fourteen years old and she comes up with that?* Most forty-five-year-olds aren't that wise. Here was someone who got her story straight from the beginning, someone with balance. Not surprisingly, Michelle's first public gesture after turning professional was to write a half-million-dollar check to victims of Hurricane Katrina. When I heard about it, I thought that, regardless of what happened with her golfing career, she had positioned herself beautifully to live a fulfilling life; it was clear that she understood, at a remarkably young age, the necessity of a good and noble premise. After that, when she and I would talk, the focus was always on playing and succeeding at golf, the vehicle for completing her Ultimate Mission; she never once talked about money or fame or anything remotely connected to them. It became clear to me why this teenaged girl found it surprisingly easy to eschew afternoons at the mall with her friends and instead go out, day after day after day, to the course or the driving range, playing hole after hole after hole: She *needed* to get better because it was only by getting better that she could achieve her purpose: *I'm playing to make a statement.*

Lately, Michelle has had her share of tough days on the tour, both women's and men's. But her full consciousness about why she's doing what she's doing, and what she represents to others—the air-tightness of her ultimate mission—not only propels her to train hard but also gives her the tremendous confidence she needs to fulfill her destiny, one that promises to exemplify deep engagement.

PURPOSE IS NEVER FORGETTABLE

As its very name suggests, a movie's primary intention is to *move* the audience emotionally. Story is the vehicle through which the movement occurs. Story is what stirs us, terrifies us, breaks our heart. A boring story fails because it doesn't move us, doesn't tap our capacity for empathy. Think of the very best stories you've ever seen or read or heard, and you remember the depth of your feeling for one or more of the characters.

That's what happens when our clients craft their new stories. These stories, finally, move their authors—and others, too—the way great movies do. We feel the potential for heroism in what the author/main character aspires to. If you're seriously going to write a story powerful enough to get you to do things like quit smoking for good, or be more positive in your outlook, or spend at least a half hour each night communicating meaningfully with your spouse, or henceforth turn off your cell phone on weekends, then you've got to create a purpose and a story so compelling that you are moved to make those corrections in your life, and make them for good. Remember that tremendous feeling you got, when younger, after seeing a movie that spoke to you so profoundly you were all hyped to make major changes to your life—travel the globe, join the air force, tell someone you were in love with him or her? That's the kind of action your own story must move you to take.

The only way a story can achieve that level of transformative power is when it supports an unassailable purpose. An example: From time to time, we have the opportunity to work with men and women from law enforcement—police, FBI, SWAT teams, elite anti-terrorist units, Navy SEALs. I'm always so impressed with—so moved by—their willingness to risk their very lives to do what they do. And why do they do it? How can they possibly do it? Well, if they're telling the truth, and I believe they are (at least by the end of the workshop), then they never do it for money (it's not exactly hedge-fund management anyway) or even power. Certainly they do it, in part, for the excitement and adventure. But primarily they do it to protect their families, their communities, their countries. This purpose is large enough, sustaining enough, that they can get up every morning, knowing it may be their last, knowing they may meet a violent death, knowing they may be crippled for life. The knowledge that they do it for their loved ones moves them to assume this extraordinary risk and responsibility.

If I asked you what your purpose was, how would you know if you had got it right? First and last, Does it move you? Really, *really* move you? Some purposes are so obviously faulty (*I train hard so I can have nice cars*) that the individual can smoke it out by himself or herself (perhaps with a little prodding). But other purposes sound very, very good, so neat, so on-message—and yet they're not quite *the* purpose. That's why finding one's true purpose is an exercise that requires real thoughtfulness and the courage to be honest with oneself. Lance Armstrong, seven-time Tour de France champion and cancer survivor, once said that if he had to choose between winning the tour and getting cancer, he would choose getting cancer. Why? Because cancer gave him true purpose. But hold on: Didn't wanting to be the best cyclist in the world *also* give him purpose, a purpose so powerful that it spurred him to train harder than anyone else every day for years and years? Yes—but not in the way cancer gave him purpose. The fruits of his cycling purpose (victory, glory, even deep fulfillment) can't stack up against the ones his cancer purpose gave him (survival; a commitment always to give every last bit of himself—physically, emotionally, mentally, spiritually; to inspire other cancer patients, especially children). In the hierarchy of purpose, it's no contest. Armstrong understood that; he knew that it was getting and overcoming cancer that made him the greatest cyclist ever, not being the greatest cyclist ever that helped him to overcome cancer. Not only was he the Tour's winningest champion but he was legendary for his awareness of the big picture of that grueling race—understanding precisely when to make his charge; knowing if and when to go for a stage win if it would further his ultimate goal of winning the Tour or sometimes *refraining* from going for a stage win if holding back on Tuesday furthered his ultimate goal of winning on that final Sunday. In short, he, as much as any athlete I have ever witnessed, understood that a story around competition will only have the right ending—victory—if the purpose is the *ultimate* one. If it could also work on one's tombstone. *He was a survivor. He gave every last bit of himself.* Those are words worth writing in stone, aren't they?

An ultimate purpose is never small. It is never minor. It can't be, by definition. It is grand, heroic, epic. You don't successfully walk a tightrope between buildings knowing that if you fall, this was the dumbest thing you have ever done. You should never put your life on the line for something not fully aligned with your Ultimate Mission.

Same goes for a company's purpose. To thrive in all the ways a company ideally should—profitability, sustainability, employee morale, superior standing in the eyes of the various communities it serves (end-users, vendors, investors)—requires a purpose that goes deep and wide, not simply a mandate to move as much product as possible and to keep costs down. In the same way that personal stories must move us if they are to work, so, too, a company's story must move people—management, employees, customers, investors. Its purpose might be, say, *We strive for everyone who walks through our doors to have the best possible Mexican food experience they've ever had*, or *Ours is truly the userfriendliest database management software around.* JetBlue and Ben & Jerry's, I have long thought, are especially obvious examples of companies (there are many others, of course) whose success is in no small part attributable to the way their storied purpose permeates the culture—their own and the ones they serve. By motivating its employees to reach for something higher, these companies appear to be doing something that transcends, respectively, mere air travel and mere ice cream. (And by "purpose" and "culture" I mean more than company slogan or mission statement. Many companies have nice slogans. That in no way guarantees that they also have an ultimate purpose, or that their workforce cares.)

Recently, I saw one of the most moving TV commercials I've ever seen, for Dow Chemical. I was so inspired by the arresting, beautiful images, music, and message that I immediately went to the company's website to learn more. What I found was a brilliant reformulation of organizational purpose. Their stated intent was to change the face of chemistry by adding the Human Element ("HU," as it's dubbed in the campaign) to the periodic table of elements. By doing so, the power of chemistry would be put to work to solve many of humanity's most pressing problems. Dow's new Ultimate Mission was to use the power of chemistry to make the world safer and cleaner, to put food on every table, to provide safe drinking water for every human being on the planet.

Now I realize what you may be thinking: Chemical company . . . isn't that synonymous with "polluter"? I realize that there's "spin" behind almost everything (more on that in Chapter 4) and that our visceral response to powerful images and evocative music can make us suspend our critical faculties. But in spite of my skepticism, I couldn't help thinking: Now *that's* a story with a great purpose (the first pillar of good storytelling), a purpose noble and aspirational enough that Dow's employees can't help finding renewed meaning and engagement in this corporate realignment.

For the story ultimately to succeed, though, it has to be true (the second pillar of good storytelling) and lead to real action (the third and final pillar), anchored in real accountability and verifiable commitments. The more I learned, the more impressed I became. Of course, their stated, noble purpose must come with measurable outcomes and objectives—like, say, the availability of safe drinking water for every man, woman, and child by 2010.

Situated somewhere between my skepticism and a deep wish to believe, I wondered what Dow's shareholders felt when they heard this message. Did they get goose bumps? Did they feel they were being spun? If I, an outsider, could become this moved by their story, what was its impact on insiders, the thousands of employees within the Dow organization?

Who knows if this spectacular purpose and promise will become Dow's legacy. Only time will tell. What it does help to show, though, is this: To have a magnificent story—be it a company's or an individual's—you must first have a magnificent purpose.

QUESTIONING THE PREMISE

Maybe you're thinking: *Hey, I may be tired and stressed out but I know what I live for. I may feel depleted and my life is chaotic but it's not as if I don't understand what keeps me going.*

Pardon my nerve, but I'm not sure that's as true as you may believe it is. In the next two chapters, as I discuss in detail the second rule of storytelling—truth—I hope to illuminate the amazing, scary extent to which we often *think* we know who we are and what story we're telling when in fact we're telling something very different.

To prepare for that discussion, here are two exercises. The first is to get you in the habit of extrapolating a real situation into an imagined one, which is exactly what you're doing when testing to see if your stated purpose holds up (*What will my epitaph be?*). The second exercise is to make you more conscious generally of how purpose—sometimes good, sometimes bad, sometimes honest, sometimes manipulative—may lurk in the shadows, yet its influence is atomic.

Exercise 1: Change a story in your mind and your emotional response changes immediately. Here are two examples.

You're driving behind an elderly lady. She's slow and indecisive. You're getting angrier by the second.

Now imagine—really imagine—that the elderly driver is your struggling mother. Or your grandmother.

How do you feel now?

Chances are your emotion has changed dramatically. Your brain chemistry has shifted; interestingly, your brain can't tell the difference between something that is actually happening and something that is vividly imagined.

The second example: You light up a cigarette, as you've done thousands of times. But as you strike the match this time, imagine the faces of your children and what they will go through if you die young. Train yourself to do this every time you light up, or are tempted to.

These are seemingly minor mental tricks I'm asking you to try. But they're important first steps to take in finding the larger purpose, the one you must have if you're to get your story straight. To discipline yourself to do that, as will be outlined in the next chapters, it helps to start small.

Exercise 2: To evaluate an action or event fairly, determining its factuality is not enough; you must try to divine its purpose, too. To keep ourselves from being seduced, we need to work at understanding the *why* behind the *what*.

In 2006, a large American metropolitan newspaper decides it's not going to report any good news out of Iraq. Its stories will highlight the deaths of American servicemen and women and Iraqis (sadly, there will be no shortage of material); the factionalization and anger and chaos over there; the staggering cost and costs of war. There will be no mention of schools being built, of tides turning, of general progress, if any, being made.

Okay, so maybe it's not quite hypothetical. Certainly media outlets make such "decisions" all the time, even as they believe they're providing a "true" picture of the world.

Now, as you read any one of several daily stories about Iraq in this newspaper, you should ask yourself two fundamental questions (at least). First: Is the story true? Are the details provided in the story true?

And, second: What is the newspaper's purpose in telling this particular story (and not, for instance, telling another Iraq-relevant story in its place)? Why did their editorial staff feel compelled to lead with this report?

To the first question, your answer appears to be: Yes, it is true. The facts are pretty much true as far as you can tell.

How about the second question? What was the newspaper's *purpose* in covering this aspect of the war? *They* might claim that their reporting is objective, and that, unfortunately, the events unfolding in Iraq are almost wholly negative. (How could any thinking, feeling person find otherwise?) They also may believe that their coverage is in the best interest of the public: Citizens need to know how badly the war is going. And anyway, if people object that the paper is not painting a full picture, they should realize that comprehensive coverage doesn't exist. There is no such beast. And any media outlet that claims its coverage is comprehensive is making a preposterous claim.

Now, if the paper's true purpose for covering the war as they do is to educate (and ultimately protect) the public, then their story is authentic, perhaps even noble, if arguably patronizing. On the other hand, if the real purpose for their overly negative coverage is to advance the newspaper's political agenda, or to create as much chaos and doubt as possible for the Administration or its political party, then the story becomes quite ignoble and inauthentic.

My place here is not to suggest that this hypothetical newspaper is right or wrong. I chose this example to show how *we need to train ourselves to build the muscle that enables us to examine the influences on us and our stories.* Only by doing this can we be sure, eventually, that the story we are living is ours and no one else's. Only by doing this can we be sure that the force driving our story—our purpose—is profound, sustainable, noble . . . and true. If you do nothing else that I suggest throughout this book but ask these two questions about events in your own life, then you will already have brought a level of consciousness and engagement to your life story that can have meaningful and positive effect:

1. *Is the story true?*
2. *Why is the story being told?*

Now let's turn these questions on ourselves and our own motives. Say you choose to reveal a true story to your wife knowing full well that it will be painful and disturbing. You tell her that last week you missed movie night with her because after another mind-numbingly busy workday you ended up having dinner with your secretary—a totally benign dinner—and neglected to mention it then. Or you tell her that your combined retirement account took a bad hit in the last six months, worse than you let on. When she asks why you chose to tell this story now, your reflex response is that it's something she needs to hear.

Is the story true? Well, yes. It actually happened. That's a fact.

Why is the story being told? Well, it turns out that you haven't been entirely honest with yourself: Upon more courageous reflection, you realize that your *real* purpose for telling the story now was to inflict pain; earlier in the day your wife did something that hurt you deeply and you were looking to retaliate.

When your real purpose is exposed and examined (*I need to hurt her back*), your choice to tell her the story at that moment is rather ignoble.

Exposing the *real* purpose in our storytelling may be embarrassing or indicting. It may bring shame or tears. But pushing yourself to uncover true purpose can and will pay extraordinary dividends.

Once, I was invited by a well-known though—at the time—struggling financial services firm to sit in on a half-day session in which senior management wanted to revise their mission statement, which they thought had grown stale and unpersuasive. Soon after they started tossing out smart, clever, even brilliant concepts to touch the heart, mind, and soul of customers new and old (and perhaps their own employees, too), it became clear to me that their intent was to come up with words solely for the purpose of driving investment. They wanted a better image, that's all. Several of those in the room had already been through our workshop, and had impressed me with their grasp of the need to put purpose at the center of one's story. But now, in this boardroom, over corporate fruit salad and finger sandwiches and bottled water, they spoke as if all they needed was to find the right words and massage them, and the firm would magically become inspirational, and once again very successful.

"We want to craft a story that says we can be trusted," said one of the executives. "That we care about our people."

I had to pipe up. "I think you're going about this backward. This is the reverse of what you should be thinking about here. First, you should ask yourself, 'Who do we ultimately want to be?' And, second, 'Who are we now?' *Then* you come up with a plan to bring the two together."

Things quickly deteriorated from there. Even as a few people in the room claimed to agree with me, my contribution as a consultant to them was pretty much worthless. As one of them said, making no attempt to conceal his patronizing tone, "There's a reality out there, Jim. I don't know that this is the time to be worrying about who we want to be deep down."

LINING UP

Although Ultimate Mission is synonymous with "purpose," it is also close to synonymous with "theme," a word with which every accomplished storyteller is familiar. Every story has a theme, usually a very simple one. You should be able to identify it, though often you may have to think about it a bit, to make sure that you have sorted out the overall theme of the story from other, less profound themes. In every great story, the overall theme is reiterated in almost every scene, in ways we usually process not intellectually but very much instinctually. Thus each scene is, thematically, a microcosm of the whole story. For example, if the overall theme of *The Wizard of Oz* is "there's no place like home," then each scene—Dorothy running away from Miss Gulch, the witch of a neighbor who wants to put Toto to sleep; Dorothy with her friends in the dark, ominous forest; even Dorothy being dazzled by the eye candy of the new world she's fallen into, the place that suggests to her "we're not in Kansas anymore"—is also about that very same idea: There's no place like home. If the overall theme of *The Godfather* and *The Godfather Part II* is that you can never escape your past (interestingly, a variation on "There's no place like home")—despite Michael Corleone's continual, deluded belief that the family business will soon become "legitimate"—then almost every scene reiterates this idea: the moral compromise young Vito Corleone makes in the New World to become "godfather," a position not unlike that held by the man who killed his family back in the Old Country; his hot-headed son's falling into a trap and being gunned down at the toll plaza; his youngest son and heir apparent, the cold-blooded Michael, eliminating all his enemies on the very day he stands before God to become his nephew's godfather. In many ways, it is this echoing or "alignment" between the overarching theme of a great story and all the scenes, characters, and moments that make up that story—be it *Madame Bovary* or *High Noon* or *Moby-Dick* or the Harry Potter books or the New Testament or countless others—that makes these stories stay with us forever. Great stories are never made up of far-flung elements. They are never about petty concerns. They are always tight, streamlined, deceptively simple. Indeed, they are *unified*.

Unity—alignment—are hallmarks of persuasive stories. A good story is consistent. It has an internal logic. Every thought you share, every word you utter, every expression you make can't help revealing some aspect of your unique story.

As with great stories, the theme (Ultimate Mission) of your life story is simple—touching on ideas like family, honor, benevolence, continuity—and each subplot reiterates the theme. Without this echoing or alignment, your mission is going to fall apart somewhere. For example, if you wish to be an extraordinary father and husband, then that entails a certain level of moral integrity; you can't at the same time be a businessperson of dubious integrity, because that runs counter to who you profess to want to be as a father and husband. There's serious misalignment in your Ultimate Mission. Or if one of the goals in your Ultimate Mission is to "empower as many people as I can over the longest time possible" (as one client wrote)—yet you are yourself closed to new learning, incapable of improving and further empowering yourself—then there is something askew in your Ultimate Mission. Or if one of your ultimate goals is to be a person who treats people with compassion and dignity—true enough of the way you treat your superiors and colleagues, say, but only intermittently true of the way you treat those beneath you on the corporate ladder—then there's misalignment. Without alignment, you can't achieve what you set down in your Ultimate Mission. This is true in other aspects of life, too. Athletes must have every part of their body moving in alignment or they will not achieve their ultimate potential. Every great tennis player must move his or her feet in a certain way, must turn the body, must get the racket back, must see the ball early, must weight and unweight in a certain way, must follow through, if he or she is to be great.

Your story can't work without all the important elements being aligned. It's no accident, I think, that a colloquial way to describe being aligned with someone is to be "on the same page." If Francis Ford Coppola and Mario Puzo, co-authors of *The Godfather* movies, had added a scene or two showing Michael Corleone genuinely feeling as if he had been absolved of all his sins by God, his family, and the "legitimate" outside community, even as he continued to preside over his crime operation, the story would fall apart; such a scene, in being at complete odds with the overall theme of the story, would make a mockery of it. We would not be drawn nearly as much to watch these movies and revel in their human truths, because now they would strike us as false. Simply put, the story would not work.

If your Ultimate Mission is to inspire you—truly inspire you, the way a great, consistent, seamless story moves and inspires you—then everything in it needs to be aligned. The values it professes need to dovetail with each part of your mission. If something in your life is not aligned with your Ultimate Mission—some behavior, some habit, some relationship—then you need to examine it and change it or eliminate it until things *are* aligned.

FLAWED ALIGNMENT → FLAWED ENDING

"Senseless" is the word we usually trot out when we speak of someone dying young and without apparent "purpose"—a bizarre accident, being at the absolute wrong place at the wrong time. *She died senselessly. He died a senseless death.* But "senseless" applies to more than just death. It can be applied, though it far more rarely is, to nearly everything that matters. A divorce may be senseless. Or the loss of a business or job. Or the loss of a friendship. "Senseless" simply means: *The rotten ending to this story could absolutely have been averted.* It just didn't have to happen. You may come to believe it was unavoidable: *It was meant to be . . . God has a plan . . . I couldn't help myself . . . There was a combination of factors . . . Circumstances dictated . . .* But that's just after-the-fact spin, somewhere between an excuse and an apology to yourself. It's comforting. But when you confront the painful truth, was the personal bankruptcy really fate? Or was it set in motion by the hundreds of misguided decisions you made, supported by dozens of misguided stories?

If you lose your marriage because of an affair; if you lose your family because of your obsession with money and power; if you lose your self-respect because you cooked the books to avoid a shareholder crisis, would you not consider these developments senseless? Are the endings of these stories okay? We far too often fail to finish the story in our minds, probably out of fear or complacency. But our failure to think through the reasonable conclusion to our stories is perilous. (Another reason to envision your own funeral and what might be said about you, or go unsaid.) If only we had done so, we might have recognized how our purpose and our actions were horribly misaligned, preventing us from getting what we wanted from life while also undermining so many of the good things we already have. "To find integrity in life," writes Dan McAdams in *The Stories We Live By*, "you must look back upon your personal myth and determine that, for all its shortcomings and limitations, it is good." Only one problem with that: Many of us fear that what we will find there will *not* be good . . . so we ignore it.

And by ignoring, we pretty much guarantee "senseless" conclusions to many of the subplots in our life.

We've talked about how a faulty purpose always leads to a bad ending. But you may have a good purpose—like those admirable, heartfelt purposes so many of the executives fill out on the questionnaires, about how they live for their family, how they want their legacy to be something that others can benefit from—and yet suffer from a monstrous misalignment between your purpose and your day-to-day actions. It is imperative to consider whether your actions and purpose are aligned; "Suit the action to the word, the word to the action," Shakespeare wrote in *Hamlet*. It is a fact, I'm sorry to say, that the ramifications of such misalignment will make their appearance—divorce, heart attack, estrangement, shame, maybe prison. Perhaps they're dormant now, or in shadow, but they will emerge at some point—a year, ten years, who knows. Bookies don't take bets on such certainties. Without examining and resolving this misalignment, no hiding, no pretending, no denial, no wishful thinking on your part can derail these unfortunate happenings from finally paying a visit, like the ghosts in Dickens's *A Christmas Carol*. If you consider yourself a moral person and yet your willingness to compromise is only growing fuzzier, what do you think the ending of that story will be? Is it one you want for yourself or those you care most about? If you continue not to work out and to eat and sleep terribly, can you not make a reasonable guess about what the ending will be? Is that an ending you can live with?

After working with us, one Fortune 100 CEO, one of the most high-profile executives in America, helped to reshape his company's culture so that its commitment to workers and its way of operating were finally more aligned with their stated values . . . then realized he himself couldn't fulfill the ultimate mission he'd set for his family and community, while also carrying the intense work, responsibility, and travel load that his job required. What did he do? Resign.

Look, work is necessary, and work can be vital, and work can be glorious. But one must beware, like the CEO just mentioned, when work is harming one's most important life stories more than helping them. A December 2006 article in the *Harvard Business Review* titled "Extreme Jobs: The Dangerous Allure of the 70-Hour Work Week," listed characteristics of "extreme jobs" (referred to in the story as "the American Dream on steroids"):

- unpredictable flow of work
- fast-paced work under tight deadlines
- inordinate scope of responsibility
- work-related events outside regular hours
- availability to clients 24/7
- great amount of travel
- physical presence at the workplace at least ten hours a day

Research showed that extreme jobholders, rather than feeling burned out and bitter about their work, reported that they loved their jobs (66%) and felt exalted, not exploited, by the extreme pressures. When asked why they loved their jobs, the most frequent response (90% of men, 82% of women) was that they found the work stimulating and challenging and that it gave them an adrenaline rush.

When queried about the fallout from their intense jobs, however, significant numbers agreed that their work clearly interfered with important dimensions of their lives. Sixty-six percent of men and 77% of women reported that their job interfered with their ability to maintain a home; 65% of men and 33% of women felt their job hindered their relationship with their children; 46% each of men and women said their job harmed their ability to have a strong relationship with a spouse or partner. When these men and women were asked whether, as a consequence of their extreme jobs, their children experienced problems with watching too much TV, with discipline, with bad eating habits or with underachieving at school, a significant number of respondents said yes. I find this study, and these extreme jobholders, fascinating; just as fascinating, I'm sure, would be an exploration of the stories these women and men tell themselves every day to justify the deep misalignment that exists between their work and their personal lives.

Without courageously confronting whether your purpose and your actions are aligned (are truthful and mutually supportive) in every aspect of your life, in every mini-story—your story around your marriage, around your friends, around your job, around your health, etc.—you risk flawed, senseless endings to every one of them.

Three

HOW FAITHFUL A NARRATOR ARE YOU?

When we experience the world *directly*, our conclusions have immediate credibility. That's not to say that our interpretations are free of distortion and inaccuracy; we are, after all, spectacularly subjective creatures. But we trust that personally experiencing a situation yields a certain baseline of accuracy and insight.

Because of our unique capacity for language, however, human beings needn't experience something directly to understand it, partially or sometimes even fully. Unlike other living creatures, which learn solely from their own experiences, man learns both from his own experience as well as—through storytelling—the experiences of others. Someone tells us a story and we are touched, we sympathize, we empathize, we are outraged, we understand. We come to conclusions.

And that's also where we get into problems.

FAULTY ASSUMPTIONS

Your story is made up of elements of which you had no direct experience; it's partly built, if you will, with bricks that aren't your own: You didn't buy them, you don't know where they came from, you don't know what's inside them. That is, *much of the material of your life story is based on assumptions*—in short, on information whose factuality and/or truth you cannot, to an extent, verify.

We all make assumptions. We have to or be paralyzed by our lack of certainty. David Hume, the Scottish philosopher known for his skepticism and utilitarianism, once famously asked, "How do we know that the sun will rise in the East tomorrow?" In the end, he said, it is unprovable, yet the sun has risen every morning so far, so it's reasonable to assume that it will rise again tomorrow. To live without that assumption, and ten thousand others, would be madness, not to mention unsettling and utterly exhausting.

Even when we know we make assumptions, we continue to do so, unconsciously. Our brain does it for us. For example, read the following paragraph (much traveled around the Internet and used occasionally in schools):

> i cdnuolt blveiee taht I cluod aulaclty uesdnatnrd waht I was rdanieg. Bsceuae of the phaonmneal pweor of the hmuan mnid, aoccdrnig to a rscheearch at Cmabrigde Uinervtisy, it dseno't mtaetr in waht oerdr the ltteres in a wrod are, the olny iproamtnt tihng is taht the frsit and lsat ltteer be in the rghit pclae. The rset can be a taotl mses and you can sitll raed it whotuit a pboerlm. Tihs is bcuseae the huamn mind deos not raed ervey lteter by istlef, but the wrod as a wlohe. Azanmig, huh? And I awlyas tghuhot slpeling was ipmorantt!

Maybe it's going overboard to say we're assumption-making machines, as if that's all we do, but we're pretty darn good at it. Some of our assumptions are shaped by narrative templates we've grown up with. For example, we'll take selected facts from our lives and assume we're inevitably living one or another kind of classic story. "While each life story is unique, many people stick to culturally sanctioned scripts," writes *Psychology Today*'s Carlin Flora, who notes that Dan McAdams, author of *The Stories We Live By,* has identified how "Americans, especially successful ones, often spin tales of redemption." Alternatively, Americans often imagine themselves victims living the "contamination narrative": Once everything was perfect, then something happened—divorce, accident, death—and things were never the same. A small but vocal subset of people spin assumptions wildly to create conspiracy theories—e.g., the U.S. government detonated the Twin Towers from within, there was no Holocaust, men never landed on the moon, etc.—and then seek out and manipulate facts to support their view. A larger subset among us will spin assumptions to create conspiracy theories on a more personal level—My boss is out to get me, everyone's out to get me, all men are untrustworthy—and then seek out allegedly incontrovertible facts to support their view. While there are numerous reasons why such fantasies develop, one of the most basic is that they deflect the storyteller and his audience from a more troubling truth. The entertaining, if fanciful, story meets a need, plain and simple, and its falsity becomes almost an afterthought. Such is the potential danger of crafting stories before having all the facts, and without making an honest attempt to assess them somewhat dispassionately. "A man hears what he wants to hear and disregards the rest," wrote Paul Simon in his song "The Boxer."

Some of our assumptions, maybe most of them, turn out to be right. Christmas Day comes along and your sister doesn't show up for the traditional family meal, leaving only a voicemail message that she's staying away because she's come down with a head cold. But you make the assumption that Sis doesn't have a cold at all, but just needed a socially acceptable excuse; after all, she finds a way to miss virtually every family get-together because she's unmarried and hates the looks and questions she gets from everyone, almost all of whom show up with a partner, often with kids. Probably your assumption is right.

Some of the false assumptions we make are of the innocuous, "no harm, no foul" variety. For example, you always think, *We're leaving too late for the movie so we'll get terrible seats,* and only some of the time is that true. Some false assumptions (as mentioned above) are less innocuous. For example, after leaving several phone messages for an important client, you still haven't gotten a return call, so you assume they've taken their business elsewhere, and so your weekend plans with your family are ruined . . . only you find out the following Tuesday that the client had been on vacation for two weeks and was unable to return any calls. Or this: Because of your personal friendship with a client, you assume he'll never take his lucrative business to someone else . . . yet he does precisely that because your assumption made you complacent.

When we make faulty assumptions about major issues, it can have devastating effects on our lives. When our clients start unearthing their old stories, a Pandora's box of faulty assumptions spills forth—about work, family, health, happiness. A sampling from executives who have attended the program:

Faulty assumptions about work:

- Most of my problems in life stem directly from my demanding job. Without all the stress of my job, I'd be a more responsible and engaged father and husband.
- The only way I can meet the demands of my job is to work longer and harder.
- I'll lose my job if I don't keep my cell phone on and constantly check my e-mails at home.
- My job controls me—not the opposite. I'm not the boss!
- Investing the lion's share of my energy at work and not at home will be worth it in the long run. I'm doing it all for my family.
- My job is who I am. Without my job and my money I'm a nobody.
- My drive for fame, power, and wealth is what gets me out of bed in the morning. Nothing else will.
- If I get the promotion and salary increase, I'll be happier and feel better about myself.

Faulty assumptions about family, marriage, and relationships:

- My family understands that the reason I work so hard is because of them. Everything I do is for them.
- It's okay with my family when I come home from work exhausted and disengaged. They appreciate all that I do for them at work.
- Once I make partner I'll have a better chance of finding a mate.
- I bring home the money and my spouse raises the kids. That's how it has to be right now.
- We simply couldn't survive on any less money. That's why I feel like a slave to my current job.
- My father was pretty rough on me and I came out okay. I rarely saw him. What was good enough for me should be good enough for my kids. I actually spend more time with my family than my father ever did.
- Thank God I don't have the responsibility of a family or a serious relationship. I'm pretty one-dimensional, which gives me a competitive advantage, allowing me to achieve my goals and

reach happiness a lot quicker, because I can devote everything to being the best at work.

- It's predictable that my family is always on my case because I spend so little time at home. That's just the way it has to be for now.

Faulty assumptions about health:

- Heart attacks happen to lots of people who eat the way I do, never exercise, and are overweight. But it won't happen to me.
- I feel good so my health must be okay.
- I'm still young so I can get away with doing things that are bad for my health. Someday I'm going to have to significantly change or face the consequences. I've still got time.
- I have no time or energy to exercise.
- Taking care of myself is a luxury I can't afford right now.
- I devote what little time and energy I have to the areas of my life that matter most—my family and my job.
- Working out is selfish.
- Choosing not to exercise demonstrates my love and devotion to my family.
- Taking care of my body is personal and has nothing to do with my responsibilities as an employee.
- Healthwise, if I do everything else right, I can still smoke and get away with it.
- We're all going to die of something someday. If I die a little earlier because I have a steak four nights a week with a half bottle of wine, it will be worth it.

Faulty assumptions about happiness:

- I will never find real happiness in my lifetime. I just know it.
- I can't be happy and be under so much constant stress. Happiness is freedom from stress.
- No one in my situation could find happiness.
- My happiness will come when I achieve financial freedom. I know it sounds ridiculous but, for me, it's absolutely true.
- I sacrifice my happiness for my family.
- Success and happiness go hand in hand.

Exercise: Identify three possible faulty assumptions you're probably making right now in each of these four main areas of your life.

Work (for example, I'll lose my job if I take time to exercise during the workday or leave early to see my child in a school play.)

1. _____

2. _____

3. _____

Family (for example, Though I'm completely disengaged when I return home from work, my family knows I love them.)

1. _____

2. _____

3. _____

Health (for example, Taking care of myself is a luxury I can't afford right now.)

1. _____

2. _____

3. _____

Happiness (for example, My happiness will improve when all this financial pressure is off my back.)

1. _____

2. _____

3. _____

All assumptions have consequences in our storytelling. Faulty assumptions always lead to faulty, dysfunctional stories. If we're to get our stories right, then we must acknowledge that much of the material we base our lives on is assumptions. Then we must verify the truth or falsehood of those assumptions.

Some faulty assumptions are easy to identify and easy to change. Incorrect assumptions like *I do not have spinach between my teeth* or *My face is not bleeding from shaving this morning* or *I have enough money in my checking account to cover this month's car payment* will soon enough be identified, at least, and probably remedied quickly, too. But some assumptions like *No one in my situation could find happiness* can be devilishly difficult to verify. It may have an almost timeless ring of truth to it.

So where did these faulty assumptions come from and how do we know for sure that they're faulty? It can be extraordinarily difficult to trace the origin of our beliefs about the world, and coming to terms with the truth of our assumptions is a lifelong, never-ending pursuit. After all, haven't we been telling ourselves a story for a very long time?

"BECAUSE I CAN" SYNDROME

Why do you check e-mails at home, smoke, not exercise, and talk on the cell phone during dinner? Because you can! No one tells you you can't. Or, if they do, then they don't really back it up with the hammer of immediate, obvious, dire consequences. No one has laid out for you a really, *really* convincing argument for why you must stop smoking *right now*, or why you should get up at five in the morning to exercise. In fact, according to your story, talking on a cell phone during dinner is *more* than okay—it's actually *normal*, it's necessary for you to do your job, it's productive, and it's not even *that* invasive. After all, you're physically sitting there with your family, aren't you?

For those who suffer from "Because I Can" syndrome, here's how some of you think about smoking: *Smoking is my choice, my right, and no one is going to take that away from me.* (You must be right. After all, nobody really *does* challenge you.)

Your thinking about sleep vs. exercise: *I need sleep more than I need to exercise. Exercise is a luxury, sleep a necessity.* (How can this be wrong? Wouldn't someone point it out if there was an ounce of faulty logic to this thinking?)

Your thinking about working late: *Everyone in my department works late, typically misses family dinners, and brings work home. This is just the way it has to be to keep our jobs and drive success.*

Nobody questions your conclusions. On this last point, your boss *clearly* won't be disabusing you of any faulty assumptions. Instead, he or she will just continue to churn out the directives: *Schedule a department meeting on Thursday . . . Complete the customer service report by the 10th . . . Fly to New Jersey and meet the client face to face . . . Poll all the department heads and summarize their feelings about the loss of the client; I want to know who is spreading all the doom and gloom around here.*

What if, instead, your boss churned out directives like these? *Exercise at least thirty minutes before leaving work today . . . I want you eating healthy lunches and never going longer than four hours without food while at the office . . . I want you home with your family for dinner at least three times every week . . . I want cell phones off during dinner with your family and no job-related work until your children have gone to bed . . . I want you in bed, lights out, by 11:30 at the latest, Monday through Thursday . . . Oh, yeah, and kill the smoking before it kills you!*

Suppose your boss *did* say such things? You'd probably conclude that he'd lost his mind or that she's somehow screwing with your head and playing power games, or that he or she has no right delving into your personal life.

The truth is, no outside force really holds others accountable for the way they live their private lives (with the exception of parents of young children). So it's easy to have all kinds of rotten assumptions and lousy habits that support misguided stories, *because we can.*

So many clients we encounter refuse (at least at first) to open their eyes, largely because they suspect what they would see if they did. They're brilliant at business—truth seekers, impossible to hoodwink, cutting through what's unimportant, spotting trends as they're happening, identifying problems, figuring out solutions—yet they're fantastically unaccountable for the stories they tell in their personal lives. And why not? No one calls them out for their lousy stories. So rather than get tough on themselves—the one real solution—they keep their eyes closed. *Hey, it's personal. I don't need anyone infantilizing me by telling me something as obvious as "Eat a solid breakfast before you get to the office." That's just insulting.*

The brutal, undeniable power of actual documentation is one

effective way of pointing out just how far "Because I Can" syndrome has taken you. For example, you stay late at the office because you can, but do you realize just how late you typically stay? And how consistently? One client, head of brand management for a national supermarket chain, said she had no idea she was abusing her "freedom" to stay late until (as we'd suggested) she began each night to log the time she walked out the door. "It was shocking," she said. "Until I had three weeks' worth of actual data, I didn't realize just how bad it was. Eight-thirty, nine, nine-thirty at least four nights a week. There was no good reason for me to stay that late *every* night." She routinely got home long after her young child was asleep (and she herself was exhausted, and her husband angry), but she rationalized it because she got to spend time with her son early in the morning. "If I hadn't logged what I was doing, to this day I still wouldn't have realized that almost every week I could get home several times to see my son before he's down for the night, and play with him, and that I can spend a whole, relaxing evening or three with my husband. I'd still be staying late."

To keep herself from slipping, she still logs her departure time every night. "My staff will say, 'I know you're about to leave,' because they see me take out my little book."

> **Exercise:** Parts of your story get perpetuated simply because they have no immediate consequences, because you don't have to justify them, because no one calls you on it, *because you can*. See if that's still true after you call yourself on it.
>
> Keep a daily log of five things you suspect you do because you can get away with it. So, for example, log every time you turn on and turn off the TV (calculate the hours it's on), or the frequency with which you check e-mail or go online, or go to the bathroom, or drink soda, or yell at someone (and apologize). You may be surprised by what the results look like, in black and white:
>
> 1. _____
>
> 2. _____
>
> 3. _____

4. _____

5. _____

COOKING THE BOOKS

There have been more wise, oft-repeated things said on the subject of perception than about perhaps almost any other subject (or maybe it just seems that way). *Beauty is in the eye of the beholder. Don't make a mountain out of a molehill. The grass is always greener on the other side of the fence. Don't judge a book by its cover.* There are countless more. But perhaps the best, most elegant, line of all is a little-known kernel by British philosopher Erich Heller, who observed, "Be careful how you interpret the world; it is like that."

We live as if our perception is not merely our current reality but everyone's reality, now and always. Thus, it is difficult to separate out the false assumptions that pepper our story and in many ways define it. If we don't exhibit the courage to look at things somewhat coldly and carefully, then our somewhat (or largely) false story becomes *the* story. It's not hard to keep to it because it's actually *somewhat close* to the truth, a version of the truth—it's got "truthiness," as comedian–fake newsman Stephen Colbert dubs it. Yet as we tell it—innocently enough, without seeming malice—our story may be as untrue (if not quite illegal) as the phony financial story a devious accountant or CFO "writes" when he "cooks the books."

Take this story, for example.

With two young children and a job that has no boundaries, I simply have no time whatsoever for community work. To be honest, I rarely even think about it. There's no possibility for it to happen in my life so I block it out of my mind completely. When I force myself to think about it, I get increasingly upset that I'm not giving back beyond the reach of my immediate family, but I have no choice. Giving back is an important part of who I want to be and the legacy I want to leave behind but it just can't happen at this time in my life.

Is this true? Yes, the marketing executive who wrote this has two children and a demanding job; I know these to be facts. But what about the assertion that her "job . . . has no boundaries"? Is that true or simply the way she chooses to think about it? Is it true that she "simply [has] no time whatsoever for community work"? Or is that, too, just how she's come to think about it? So many people we see at HPI are conflicted on the subject of community service. She's like most of them: They place an extremely high value on charitable service but spend virtually no time on it. Yet 10% to 15% of them, with jobs just as demanding and families just as big as hers, report that they *have* found time for it. With similar time constraints, they have somehow found ways to align their lives with this cherished value. How can this be?

Even if she was not aware of the litany of ancillary benefits associated with volunteer work and community service—improved life satisfaction, higher self-esteem, social integration, distraction from one's own troubles, longer life—she is acutely aware of her personal value system and, at least dimly, of her Ultimate Mission in life. Community service is integral to both of those. How, then, could there be such a discrepancy between what she says is important to her and how she actually lives her life? Is it really just a matter of hours in the day? Is it really just this finite period of young motherhood she's currently in the midst of? Is community service really something that can, or should, be put off to some indeterminate time in the future?

As we examine her story, its dysfunctionality, at least as it relates to community service, is traceable to the faulty assumptions she has made about her job's boundaries and about time. Once these assumptions embed themselves into her story, her "book is cooked" on doing *any* community service, now or in the foreseeable future. As long as she persists with these assumptions, then this reality, this supposed truth, will rule. There isn't a glimmer of hope that she can do anything to change her current situation. With the story she's got, I can guarantee that she will never get to community service.

THE FOUR SCENARIOS

On the Storytelling Inventory our clients fill out, we ask a number of questions to get them to portray their life in story terms: *Describe the theme of your life story; Describe your character role in it; Describe the tone of it; Describe the trajectory.* For example, one question asks:

Which is your story? *

a. A good past has led to a good present.
b. A good past has led to a bad present.
c. A bad past has led to a good present.
d. A bad past has led to a bad present.

While it may, at first, seem artificial or simplistic to ask people to reduce their entire, quite complicated, endlessly nuanced history to one of four rather blunt scenarios (elsewhere we ask—to give another example—"Is your life story a Comedy? A Romance? A Tragedy? A Fable?"), we treat it as a first step. It gets one thinking. It enables the respondent to see structure where perhaps he or she didn't before; to recognize that there is an end toward which every life, like every story, is driving. And because one's life is so obviously more complicated than broad descriptions like "good" and "bad" (and "past" and "present," for that matter) can ever portray, simple questions like these tend to promote elaboration.

Here, for example, is the more elaborated account of a respondent, an accomplished professional musician, who circled (c) A bad past has led to a good present. (For the record, 43% circle (a); 15%, (b); 22%, (c); and 20%, (d).)

The truth is I came from a home that was cold and loveless, with parents who were either never around or incapable of expressing affection for my siblings and me. As an adult, the home I've made is full of love, with a great husband and two great girls. But I have started to realize just how much I have immersed myself in my work, telling myself the whole time that creative achievement and professional advancement are incredibly important to my sense of well-being. Meanwhile, I've become less and less available to my family—and yet it is the love of my new family that I've always wanted, more important to me by far than career advancement. The truth is, if I keep on this path, I may lose it all, when it was right there in front of me.

* This formulation is the brainchild of Agnes Hankiss, who first used it in her 1981 article, "Ontologies of the Self: On the Mythical Rearranging of One's Life History."

Perhaps there's something presumptuous about asking questions like the multiple-choice one earlier, and making respondents commit to the "best possible answer" to describe their incredible stories. But another useful reason to paint it, initially, in such broad terms is that people are pretty adept at describing the *mood* of their failing story. Only then can they start to pick apart the potentially false, toxic details that have made it so.

Which are you? a, b, c, or d?

PESSIMISTS, WATCH OUT

Whether we're by nature the Little Engine That Could or Eeyore, most of us would accept that positive thinking tends to be more beneficial for us than negative thinking. This proposition is not just something grasped intuitively or suggested anecdotally; repeated scientific studies back it up. Hope-filled individuals tend to heal faster, from both psychological wounds and actual physical ones, than do their dread-filled counterparts; optimists are more likely to persist in the pursuit of their dreams and desires; they're more likely than depressives to make those around them feel energetic. A story can only work if its Ultimate Mission is positive; it won't work if its main goal is merely the avoidance of risk and pain. Even if we're wired to be pessimists, there's something about the glass-half-filled camp that appeals irresistibly. "Some men see things as they are and ask 'Why?'" Robert Kennedy famously said. "I dream things that never were and ask, 'Why not?'" If the choice were ours (is it?), who wouldn't prefer to be blessed with the latter mindset?

As I said earlier, more important than the "facts" of any life story is the meaning we attribute to the facts. It's crucial, therefore, to be aware not only of external influences on our perception—the inherent biases in information sources such as one's parents, teachers, newspapers, TV news channels, or websites of choice—but also our *internal* tendencies. Our basic natures have an enormous effect on how we see things. If you're inclined toward pessimism, perhaps no otherwise rational analysis of your situation or story will make things seem attainable or fixable. (*No one in my family has escaped addictive behavior, so what makes me any different?*) Or perhaps this negative tendency, while not based in "reality," is a valuable, if distorting, survival technique. For instance, worriers have no more control over events than non-worriers do, yet, as studies show, most of the perceived benefits of worry center around people's belief that worry helps avoid catastrophe and deeper emotional topics that they don't want to think about. Anyone counseling a worrier to stop worrying is pretty much wasting his or her breath: The benefit of worry "may also be reinforced superstitiously because the vast majority of things people worry about never happen," say psychologists Susan Mineka and Richard Zinbarg of Northwestern University, who studied the roots of anxiety and phobias. In other words: I envisioned the plane crashing; it didn't crash; therefore, every time I'm haunted by the specter of a crash, I'll make myself sick by envisioning it again and perhaps duplicate the desired result. By this circular "reasoning," worry becomes "self-sustaining" and thus "notoriously resistant to extinction."

I'm not here to advocate for blind optimism, which, in its own way, can be as indefensible and misguided as blatant pessimism, often leading to tragic outcomes (wait one more paragraph). But those naturally given to feeling off balance by the unpredictable, stressful nature of their life may suffer from something called General Anxiety Disorder, a malady whose central characteristic—worry about possible bad outcomes or dangerous events—"seems to serve as a cognitive avoidance response that is reinforced because it suppresses emotional and physiological responding." That is, once people develop compulsive rituals to neutralize or prevent obsessive thoughts, they have made it that much harder for themselves to confront the truth of their story and thus to move to greater fulfillment. Such people must find a way to move from what renowned psychologist Martin Seligman termed "learned helplessness" toward "learned optimism"—a state not to be confused with (to use Alan Greenspan's memorable phrase) "irrational exuberance," but, rather, one that is both forward looking *and* reality based.

OPTIMISTS SHOULD WATCH OUT, TOO

A human being simply cannot run the mile in under four minutes. Can't be done; physiologically impossible.

So said many "experts" in the months and years leading up to May 6, 1954, the day Roger Bannister covered 5,280 feet in 3:59:4.

By the end of 1957, sixteen other runners had also broken the golden barrier.

Hail the power of positive thinking.

The majority of studies about medical placebos support the power of positive thinking. Time and again, my own professional experience has shown me just how profound an influence positive thinking can have. One particularly memorable example from my own history: After world sprint champion speedskater and overwhelming Olympic favorite Dan Jansen suffered humiliating defeats at the Calgary and Albertville Games in 1988 and 1992, he was in jeopardy of securing a place as one of the greatest chokers in modern sports history. While training for his last-ever Olympics, he came to see me. We agreed (though not without some back and forth) that his training so hard for the 500 meters, his best event, and not fully embracing the 1,000, the other distance he would compete in at the 1994 Games in Lillehammer, Norway, would make the pressure in the shorter race almost unbearably high pitched. Since this would be Dan's final Olympics, with his ultimate legacy as a competitor on the line, sustaining maximum performance during the race would be the greatest challenge (as it always is, of course, only here it seemed even more pronounced). At first, Dan didn't buy the idea (negative assumption) that he could ever be as great at the 1,000 as he'd been at the 500. In the latter, after all, he was the only human ever to skate the distance in under thirty-six seconds, and he'd done so four times; in the 1,000, meanwhile, there were several skaters faster than he. But he was so supremely talented and strong, there was no reason that, with proper training, he couldn't dominate any of several distances if only he could change the story he told himself. We worked together for two years while he not only trained under his coach with phenomenal dedication at both distances but also worked at truly believing in his new 1,000-meter story. Finally he felt that this, too, was a race he was born to skate and win. In his final Olympic go-round, Dan, still world 500-meter champ, skated in his beloved event . . . and again came up short, finishing a pedestrian, almost unthinkable eighth place. His reputation as a choker almost assured, he had one last race in which to rewrite his Olympic story—

and it was the 1,000, a distance he had for so long not fully accepted as his, but around which he had now told himself a great new story.

Dan won the gold.

The medal and the moment that had eluded him for years were his, and he captured them by skating the fastest 1,000 meters of his life—or anyone's, for that matter. He broke the world record.

I'm sure you can think of dozens of examples from life—those around you and, one hopes, your own—in which optimism and belief (positive assumption) led to the achievement of great things.

There are two popular definitions of optimism. One, identified by psychologists Michael Scheier and Charles Carver as "dispositional optimism," is "a global expectation that good things will be plentiful in the future and bad things scarce." In this definition, optimism is largely objective, the inescapable response to a world of bounty and virtuous elements.

The second definition, largely subjective, is that optimism represents a constructive way to partly neutralize bad events. For now, I am more interested in the latter definition because a natural tendency toward optimism can be a surprisingly destructive force, once it strays far enough from reality.

A 1987 study by Neil Weinstein showed that people consistently underestimated their risks in eating bad foods, not exercising, and following generally poor health habits. The story they told themselves was that others behaving in such a way were likely to suffer serious health consequences but that they themselves would not. *I won't have a heart attack from smoking but lots of other people will . . . I won't have an accident so I don't need to wear a seat belt.* Such a worldview becomes a license to do anything and to do nothing, without regard for consequence. While paralyzing worry may be rooted in superstition, behaving in ways that you believe are consequence-free is rooted in delusion.

Of course, such "irrational exuberance" (the phrase seems appropriate now) may quickly extend to areas beyond health, into other meaningful aspects of one's life. *My wife will never leave me no matter what I do . . . No matter how much I work, I will never become estranged from my kids . . . Even though my debt has built considerably every year for the last several years, I do not have to change my lifestyle patterns . . .*

Another study also corroborates the danger that a positive,

forward-looking temperament, an outlook we otherwise tend to admire, can undermine reality. When there's too much negativity, the environment becomes toxic, granted, but when there's too much positive feedback, the environment departs from reality. Several researchers have concluded that "bad is stronger than good"—meaning that positive experiences may need to outnumber negative experiences if human relationships, including business relationships, are going to flourish—but only up to a point. Dr. John Gottman, one of the leading voices on why marriages succeed and fail, conducted two decades of observational research on marriage and determined that unless a couple is able to maintain a ratio of at least five positive messages (praise, encouragement, affection) to one negative message (complaint, critique), it is highly likely that their marriage will fail. (Very little that comes out of our mouths can be called neutral: Almost every utterance has either a positive or negative aspect in content, tone, or suggestion. If you merely say it's sunny outside, it likely registers as a positive message—or negative, if you're in the middle of a drought; if you're looking for a good deal on a used car and simply read aloud a newspaper ad about a cheap car, it registers as positive, whereas if you read aloud an ad about an overpriced vehicle, it's negative.)

But that's not the entire story. Not only does excessive negativity (a ratio under 5:1) threaten to undermine the marriage, excessive positivity does, too. Disintegration of the relationship also begins to occur when a positive to negative remark ratio exceeds 11:1.

Barbara Fredrickson from the University of North Carolina and Marcial Losada from Catholic University of Brazil, studying the dynamics of business relationships, concluded that business teams flourish with positivity ratios above 2.9 and begin to disintegrate at positivity ratios above 11.6.

Such findings corroborate what I had already gathered from my early experience in coaching tennis. When working on stroke technique with young tennis players, I largely eschewed offering positive feedback and went right for what was wrong. I assumed that was what good coaches did, and the most efficient way for my pupils to acquire sound mechanics. Wrong. I gradually came to see that my relentless focus on what was faulty in my student's technique was blocking the overall learning process. I grew more aware of the need to temper criticism with affirmation (since I'd already been a parent for many years, you'd think I would have figured out that the same general balance that held true for my kids might hold true for other young people). It struck me (years before scholarly studies provided corroboration) that this balance worked out to roughly 4:1. For every one correction I would make to the player's stroke, I had to offset it with four comments about things the player was doing well. I had to be four parts cheerleader to one part critic.

It becomes obvious, then, that the balance between truth and optimism is a delicate one. An optimistic bias, if it departs sufficiently from reality, can be as harmful to one's story as a pessimistic bias. When we depart sufficiently from reality, the optimism that ushered us there deserves a new name: denial.

As the author of our own story we determine not only content but tone. Although I suggested a couple of pages ago that, given the option, most of us would choose optimism, it's not necessarily our nature to be optimistic. Indeed, while countless studies have confirmed the utility and benefit of placebos, less well-known studies of "nocebos"—the placebo's evil twin, an inert drug that the patient believes can cause harm or unpleasantness—show that they *also* tend to work. The mind, needless to say, is a powerful instrument. One may be as easily given to unjustifiably negative storytelling as delusionally positive storytelling.

To undo old, bad stories, then, we must move forward within a positive framework, yet maintain a capacity to confront our stories with dispassionate eyes and ears: to detect lies and manipulations; to recognize our tendency to make assumptions, and often false ones, at that; to appreciate our predilection for optimism or pessimism, which may skew the tone of our stories.

Easy to say, harder to do. The problem to accomplishing that evenhandedness? Our early training, which is so powerful, so hypnotizing, so subconsciously digested and integrated, it's often hard to know if the story we're telling is even, in fact, our story.

Four

IS IT REALLY *YOUR* STORY YOU'RE LIVING?

He was everybody's idea of the perfect guy: California handsome, captain of his own multimillion-dollar business, great wife and kids, Harvard-educated, scratch golfer, licensed pilot, a person of boundless energy. Whatever he tried, it seemed, he conquered. Businessman, family man, man's man. In so many of the people he encountered he inspired envy, because he embodied the ultimate: to fully live one's own life, which is really all any of us want.

When Steve B. came to us in December 2005, he and I hit it off immediately. He was one of those rare people who's exciting just to be around.

But I'd read the bio that he, as everyone, had provided us, and during a break on the second day I couldn't help making an observation.

"I could be way off base, Steve," I said. "I get all your accomplishments and your vision and your amazing capacity to persevere. I get all that. What I don't get is any joy."

Had I been a surgeon, it was the equivalent of hitting an artery. He was silent. His eyes could not have looked more startled. Later, after he'd had time to digest my critique, he would tell me that it was as if a laser had penetrated skin, bone, and heart, and gone right to his soul.

When we found the opportunity over the next two days, he and I talked about the absence of joy in his life. I told him he needed to be as scientific as possible about it—that it was necessary to get to the root cause of his joylessness before any meaningful corrective action could be taken. I pushed him hard. I wondered why, with such a seemingly blessed, spectacular existence, he could appear at times to lack feeling, even to be robotic. The outer and the inner just didn't synch up. With all he'd accomplished in his fifty-three years, I asked, why couldn't he sit back with a big fat Cuban cigar and contemplate the joy in his life?

I pushed more. Something was behind this, of that I was certain, but I wasn't sure what. I've met scores of successful, driven people, and with most of them I could soon enough grasp some sense of where the intense drive came from: Maybe it was spurred by low self-esteem, or an ugly divorce at the absolute worst time in his or her childhood, or a bad relationship with his or her parents, or not being picked for the All-Star team . . . none of that was true with Steve. What was it? As he talked and I pushed, I remembered what he'd written in his bio about his father. Steve constantly found a way to work his dad into the conversation. His father had been his mentor, role model, best friend; there seemed to be no person in his life for whom he had greater love and respect. They'd golfed together and shared friends, and Steve worked for, and eventually took over, the rubber-molding business his father had founded thirty-five years before. In the twenty years since Steve's father had died at age sixty-eight of cancer, the business had grown significantly, yet you'd hardly think that Steve, president and CEO during that whole expansion, had contributed very much to it— certainly not nearly as much as his deceased father had.

"Steve," I asked, diving in again, "whose voice is it that's constantly admonishing you?"

Another nicked artery, another deer-in-headlights expression.

"What do you mean, 'Whose voice?'" he said weakly.

"That tyrannical voice, that relentless critic," I said. "It comes from somewhere."

We had to stop just then because his group had a gym session scheduled, and Steve went off, shakily, for a workout. A half hour later as I worked in my office, Steve poked his head in. He was on the verge of tears.

"It's your father's voice," I said, as gently as possible.

"Yeah, it is," he said, the tears coming.

He sat down heavily. I told him I thought he was either too afraid to confront the fact that his father was dead, which is why he was trying to live the golden years of his father's life, which his father didn't get to; or maybe he was doing it for the Oscar he expected to win when he got to heaven, for playing a role all these years that wasn't him. The echo of his father's voice dominated, and eventually became Steve's "private voice," obstructing him from experiencing any joy or fun in his life. It wasn't that Steve's father was a scary guy; but when he died, his son had saddled himself with the belief that the only thing that mattered was keeping the family business successful. Steve seemed spiritually, psychologically dead because, for all his fabulous outward accomplishments, he'd been pursuing a life at the heart of which was an inadequate purpose, a flimsy storyline that did not and never could infuse him with joy. I recalled a story that Steve had told me, offhandedly, about a recent golf tournament he'd competed in. A top amateur golfer, Steve had finished second in the tournament but didn't bother to attend the award banquet. If he didn't win, then the only way to characterize what had happened was that he had lost.

"If you keep on in this way," I told Steve now, "I fear you're going to die a deeply unfulfilled human being. With all your accomplishments. You've got to start living your life."

The manipulations on our lives are numerous, often impossible to recognize or calibrate, and by no means always or wholly destructive. But because outside influences have the capacity to exercise profound, at times paralyzing, sway over us and how we live our days, it is imperative—at least for the vast majority of us who have ever felt a "misalignment" in our lives, a gnawing lack of engagement and joy—that we work at figuring out how we ended up doing what we do and being who we are. I am not advocating four-times-a-week psychotherapy or anything like it (not that there's anything wrong with that) but an exercise in self-discovery, one of which we're all capable, one whose benefits go a long way. We wake up one morning and feel rotten, not knowing it's because we've become so dogmatic, and our story so inflexible, that we're impervious to change and even fresh input. We stare midday at our computer screen, cataloguing our life, unaware that every important decision in it has been triggered by one goal: the avoidance of pain and risk, professionally and personally. We look out the airplane window and review silently our rock-solid belief system, unconscious to the truth that it's really an *anti*-belief system, a rejection (say) of all things sacred. We lie in bed at night and think, *Personal integrity has always been a non-negotiable principle for me . . . I work for Enron . . .* and don't understand how we've just gone through another bottle of antacid pills.

To quote the Talking Heads' song: *How did I get here?*

In many cases, it's because we've been manipulated there. But whether external influences on us are intentional or accidental, malicious or well-meaning, my experience with all kinds of professionals, be they athletes or CEOs or cardio-surgeons or salespeople, is that the terrible traps that people get into, the flaws in our stories, *simply cannot happen unless we let them happen.* And we let them happen by remaining unalert, often willfully. We look the other way until we can't. "How did you go bankrupt?" one character asks another in Hemingway's novel, *The Sun Also Rises.* "Two ways," answers the other man. "Gradually and then suddenly." The "slippery slope" that serves as a metaphor for almost anything—morality, the passage of time, commitment—gets an unfair rap: We see the mountain, often from a considerable distance, but when we find ourselves "suddenly" sliding down it, then of course it's the slope that's to blame. Your boss asks you to do a little tiny thing you're not comfortable with—to refrain from reporting something that maybe ought to be reported, say, but which technically isn't even lying, right?—and you do it . . . and soon enough you're committing acts way over the line, crimes even. Ladies and gentlemen, welcome to the Nixon White House. Or let's not blame it on the boss: Say you're a journalist who needs juicier quotes to make your story really sing, so you start massaging your sources' words; after you've done it once, what's the difference in doing it a second time, or a one hundredth? Soon enough you're actually fabricating thoughts, people, events. Ladies and gentlemen, meet Jayson Blair, the *New York Times* reporter who banged out stories about colorful happenings and characters from around the country, often while sitting in his Brooklyn apartment and lifting passages from other newspapers or just making stuff up. *How did he get there?*

Those people were at least lucky enough to get caught. They got caught because there were people out there with sufficient incentive to catch them. Is there someone out there to call you out on the phony, self-sabotaging parts of your story? Do you have someone who cares enough to do that, and is himself or herself unentangled? Who sees you and the world with some measure of objectivity? Whom you trust and respect? If you have such a person or persons, that's good. Great, in fact. But even if you do, you don't want to rely on others to police yourself. *Individual and collective disasters happen when we don't examine our story to see if it's really ours anymore,* when we don't look hard to see if perhaps someone or something else has infiltrated it without our conscious knowledge or consent. If you don't activate your built-in bullshit detector (more on that later in this chapter), if you don't start listening to your intuition, you make your evolving story vulnerable to hijacking, to rerouting, to programming. That's why it's vital to work at understanding how external forces help us to *form* our perceptions and values; that's why it's vital to waken ourselves to the brilliant, subtle, often nefarious methods that individuals and institutions use to indoctrinate us, be they parents, corporations, media, religion, schools. We are, after all, easily indoctrinated, amazingly easily; worse, once indoctrinated—or "frozen," to use the term coined by Edgar Schein, author of a study on interpersonal dynamics in corporate America—it is extremely difficult to unlearn. To unfreeze.

Although "indoctrination" has come to have a largely negative connotation, it does not always manifest itself as a dark force. Quite the opposite, in fact. "Mind control" can be used beneficially, for example, to cure people of drug addiction; Reverend Jim Jones, who would later lead almost a thousand people to commit mass suicide in Guyana, started out as a drug counselor. Parents use indoctrination every day for positive ends: to convince their kids never to get in a car with strangers, say, or always to look both ways before crossing the street, or to stay away from drugs, or to love music and art. (Of course, negative applications of the indoctrination process are at least as endless: embedding intense racial hatred or prejudice, or the belief that the intentional killing of women and children in suicide bombings is justified and even noble, or the belief that defrauding customers is nothing more than smart business, and on and on and on.)

Nor must one be, or teach others to be, excessively wary of outside influences, via an overactive crap detector, in order that we remain, now and forever, a blank slate (*tabula rasa*). How boring and joyless would *that* be? After all, Earl Woods did nothing less than "manipulate," if you will, his son, Tiger, into seeing balls in high grass and behind trees and in sandtraps not as lamentable misfortunes but rather invitations to greatness, golf shots for the ages just waiting to happen. Earl Woods spun this "positive illusion" for Tiger as his loving coach and father. Nothing nefarious about that.

What's important, then, is to understand the astonishing *power* of influence and indoctrination, so that we may be better equipped to fend off the diabolical paradigms and theories (or discard those already embedded in our belief system), "new stories" that are usually gift-wrapped as panaceas, as promises of eternal happiness, as life-altering revelations of calm and vision. What's important is to stay connected to reality and, by so doing, maintain the ability to evaluate whether our story is a reasonable one, a neurotic one, or a downright psychotic illusion. What's important is to be flat-out *conscious*, lest we find ourselves drinking the Kool-Aid and living a story that someone else has manufactured for us (e.g., perpetual consumer, cog in a corporate wheel, religious fanatic, overly responsible son).

Of course, doing what I'm suggesting—unerringly knowing what is good for you versus what is bad for you—is anything but easy. The oft-tossed-out retort, *It's my story and I'm sticking to it*—tongue-in-cheek though it's usually meant—slyly speaks, I believe, to this very difficulty. The snappy comment suggests two things simultaneously: First, *My story is an unchangeable story*; and, second, *My story may well be wrong but I will never abandon it so long as it's mine.* There's honor simply in clinging to the "mine-ness" of it; better to propagate a false illusion one can call one's own than rent out a truth belonging to someone else. A culture where such an idea is deemed honorable is one that may now and again muddy the concept of truth.

To understand the indoctrination process, then, will require more than a passing acknowledgment that, yes: Indoctrination does, in fact, exist. "If I, as a young woman, had had someone explain to me how indoctrination works," said Deborah Layton, "my story might not have been the same."

Who, you might ask, is Deborah Layton? One of the thousand who followed Peoples Temple founder Jim Jones to Guyana where, in 1978, 914 of them died, many of them when they quite literally drank the Kool-Aid, laced with cyanide. Deborah Layton survived but we can only guess at the damage; and she never would have followed had she only been aware that she'd been manipulated.

BIG BATTLE FOR A LITTLE VOICE

You have a story right now, a story that is by definition the story of your life. Who owns it? Is it a story your parents gave you? The one your uncle or preacher gave you? The one your peers gave you? Who owns the billions of neural pathways in your brain that determine your personal reality? Who has been the principal architect of the one reality you know and the stories you tell to support that reality? If it's not you, then are you comfortable relinquishing control of your reality to forces outside yourself, particularly considering what's at stake—namely, your life?

If your values and beliefs are the prism through which you see the world, and the guiding force for the choices you make, then where did they come from? Was your mother a flower-child during the sixties whose values inescapably influenced yours? Did your dad's Depression Era mentality about money so profoundly affect your worldview that you don't travel as much as you might, don't treat yourself to the good food and wine you now enjoy only infrequently, never spontaneously call your siblings who live in other cities—as you'd like to—unless it's after eleven at night and the phone rates have dipped? Who or what influenced your view of family, of women, of men, of love? Of sex? of morality? of good and evil? of America? of what's worthwhile in life?

The little private voice inside you that seems to have been there as long as you can remember—the one that insists, say, that everyone has it better than you do, or that women are no good, or that someday in the indeterminate future everyone will realize your brilliance—where'd that come from?

No matter how admirably you wrestle to unearth the origins of these ideas of yours, getting to the answer is devilishly elusive. Influence mostly operates in the murk of unconsciousness.

But one thing you can be certain of, and conscious about: Someone is vying for your story all the time. Lots of people have an interest in owning part or all of your gray matter, that part of the brain that is home to the raw material where your story was born and lives. The world is full of people whose sole professional purpose is to get you to say yes to their requests, suggestions, commands. And if they get to "own" your gray matter—that is, to own the configuration and directionality of your brain's pathways—then they get to determine the vigor or sickness of your stories, and thus the success or failure of your life, your destiny. If we own our neural real estate, then we have control; if others own it, then they have control. Control of what we think, feel, say, do. And if *that* happens, then we've been complicit in identity theft . . . only the identity we've allowed to be stolen is our own!

For some of those who seek ownership of our gray matter, their motivation is noble; for others, sinister. Politicians have an interest. Corporations. Media. Friends and enemies, competitors and salespeople, parents and teachers and clergy, TV producers and casino operators, bosses and military leaders, the list goes on and on. Everyone is fighting to get *your* belief system to conform to *their* needs and wants.

How do they get to own it? Often by deception and seduction (seduction, one may argue, is merely a subset of deception, or—better yet—its prettier, but no less manipulative, twin). Let's deal first with deception. So many forces out there are intent on tricking us. Take, for example, the source of much of our daily information. Every newspaper we read has spin, obvious to us or not so obvious. *The Wall Street Journal* has one spin, *The New York Times* another, *USA Today* still another. They don't give you the "facts" or the "news," but their version of them; they give you a story. "If you don't read the newspaper, you are uninformed," said Mark Twain. "If you do read the newspaper, you are misinformed." Whether we absorb a story's "angle" consciously or not, it means everything that one paper's lead, in big type and accompanied by an above-the-fold color photo, is another paper's one-paragraph item on page sixteen, just next to the advertisement for a big linen sale. Every magazine, TV channel, radio station, and website is spin. Every book is spin. This book has spin—one you may or may not be aware of, one *I* may or may not be aware of. Spin simply means agenda, and it is everywhere.

But for their vast ideological differences, the sources of indoctrination catalogued above all share a desire to shape your reality. What they want, for better or worse, is influence: influence over what you value, think, feel, say, or do. For our parents, the agenda may be our happiness and well-being; for our boss, our team spirit and productivity; for casino operators, our money; for politicians, our vote; for TV producers, our viewing loyalty; for clergy, our religious beliefs and practices, and weekly attendance.

All too often, unfortunately, the "property rights" to our minds can be purchased outright for money. Many of us are only too willing to sell big chunks of our reality for the right price. Our values, beliefs, thoughts, and actions go to the highest bidder. Maybe we choose friends because of their station in life, or we'll work for a company whose values we disagree with but whose compensation allows us to make that trade-off, or we take a position we abhor because we've received financial support from backers of that position, or we marry for money.

What happens, though, when interested parties are unable to purchase our gray matter directly? In that case, they're forced to seek alternative strategies for ownership.

The word that best embraces the full range of these strategies is "indoctrination."

Indoctrination, according to the dictionary, is any instructional process whereby a targeted change in thinking, values, beliefs, or identity is attained. *Successful indoctrination actually changes one's neurological structure.* Broadly speaking, brain mapping shows that neural architecture is shaped by each stimulus experience. Many neuronal pathways appear "well paved" because electrical impulses travel them regularly and often—in response, say, to the faces of our family, tasks we do at work, habits we follow or hobbies we love. With each repetition of these familiar experiences (often habitual, often subconscious), the pathway further increases its load capacity. So long as these roads continue to be well traveled, they will continue largely to define who we are—until new pathways form for energy to travel more easily, which would bring with it a change in our feelings and actions, a change in our reality, and ultimately a change in the story we tell.

The indoctrination process can be completely conscious or unconscious, self-directed or other-directed. If we remain unaware, indoctrination can proceed against us unabated.

While some indoctrinations, according to psychologists Philip Zimbardo and Susan Andersen, use " 'exotic' technologies such as hypnosis, drugs, and intrusive assaults directly on the brain, most forms of mind control . . . are more mundane." Generally, the persuader wants to keep the physical setting and social situation as normal as possible, so as to move you quite gradually toward a moment of cognitive confusion, at which point some response from you is required. Very often the persuader relies on emotional appeal, where feeling and sentiment trump reasoned consideration; this is the modus operandi of most religious evangelists. Some indoctrinators attempt to arouse guilt and fear. In most cases, the persuader tries to disguise his intent by first ingratiating himself, thereby increasing the chance that his audience, later on, will consider his point seriously, whereas at first they might not have done so. In this way, a cult is comparable to a card shark who allows a newcomer to win a few games at first in order to take their whole stash in the long run. It has been pointed out that the opening salvo in Mark Antony's famous oration to his fellow Romans in Shakespeare's *Julius Caesar*—"I come to bury Caesar, not to praise him"—brilliantly disarms those in the audience who had pegged Antony as a lockstep defender of the flawed Caesar; only then, having edged the crowd toward him—by identifying with them—does Antony slowly and surely work toward his real argument, which is precisely as Caesar's loyal defender; only then can he whip them into a mob that feels as he does: that Brutus and the other conspirators who murdered Caesar deserve to die.

Of course, some organizations *do* use unabashedly "devious psychological techniques," in Zimbardo and Andersen's words. For example, the Scientologist policy regarding "suppressed persons"—those who are *de facto* excommunicated from the group for, say, quitting the church without undergoing an extensive security check (such as an extremely invasive exit interview)—prevents former members from telling any story about the organization except the one the church tells. Some brainwashing brilliantly exploits basic human physical and psychic needs—for example, subjects may be forced not to move or use the bathroom for extended periods, or they're deprived of liquids or nourishment; with the accompanying drop in blood sugar level (to give one consequence), the subject becomes less able, and eventually disinclined, to act, speak, and even think authentically. Subjects accused of false acts over and over and over again eventually break down and confess. "Disordered brain function is indeed easily produced in any man," wrote Denise Winn in *The Manipulated Mind*. "No amount of 'will power' can prevent its occurrence." In short, no matter how much we believe in ourselves, our independence, our intestinal fortitude, it turns out that our beliefs and actions are, in fact, deeply influenced by circumstance; to an extent, they are for sale. How else to explain the phenomenon of Stockholm syndrome, in which hostages often come to identify with their hostage takers, no matter how illogical and potentially self-negating such identification may be?

But here's the startling and unseemly truth about really good brainwashers: Most of the time, they're not lying to you but, rather, telling you only truths they think will be acceptable to you. The persuader says or does something meant to influence your beliefs . . . *yet the actual controlling of the mind is done by you, the subject.* Thus the term "mind control" can be misleading: It suggests that a person's mind can be robotically manipulated by some outside agency, or that thoughts can be somehow hypnotically implanted in a person's mind. But that's not really how it happens. *In cult mind control, it is the belief system itself that is the primary active agent; effectively, a cult uses a person's own energy and aspirations against him.* In the 1960s, after social psychologist Stanley Milgram did his legendary experiments in which volunteers were asked to administer near-lethal electric shocks to subjects—and did so (or thought they were doing so) at an alarmingly high rate—it was concluded that this didn't so much prove that man desires to inflict pain on his fellow man but that we are so obedient to authority and oppressed by groupthink that we can be dangerously manipulated. Broken down further, the experiment may be said to show that, out of mere politeness, out of a mere wish to keep one's promise and merely to avoid embarrassment at backing out and discomfort at standing alone, few volunteers were willing to take reasonable, independent, perfectly available action to stop the experiment and do the right thing.

Ladies and gentlemen, welcome to the culture of Tyco, of World-Com, of Enron.

In the end, *brainwashers and cults very often simply allow us,* admittedly under their guidance, *to bring about change on our own, usually through small, continuous modifications.* They use our deeply ingrained belief in etiquette, protocol, and social convention against us. They use deception—unquestionably—but deception that would be ineffectual if human nature were not as it is. But is that a satisfactory explanation for our actions or inaction? For example, while it was beyond reprehensible that federal officials failed to warn the American public about the risks of radioactive fallout during the atomic-bomb tests in Nevada in the 1950s, evidence did exist—such as "frost" on surfaces that were not cold to the touch; heightened incidence of cancer and cancer deaths in area residents—that something very wrong was happening. Yet most residents, burying alarm and embracing ignorance, remained in the region for a very long time, with further widespread tragic results.

Ignorance can be bliss, for a while. But a life that deeply engages and fulfills us demands that we remain vigilant and conscious about the powerful, unseen forces working to influence and even steal away our sense of who we are, our values, our beliefs, our vision of the future. In simple words, what we're fighting against is the most tragic form of identity theft.

LESSONS IN STORYTELLING 101: COMMUNIST CHINA

To understand the process by which an actual indoctrination takes place, let's look at a sinister application that affected tens of millions of people. The closer we examine how this particular indoctrination occurred, the better equipped we'll be, I think, either to accelerate the process on our behalf (when it's good for us) or rally our forces against it (when it's bad for us).

In his 1951 book, *Brain-Washing in Red China*, Edward Hunter describes in great detail how the Communist Party of China set out to reform the hearts and minds of an entire nation. In September 1949, China's ruling party implemented a powerful indoctrination program to restructure the thinking of every man, woman, and child. Under the leadership of Mao Tse-tung, the program was designed to alter the reality of the Chinese people in three ways, by getting them to (1) fully embrace Soviet-style Communism; (2) abandon religious beliefs, particularly Christianity; (3) develop an intense hatred and distrust for anything American.

Was the program successful?

The good news is that no foolproof way of brainwashing, according to those involved in the CIA's mind-control unit, has ever been found. The bad news is that a vast number of people, easily the majority, are brainwashable. And the method the Chinese government chose to transform the core beliefs and values of its then half-billion people?

Storytelling.

The Chinese indoctrination process focused fundamentally on two things: (1) controlling what people said to others—that is, their public stories; and (2) controlling what people said to themselves—that is, their private stories. Of the two, controlling the private story was considered by far the more important. Typically, the control process began with "Idea Training." It was here that beliefs about Communism, religion, and America were systematically laid out, in a simple story-rich lecture. After each lecture, the inductees (as I'll call them) would be broken into small groups, where each person had to express the ideas just told to him or her. In effect, they were to retell the story they'd just heard. Inductees then had to write a report about the lecture, a report that would be graded for accuracy of content and sincerity of expression; a poor grade meant repeating the lecture until they got their story "right."

To me, it is this "grading for sincerity" part that was the truly ingenious ingredient: In this way, the government could gain control of the inductee's private voice.

Idea Training was designed to build the neural pathways that would profoundly alter the beliefs and values of every inductee, no matter the content or apparent strength of his or her old stories.

Another strategy for controlling the inductee's public and private voices and their emerging new stories was to require everyone to maintain a detailed daily diary. Again, the diaries were collected and reviewed for both accuracy of content and sincerity of expression. Repeated failure to meet the standards meant a return to more Idea Training, more lectures, more reports. Inductees came to dread returning for more Idea Training.

Inductees were also required to make regular, public confessions of guilt. Standing before peers and Party officials, they would confess to thoughts and feelings that were contrary to the best interests of the Communist movement and the Chinese people. These public confessions gave indoctrinators access to the inductee's "faulty" old story and the public and private voices they used to support them. By suffering public humiliation for allowing any remnant of his old story to surface, the inductee eventually silenced himself. Successful indoctrination required that the old, unenlightened stories about Communism, religion, and America be totally extinguished and replaced with the carefully crafted new doctrines.

Yet another ingenious component of the indoctrination process was the policy of making every inductee the keeper of everyone else's thoughts. Inductees were instructed to listen carefully to what others said and, if any idea or thought expressed was contrary to the Party line, the listener was to correct it immediately. If violations continued, inductees were required to notify Party officials, and the wayward member was made to return to basic indoctrination school.

Indoctrinators also used skits and plays to accelerate the brain reform process. Inductees wrote and acted out themes like "the stupidity of religion" or "the ugly, self-centered American." However crude and clumsy the acting and writing skills of the inductees, the skits stirred powerful emotions in the actors and audience both, which reinforced the targeted neurological changes. The repetitious singing and chanting, a frequent element in the plays and skits, accelerated the indoctrination process.

The last but perhaps most critical step in gaining control of the inductee's mind was the constant linking of the Communist movement, and this new methodology for thinking and acting, *to a noble purpose*, one that transcended mere self-interest. The Communist movement was "for the people of China," so that all Chinese people could experience "a better life." Sacrifice and hardship were to be endured for the welfare of future generations. Thus, they felt that what they did was for the well-being and happiness of their own children. The new story was orchestrated so that nothing could seem more noble, just, and worth fighting for than Communism.

How successful was the indoctrination program?

The numerous interviews that Hunter conducted for his book confirmed the power of the government's techniques. Here's one representative fragment from a subject who'd been exposed to the techniques for just ninety days:

> *I finally decided that religion was altogether bunk. We don't need any religion . . . At last I had rid myself of the poisonous thing called religion. I was convinced that religion was selfish . . . so at last, after 2 or 3 months, I have given up my religion, something which I had held sacred and had cherished all my life . . . Christmas came, and for the first time it held no meaning for me . . . I always had spoken so highly of the United States . . . now I have developed an extraordinary hatred for America, which I now consider to be the worst country in the world . . .*

Obviously, the program worked in the short term. What about the long term? Well, anyone who has spent time in China, as I have, can feel that more than a half-century later the effects of this widespread indoctrination continue to permeate Chinese culture, particularly among the older generation. As expressed personally, in their culture and in their literature, the views of many Chinese on religion (particularly Christianity), Communism, and American culture still reverberate with beliefs instilled generations before.

EVERYDAY INDOCTRINATIONS

Many elements central to the Chinese system of indoctrination, as well as other "extreme" programs of "mind control" (such as est or pyramid schemes), also happen to be cornerstones of training and education programs that most of us hardly consider "out there," social and cultural institutions of great value and integrity, of noble purpose. We've all encountered one or more of these institutions. Belief in them and their tenets can be healthy, constructive, transforming.

And yet the parallels to the indoctrination program just discussed are striking.

Higher Education
- Idea Training (new story preparation and public/private storytelling voice control) through lectures, small group discussions, and the requirement that each person express the idea and then write a report, which is graded for accuracy and, in some cases, sincerity
- If you don't acquire the learning, then you must return to basic indoctrination school (if the student fails, he must return to retake the class)
- Linking the indoctrination process to a higher purpose; education in itself is a noble pursuit

Alcoholics Anonymous's 12-Step Process
- Public confessions: identification of old story, confrontation of truth
- Peer support, personal coaching, peer pressure
- Public expression of new story
- Spiritual anchoring: enlist support and help of Supreme Being

- Make each recovering alcoholic the guardian of his fellow brothers' thoughts
- Repetition of meetings: weekly/monthly meetings for life

Military Training
- Immediate control of public and private voices: quick punishment for showing any dissent, negativity, cynicism, anger, or fear (new story)
- Repetition (new story)
- Peer support and peer rejection
- Idea Training (new story formation)
- Linking entire indoctrination process to higher purpose: protecting family and country

Religious Training
- Idea Training—using the Bible, Koran, Scriptures, etc., as basic content of new story; churches, temples, mosques, and synagogues are primary indoctrination centers
- Public and private confessions (old story)
- Repetition—reading, discussing, singing, chanting (new story)
- Make each person the guardian of his brothers' thoughts
- Peer support and peer pressure
- Indoctrination starts immediately following birth, the younger the better—for example, in Muslim madrassas, Catholic catechism classes, parochial schools
- Linked to a cause beyond oneself: Supreme Being

Then there's corporate training, whose doctrine, while somewhat more varied perhaps than those above, still hews to a powerful orthodoxy.

Corporate Training
- Idea Training—corporate vision, mission, values, ethics, product superiority, rules of engagement (new story)
- Leadership training—lectures, small group discussions, reports; advancement requires successful indoctrination in company's party line thinking and politics (new story)
- Peer support (mentoring) and peer pressure

- Chief learning officers are indoctrination specialists who help to disseminate key learning elements
- Corporate retreats (special indoctrination events) promote renewal and repetition (skits, plays, games, ropes courses, adventure events)
- Daily diaries—many firms employ corporate coaches who recommend the practice of keeping a daily diary; coaches periodically review written entries for evidence of learning and provide constructive feedback

Now I'm not suggesting that because the institutions above use many of the methodologies used by cults, they are the moral equivalent of cults. I *am* suggesting that being aware of these similarities allows us to understand how our stories and ourselves often morph, typically in undetectable increments, into things we don't want or like.

Take the business world. The leaders I meet every week hardly lose sleep in fear that they will turn into ideological monsters à la Mao or Reverend Jim Jones. But the ones who are committed to improving themselves and their corporate environments become (more) aware of their potentially fanatical behavior. Yes, fanatical: After all, the roots of fanaticism are found in mere intolerance, intolerance for any thinking or belief contrary to one's own. For example: "I know I'm right and I'm not going to allow any contrary discussions about it." Ever hear any leader express that thought, explicitly or implicitly? Have *you* expressed it? Felt it? And when it's expressed, what message is the employee/listener getting? Probably this: "Adopt our thinking without question or get out of the organization."

If, in your professional life, you express to others, or even just to yourself, one or more of the following, you should probably consider it a sign of a growing problem:

- Increasing intolerance for beliefs and values that don't absolutely align with yours
- Increasing rigidity and inflexibility in thinking and action
- Increasing use of fear and threat of retribution if what you say is not acted on or taken seriously
- Increasing inability to see value in opposing points of view

The examples above can just as easily be applied, of course, to life outside the boardroom and the workplace. Fanatical thought and coercive behavior are alive and well not merely in formal settings like the classroom, the office, the chapel, but in subtler, seemingly less structured environments, too. For instance, what is the true difference—when comparing net results—between a coercive Communist government using brainwashing techniques, on one hand, and an insidious, infiltrating corporate culture using mass-market advertising to sell valueless real estate, on the other? If the former deceives us into doing things we otherwise wouldn't, things that are bad for us, then the latter at least . . . wait, doesn't it do exactly the same thing? It's no great insight to suggest that, but for the hypnotic power of TV commercials and other sorts of advertising, we would not buy many (perhaps most) of the products we buy, we would not buy kids' sugared cereals, we might be less tolerant of physical violence, more intolerant of abuse of any kind, etc. But could the biggest difference between these two cultures of indoctrination simply be the content of the messages injected into the inductee? Perhaps I overstate things, for dramatic effect; after all, technically one *can* walk away from the TV (though few young children, once exposed to the Sirens' call of its content and form, have been known to pick up the remote and turn off the TV of their own power—and few grown-ups have walked away, either), while such an option clearly did not exist for the Chinese man, woman, or child who felt the government's program and message just weren't his or her cup of tea.

Then again, perhaps I don't overstate it. Many cults notoriously attempt to strong-arm their constituencies by controlling all forms of communication that could provide them with a competing message; on the other side, those of us who smugly consider ourselves independent-minded are, if not deprived of information, then *imprisoned* by it: More than half the executives we work with freely acknowledge that their means of communication and information—BlackBerry, cell phone, e-mail, Internet, TV—control *them*, not the other way around. I'm not sure that the differences between and among mind control techniques are quite as great as we'd like to believe. One man's indoctrination is another man's socialization; one woman's mind control is another woman's persuasion.

One thing is for sure, though: Whether it's called persuasion or mind control or socialization or indoctrination, getting people to formulate or change their core beliefs and values—to change the story of their life—is achievable only when it's supported by an enormously powerful premise. That's where seduction comes in.

PROMISES, PREMISES

Jim Jones ordered the mass suicide of more than nine hundred people in Jonestown. The promise to the "victims"? Redemption. The "Moonies," led by Korean-born Reverend Sun Myung Moon, recruited thousands away from their families and into their Unification Church by promising spiritual purification and enlightenment. David Koresh created his own religious sect, eighty of whom ultimately died by suicide and self-inflicted conflagration, at the Branch Davidian Commune in Waco, Texas; he, too, had promised spiritual redemption. Iran's Ayatollah Khomeini sent children on suicide missions against Iraqi fortifications with the promise of their gaining direct entry into heaven. Marshal Applewhite promised the same reward—direct entry into heaven—to his people, the Heaven's Gate cult, thirty-nine of whom participated in a mass suicide (preceded, for the men, by castration) when the Hale-Bopp comet arrived, apparently their signal that it was time.

The indoctrination process invariably begins with a story of seduction, one of great promise.

Follow me and my beliefs and you will experience the peace, meaning, and hope you've always longed for.

These beliefs and practices will take you into goodness, purification, healing, enlightenment, and rebirth.

This path will provide entry into everlasting happiness and joy.

To draw outsiders in, the seducing individual or organization must flash a damn good promise; one might also call this the seducer's premise, or purpose—at least as far as the seduced are concerned. (The *seducer's* ultimate purpose—e.g., power, prestige, money, fame, a captive audience—may well be quite different from what is being offered to the constituents.) The promise bears some typical characteristics:

- It's always presented under the guise of good.
- The "door" through which the indoctrination process typically passes is the spiritual door.
- The deeper you go into the belief, the less able you are to question its validity and truth.

Once again, the business world provides a rich vein of examples. The vulnerability to seduction and unrealistic promise helped to fuel both the spectacular rise and crash-landing death of corporate giants like Enron and WorldCom. Early on, they made explicit promises, as virtually all public companies do and must, to act responsibly and ethically with the money invested in them. I don't believe the people running these companies started out with the intent to defraud employees and shareholders, or to empty the 401(k)s and pensions of retirees, as they would eventually do. I believe they were generally decent people who got seduced by the promise of great wealth and glory—gradually, then suddenly—into doing evil deeds. Despite those very public failures, every day another corporate leader is seduced into changing his or her story about what's right and wrong—from withholding critical data to deceptive accounting procedures to falsifying shareholder quarterly earning reports. Every day, by some storytelling process, an employee is seduced into altering a fundamental ethical position and, in doing so, places himself or herself in moral peril. Every day, organizations and their people seek out and take shortcuts, seduced by the belief that there won't be a price to pay, that somehow they'll be the lucky ones to get away with it. Every day, huge, profitable companies find creative ways to lay off employees who've been with them for nineteen and a half years so they won't have to pay the pension that kicks in at twenty, telling themselves a story that it's unavoidable (it's not), that the departed worker is getting a severance package that's generous (it isn't), that the company ought not be faulted for betraying a promise the company made almost two decades ago (of course they should).

Some warning signals that may suggest you have a heightened vulnerability to seduction:

- Increasing preoccupation with securing fame, power, or financial wealth

- Lack of clarity about your values, purpose, and spirituality in life
- Tendency to look outside yourself for answers to life's most profound questions
- Very limited capacity for self-awareness and self-reflection
- Poorly defined sense of self
- Considerable inner turmoil, unhappiness, and discontent

From the hundreds of workshops I've conducted and the thousands of people I've worked with, I realize it's no small thing to ask you to step outside yourself and examine what does and doesn't work about your life as you're living it, as your story has been unfolding all these years. A fish, after all, spends its entire existence never realizing it's in water. But we're more self-aware than fish, and so it's imperative that we dive in. "It is so easy to become our surroundings, our environment," wrote Jonestown survivor Deborah Layton in her book, *Seductive Poison*. "Without clarity, we are our own deceivers." When Steve B., the man at the start of this chapter who seemed to have it all, recognized, at age fifty-three, the fundamental flaw in his story—that his private voice was not his own but his father's, that for decades he hadn't really lived his own life, that he had experienced so little joy in a life that should have been overflowing with it—he broke down. He bawled like a baby. For a good while, he was a mess. He had lost one of the most vital elements in his life: his identity. For so many others I've had the privilege to work with, an equally seismic breakthrough occurred when they realized, for the first time, how completely "off" their story had gotten, how the journey was not of their own making, though they had followed its flawed road map. On the second morning of the workshop, I ask the group whether, in doing their homework (writing their old story) the previous night, they had unearthed the authentic "voice" they were writing in and, if so, was it theirs? In almost every class, several people raise their hands to say that yes, they found the voice—and that it belonged to their mother or father. (Every now and then the infiltrating voice belongs to a teacher or a priest or another family member, but the vast majority of time it's a parental voice.) "Our brains are valuable forgers, weaving a tapestry of memory and perception whose detail is so compelling that its inauthenticity is rarely detected," writes psychologist Daniel Gilbert in his frank and insightful book, *Stumbling on Happiness*. "In a sense, each of us is a counterfeiter who prints phony dollar bills and then happily accepts them for payment, unaware that he is both the perpetrator and victim of a well-orchestrated fraud."

You may think everything coming out of your mouth is of your own formulation but it's probably not. Better to be wary of even your own ideas and words until you can examine their roots. We'd be well served to heed the endearing skepticism of media critic Marshall McLuhan, who once said, "I don't necessarily agree with everything I say."

HOW YOUR VALUES AND BELIEFS AFFECT YOUR STORYTELLING

Before you can write your new, better story, you must know who you are. Absent that knowledge, the author has no authority.

Nothing speaks to who we are and how we perceive the world more than our core beliefs and values. Inescapably, it is these beliefs and values that serve as the lens, or filter, through which we interpret our sensory experience. Many of our most dominant stories, not to mention our most dogmatic and inflexible ones—people can't be trusted; God exists; God does not exist; affirmative action is just another form of bigotry; affirmative action is not only justified for aggrieved minorities but benefits society as a whole; euthanasia can be an act of grace; euthanasia is playing God; etc.—can be traced to deeply embedded values and beliefs. To understand just how profoundly beliefs and values influence the way we create stories, let's look at one of the most loaded subjects for human intercourse: politics. And while our sleeves are rolled up, let's examine the divergent views about one of the most inflammatory issues bedeviling Americans as I write this in early 2007: the war in Iraq.

The invasion and the ongoing perilous situation over there have sharply divided the country in the stories we tell. Stories about President Bush range from those that heroize him to those that villainize him, while stories about the war itself range from those portraying it as grimly unavoidable and necessary and better now than later, to those portraying it as calamitously irresponsible, even evil. Let's hear the respective takes of Robert C. and Diane R., two representative Americans, on the subject. First, Robert:

> George Bush is the worst thing that could happen to America. His arrogance, stubbornness, and poor judgment have done incalculable harm to this country and the people of Iraq. I hate the man and all that he stands for. When I see him on television, my skin crawls. In the grand scheme, he's more dangerous than the terrorists themselves. I personally believe that he knowingly lied to the American people—but even if he didn't, he's guilty of other lethal sins: willful ignorance; abominable lack of preparation for Iraq after the capture of Saddam; and an inability to assess how the situation is *really* going, by some objective, nonpartisan, nonpolitical measure of reality, and to make the necessary adjustments so that the minimum number of lives are put at risk. He leads an administration that has really learned only one lesson from Vietnam: *This* time they're going to shut down as much daily TV and media coverage of the death and brutal destruction going on over there, to keep the issue abstract for most Americans so the war machine can proceed unimpeded. I'm absolutely certain he will go down as the worst president in this country's history.

Now, Diane's story.

> I deeply admire George Bush. Because of his courage, conviction, and determination, my family and this country have not been attacked since 9/11 and have hope for a terror-free future. His willingness to attack terrorists relentlessly, wherever they are found, and to spread freedom and democracy throughout the world, is changing the course of history in a profoundly positive way, despite the difficulties that we at home and especially our soldiers and the Iraqi people are facing right now. Really, now: Did people expect such a sea change would proceed without a hitch? Has it ever? This is an enemy that is not looking to compromise, and we kid ourselves to believe that diplomacy alone is the answer, when it so very rarely is. If we

cut and run now, what will we have done? Weaken us in the eyes of our allies *and* our enemies and, more important, put off the time when we will have to confront an adversary that is not going away simply because we want them to, and which will only be stronger, and more nuclear-ready, the next time around. In spite of Bush's declining popularity, I believe he is a man of great character and integrity, willing to make difficult decisions, which makes him precisely the right person for managing the grave crisis we now face as a nation. When the history books are written twenty to fifty years from now, George Bush will no doubt be regarded as one of this country's finest presidents.

Can they really be talking about the same man? How could such completely opposing stories be formed from the same set of facts? What could account for such divergent views of the president and his actions? It's clear that Robert and Diane each adamantly believe that the story he or she is telling represents the *real* truth—the objective reality—about Bush's actions, decisions, and very essence.

Their divergent narratives ultimately stem from vastly different beliefs and values, the keys to how they, or anyone, interpret whatever facts they're exposed to. For example, one of Robert's most impenetrable beliefs is that war is never an acceptable way to resolve an injustice or settle a dispute. According to him, war is always evil, represents a massive human failure, and never truly resolves anything. According to his belief system—his *story*—no matter how bad or tragic a situation might appear, with persistence, diligence, and prayer, an alternative to war can always be found. The intentional taking of human life can never be justified. For Robert, all wars are ill-conceived failures, leading only to indescribable human suffering and pain.

Once one knows Robert's beliefs about war and the taking of human life, his attitude and opinions about President Bush become more understandable. Every article Robert reads about Bush, every fact about the war he absorbs, every newscast he views is filtered by his powerful beliefs. Even when confronted, at one point early on, with news that elections were being held successfully and Iraqi troop strength was growing, Robert's hatred and contempt for Bush persisted. Indeed, after reading reports suggesting that the war was yielding possibilities for hope, Robert felt all the more threatened and disturbed; this good news directly contradicted his belief that war never leads to a positive outcome. Deep down, Robert secretly hoped the war would fail and that President Bush would get what he deserved: impeachment.

Diane's beliefs lay the foundation for a completely different story. One of her most important beliefs is that evil exists in the world and, if left unchecked, it can spread like a deadly disease. Serial killers, mass murderers, and ruthless dictators are facts of life and pose such serious threats to the welfare of others that physical force and even war become not only justified but moral imperatives, necessary actions to excise these cancerous threats to civilization. Violence and war are choices of last resort but may be required in special circumstances to protect the rights, freedoms and well-being of others. To support her belief, Diane cited two examples: the removal of Hitler from power; and the fact that law enforcement officers must occasionally use deadly force to protect the innocent. Even if the original rationale for the American invasion, and the most broadly persuasive, turned out to be untrue—that Saddam Hussein, who had already exhibited a willingness to use weapons of mass destruction, was gathering them for deployment against the West—Diane was not fazed. Because of her steadfast belief that life is extremely messy and complicated, full of bad people who will use all means to destroy America and its way of life, she could easily explain to herself the WMD debacle: It was naïve, she argued, to assume that our intelligence-gathering operations could ever be flawless when dealing with madmen. When the media began to report that the upper ranks of the American military and even members of the president's own party were growing increasingly disenchanted with his military strategy—or lack of a strategy with any apparent coherence or thoughtfulness—Diane dismissed it as flinching, as 20/20 hindsight; the reports only strengthened her belief that cowards are always quick to criticize but slow to act and fueled her argument that the invasion was completely justified, since numerous diplomatic attempts to bring Iraq back into the community of nations had long ago failed. For America *not* to draw a line in the sand, when the Iraqi people were being killed and oppressed and the world was in a perilous situation from which it might never return, would have been a surrender of morality and responsibility because it would serve only to embolden other madmen.

Whose version of the story is right? Or—at least—*more* right? Which one more closely reflects objective reality?

There is, of course, no answering this question. If there is an objective reality—and I believe there is—then we can hope only to approach it but never to know it fully. The only reality we know *fully* comes from the stories we create around our sensory experience; these stories are profoundly influenced by beliefs and values, the bedrock of each person's worldview; and this bedrock is formed by a mixture of influences that varies wildly from one person to the next. "There is properly no history," said Ralph Waldo Emerson, "only biography." The core values and beliefs we hold are not *the* truth, of course, but rather *our* truth, representing critical elements only to *our* story. Morality is kaleidoscopic. "We do not see things as they are," says the Talmud, the sacred Jewish text. "We see things as we are."

Robert and Diane used mostly the same facts—or perhaps "filtered" is more accurate—to build to vastly different conclusions. Facts are meaningless without a contextual story; that context is built with the bricks and mortar that are our pre-existing values and beliefs. For our purposes in this book, the crucial point in all this is to recognize that *whatever* our beliefs and values, they are powerful forces in our storymaking. For better or worse, they help us to form, modify, alter—and, yes, distort—our sensory experience. If we hold a core belief that, for example, people can't be trusted, then we will bend or distort the reality we experience to support that belief. Rather than register and consider and appreciate and finally embrace the living example of the next twenty trustworthy people we encounter, whose existence and actions might logically undermine this belief of ours, we instead wait for, and are ready to pounce on, the example of the twenty-first person, that lying, lousy, two-faced cheat who represents everything we've been saying for so long. We'll find facts or generate evidence to prove our point, to keep our belief alive. If those strong beliefs reflect racial, ethnic, or gender biases, say, then we'll find evidence to perpetuate the story we tell around it.

In short: It's our story and we're sticking to it.

WHERE DO OUR VALUES
AND BELIEFS COME FROM?

Since core beliefs and values play such a central role in our storymaking, it might be useful for us to understand how they form inside us. That's not a simple task: There are so many factors to consider, most of them invisible. But one thing we do know: *Beliefs and values are not inherited or coded in the genes.* They are assumptions about life—it's always wrong and immoral to take human life; love of money is the root of all evil; all people have inherent value in and of themselves; meat-eating is wrong; people who don't travel are narrow-minded; you have to be crazy to live in New York City; Southerners talk slow because they're dumb—that we *acquire*, in the same way that we acquire a foreign language, or learn our way around a new city, or learn to be respectful toward others, or to love our parents.

Because beliefs and values are acquired, their truth does not typically lend itself to scientific verification. Sure, we might be comforted if science, which we adjudge to possess a high objectivity quotient, could help us to confirm or dispel the truth of beliefs and values, but for the most part we can't. (How satisfying would it be to have a science experiment prove, once and for all, that a belief of yours, a belief that contradicts your friend's, is true? How long could you keep yourself from calling him up to crow, "You see? *I* was right!") Now and then, an assumption that many people have held to fervently for centuries *has* been debunked by scientific inquiry; the best example, undoubtedly, is "The world is flat." But that's the exception. Scores of attempts have been made, for example, to scientifically prove the existence of God, but to the entrenched nonbeliever, the evidence presented is neither scientific nor convincing. (And could it really ever be thus—that a mathematical proof or scientific experiment could definitively corroborate the truth or falsehood of a belief? Or do we idealize that science's "objectivity" could help us, precisely because it never could? "There are three kinds of lies," Benjamin Disraeli is reputed to have said. "Lies, damn lies, and statistics.")

If core beliefs and values are not inherited, where do they come from? How do our major assumptions about life, which play such a central role in our storymaking, get formed? To understand the process by which beliefs and values are acquired—that is, how they get embedded in our minds—is to gain control over a profoundly important tool. It is to understand that beliefs and values aren't just static tendencies we possess, but qualities that, at various key turning points in our lives, as well as in our day-to-day life, move our story this way and not that, or that way and not this. This self-awareness can then be accessed to change, modify, or eliminate those beliefs and values of ours that, upon examination, work *against* our self-interest. This knowledge can help us to answer the important question: *Do my beliefs and values help my story take me where I want to go?*

To understand the acquisition process a bit, let's revisit our friends Robert and Diane. Again, I start with Robert's story. An only child, Robert is unmarried. Both his parents are well-educated and deeply religious. Robert's father holds a doctorate in theology and has been an Episcopal priest for twenty-nine years; Robert's mother earned a master's degree in marriage and family counseling and for more than a decade has maintained a small private practice. It's no surprise to Robert that his core beliefs are so similar to his parents'. He has vivid memories of how his parents used every opportunity to instill their beliefs that war is never justified and the taking of human life is always wrong. "They were relentless," says Robert. "At times, I guess they were over the top with their indoctrination of what they believed. Their intent was good and, in the end, what they did worked. I believe I'm a deeply principled person and I credit them for who I've become." Robert graduated with honors from a small West Coast college within driving distance of his parents, then went on—against the wishes of his conservative parents—to receive a master's degree in political science from that famously liberal bastion, the University of California at Berkeley. While in grad school, he became politically active and an advocate for numerous social causes. His favorite and most influential teacher was, according to Robert, one of the more controversial figures on campus. Robert credits this professor with not only reinforcing some of his established beliefs but, more important, challenging many of his traditional views, spurring him to expand his thinking in ways that have fundamentally changed his life and view of the world. According to Robert, his core beliefs and values are primarily the product of the strong influence of his parents, his rigorous religious training, the many books he read as a child, and his exposure to new ideas and thoughtful people during his graduate years, nurtured most memorably in the endless discussions he had with his favorite graduate school professor.

Now Diane's story: Married with two children, ages two and four, she's a stay-at-home mother who's active in her church and a community volunteer. She received a nursing degree from the University of Nebraska and intends to pursue a nursing career once her children attend school full-time. Her husband owns a small construction company and works part-time as a volunteer fireman. Diane and her family live in the same midwestern community where she was born and raised; her parents live two miles away, in the house they moved into when Diane was a teenager. When asked about the origin of her values and beliefs, Diane points immediately to her parents as the strongest influence. Both of her parents, she says, are hard working, possess strong religious views, and take a conservative approach to almost everything. Her father owned a hardware store and small grocery. Both her mother and father worked from "dusk to dawn" to make ends meet. Diane's only brother was killed in a military training accident. Despite the pain and anger she and her parents felt over her brother's death, her positive views about the military remained largely unchanged. During her mid-teens, she rebelled against much of the religious doctrine she'd been exposed to, but as she got older, and particularly after having children, she returned to most of the same beliefs and values taught her by her parents and religious educators. Diane believes that her feelings about war and the existence of evil, and her admiration for President Bush, stem from the influence of her parents, her religious experience, the frequent conversations she has with her husband (who, according to Diane, is cut from the same political cloth as she), as well as a circle of friends—her "political buddies," she calls them—with whom she shares ideology, who watch the same news channels, and who keep each other current on world affairs by exchanging books on topics that are vaguely or explicitly political.

Both Robert's and Diane's stories exemplify how plentiful and diverse are the factors that influence the formation of core values and beliefs: parental input (particularly during the early childhood years), religious teaching, formal educational experiences, the beliefs of selected teachers, reading materials both religious and political, news reporting on television, and the beliefs and values of friends, peers, and extended family. Our core values and beliefs, then, admit to multidimensional origins and reflect complex indoctrinating forces.

But for the purposes of this book and its potential benefit to you, the most significant point to take away from Robert's and Diane's stories, I think, is not the multiplicity of influences on them. Rather, it is how—though the strongest and most pervasive influences may have occurred during early childhood—*the learning process continued throughout their adolescent and adult years.*

That's not unique to Robert and Diane. This evolution happens to all of us, if you believe the data and stories we've collected on the many clients who have attended HPI.

Why have I spent so much time, relatively speaking, examining Robert and Diane? I do it because I believe their life stories are representative; because I think that looking at them can help you to look at your *own* life and story, with a finer appreciation for the force of indoctrination in your life. By doing so, you come to see—I hope—that indoctrination, quite simply, determines the reality you experience; this reality, in turn, largely determines your hopes (and, equally important, your sense of hope), your fears, your joys, your sorrows, your feeling of accomplishment, your sense of value, your resilience through all of life's storms—in short, your destiny. As Freud and quite a few others have noted before me, the better portion of our most enduring indoctrinations occur during early childhood, when the brain is particularly malleable and critical thinking skills are developing. Once the indoctrination is complete and the brain's architecture has changed, it is unlikely that even logic and rational thinking can dissuade you from your view of the world and the story you create that reflects it. The progression works this way: A core belief is embedded, thus changing brain structure; the change in brain structure changes your reality; the change in your reality changes your stories. Perhaps truer than "You can't teach an old dog new tricks" would be "You can't unteach an old dog old tricks." While the difference between the two statements may appear cosmetic, the latter speaks more starkly, if clumsily, to origins, explaining *why* old dogs have practically zero chance of learning a new trick. Once you've formed a core belief—say, that fear drives all people, or that no one really appreciates or cares about you, or that Belgians are bad people—you will argue and defend your position against all challengers. You simply *know* your belief is right. New tricks can't be taught to you because you see absolutely no reason for them in the first place.

Outside of the sheer pleasure and fascination that comes from studying and understanding any meaningful idea, the source of the influences on our values and beliefs would otherwise merit no special scrutiny . . . *if your story took you where you want to go in life*. If your story engaged you in such a way that you were always in the process of fulfilling your most important missions in life. If your values and beliefs, deeply cherished though they were, could easily be tweaked or even overhauled whenever they seemed to be working at cross-purposes with your interests.

If, if. If only any of that were the case.

But it isn't.

THE DILEMMA OF FLAWED VALUES AND BELIEFS

What happens when our values and beliefs are seriously flawed? What if one or more of the assumptions we make about life are tragically misguided? *Flawed beliefs, I am certain, produce flawed stories; a flawed story, I am equally certain, produces failure.*

In the worst examples, the embedding of core beliefs and values of dubious or outright indefensible worth can have catastrophic repercussions on the culture—take Hitler's belief in the inferiority of Jews and the superiority of the Aryan race, for example, or the Islamic extremist's belief that nonbelievers represent the most vile form of evil and must be exterminated from the earth.

On an individual scale, the person who harbors a seriously flawed belief victimizes those around her—and damages herself, of course, worst of all. Judy L., employed by a giant company and in charge of $1 billion in sales, attended HPI in 2004 with twelve of her direct reports, nine of whom were men. Upon receiving the 360 evaluation feedback from her direct reports, Judy grew visibly upset, then defensive. Feedback from eight of the nine men was disturbing and consistent—disturbing in large part *because* it was consistent; so consistent, in fact, that Judy was convinced the men had conspired to send her the same negative message. All but one of them depicted Judy's approach as a person, as well as her management relationship to them and to others, as distrustful, cynical, angry, defensive.

After discarding the idea—by herself, to her credit—that there was a "conspiracy," Judy worked hard to figure out why the men beneath her (none of the three women drew such a portrait of her in their 360s) could feel the way they did. Finally, after taking a hard, genuine look at herself, she acknowledged to me that, yes, it was true: She didn't trust men. Then she articulated the story she'd always told herself to support and justify this belief. "Two days before my fourteenth birthday my mother and father announced they were getting divorced," she wrote as part of her storytelling inventory. "My mother had discovered that her husband of seventeen years was having an affair with her best friend. The effect on me, my sister, and my mom was devastating. Barely four years into my own marriage, I learned that my husband, whom I adored, was involved in multiple affairs. I've been divorced for five years but the sense of loss and betrayal are ever-present. I don't think I'll ever fully get over it. To make matters worse, I'm ninety percent sure my boyfriend, whom I've been dating for eight months, is cheating on me. Do I trust men? No, I don't! Why should I? I'm bitter and angry but I can't let go of it. I'm not even sure I want to. As long as I feel this way, I won't be disappointed or blindsided ever again. I'm surprised, however, that my feelings about men have spilled over into the workplace. I thought I hid them quite well. Obviously not."

YOUR CRAP DETECTOR

Asked what it takes to be a great writer, Ernest Hemingway replied, "a built-in shock-proof crap detector."

We all have a crap detector—some better than others, some exquisitely on the mark, some tragically deficient. It is our evaluative inner voice, an absolutely vital instrument that enables us—privately, at least—to see things for what they are; to know if something, deep down, is good or bad for us.

Just being able to detect crap, however, is not enough; if it were, then we'd all be doing the right thing for ourselves, all the time. There are people all over who, while capable of detecting crap, do nothing about it (for example, those who remain in abusive relationships, rotten marriages, dead-end jobs; who take no concrete steps to pursue lifelong dreams). Theirs might be called an "underactive" crap detector: It exists, it's even turned on, but it doesn't trigger meaningful action, and thus does its owner little good.

An underactive crap detector also makes us vulnerable to all sorts of deceptive influences (e.g., some of the indoctrinations mentioned earlier in this chapter). If we refuse to listen to what we know is suspect, then we are complicit in the sinister indoctrination that may happen to us. We need the crap detector to filter, to protect us from all kinds of destructive input. An underactive crap detector greatly increases the chance that we might drink the Kool-Aid.

On the other hand, we don't want an "overactive" crap detector, either—an inner voice that, metaphorically speaking, guards us so tightly against external input that nothing new is allowed in, even if new, constructive data or perspectives are precisely what we need to improve our story. The possibility that Judy L. could encounter, much less befriend or grow intimate with, a trustworthy man seemed impossible so long as she had an overactive crap detector. If you built up such a wall and, say, a colleague commented that he'd discovered a more efficient way to run meetings, or your mother told you about a movie she'd just seen that she thought you would really enjoy, or a friend you hadn't encountered in years showed up in phenomenal physical condition and described his regimen . . . you'd block it all out. Because you approached everything new with cynicism, skepticism.

If positive change doesn't happen with an underactive crap detector, with an overactive one, change *can't* happen. Yet change might be exactly what you need: By giving up your own long-held notions about physical conditioning, say, which haven't worked, and indoctrinating yourself with your friend's thinking, you'd have a real shot at turning your dysfunctional story about fitness into a constructive one. But your crap detector is having none of it. An overactive crap detector won't allow any changes in your stories to occur; it perceives everything as threatening or irrelevant. So a crap detector gone berserk doesn't help us, either.

In workshops, I often compare the crap detector to a gatekeeper: It's there to let in the good influences and keep out the riffraff. What so often amazes me, and amazes the clients themselves, is how sensationally well developed their gatekeeper is in their business life—knowing the good people to hire and the bad ones to eliminate; jettisoning superfluous or destructive ideas and embracing constructive and necessary ones; focusing always on the fundamentals—and yet how sensationally *under*developed their gatekeeper is in their personal life— neglecting their health and their relationships with loved ones; getting caught up in what doesn't really matter; not focusing on the fundamentals. I often say that if the gatekeeper they employed for their personal life were hired to do the same for their business life, they'd have gone bankrupt years ago.

You need a built-in, shockproof crap detector to help you, but not just to know when to let in the good external influences and keep out the bad. It's also valuable in allowing you to distinguish between two things very much within you: your public voice and your private voice—the latter, the very force that provides a running narrative of your life and, in many ways, determines its success.

Five

THE PRIVATE VOICE

I don't mean to suggest that because you, like all of us, are subject to the effects of subtle indoctrination, you're but one small step away from succumbing to a cult and relinquishing all control over your thoughts, your money, your life. Still, distasteful as it may be to accept, there *are* parallels we can learn from. And perhaps it's in the unabashed, unnuanced nature of extreme indoctrination to let us peek behind the curtain and understand a little better how all indoctrinations work *inside* of us, how they can seep in and help to create storylines for us that can be at once fantastically seductive and destructive. This knowledge may prove extremely useful to us even for everyday situations, even for those of us who could never imagine ourselves, in ten lifetimes, capitulating to cult-think of any sort.

To embed beliefs in us, precisely which part of our story are "they" trying to infiltrate and transform? Two parts, really: our public, outer voice—the one we use to account for ourselves (i.e., tell stories) to others—and especially the private, inner voice—the one we use to narrate our life story to ourselves. Years of indoctrination can result in the partial or complete loss of ownership of that private voice. It's an extremely disturbing loss because it means you no longer own your stories (if you ever did); these stories are someone else's now. *In your own body, in your own life, you have been usurped by another.* This inner, private voice may belong instead to your mother, father, relative or anyone who played a powerful role in your life. Your teacher or preacher maybe. For Steve B.—the outwardly confident, inwardly joyless CEO who ran his family's multimillion-dollar rubber business and otherwise seemed to have it all—his private voice belonged to his late father, a revelation Steve experienced only after coming to see us. That Steve's voice was not his own—no matter how much he may have respected and loved his father, which he did, abundantly—prevented Steve from experiencing genuine pleasure and fulfillment in his life. When he realized the inauthenticity of his voice, and how many years it had been not his own, he broke down.

Is your private voice still yours? You're sure about that? To help determine this, and whether your private voice is working for or against you, here are a few questions to ask yourself:

1. What's the general tone of your inner voice? Harsh, bitter, and critical? Or supportive, kind, and encouraging?
2. Estimate how much of the time your inner voice is a constructive force in your life, and how much a destructive one. To what extent does it instill you with confidence and hope? To what extent does it terrorize you with messages of inadequacy, incompetence, and regret?
3. Ever feel that your inner voice is not really you speaking? If it doesn't feel like you, whose voice might it be? Consider both content and tone.
4. To help you achieve real happiness and to leave the legacy you desire for those you care about most, what changes would you make in the content and tone of your private voice?
5. To what extent is your private voice aligned with your ultimate mission in life? What seems to be the driving force behind your private voice? Where is it taking you?

Because everyone possesses both a public and private voice, and because the stories we tell and hear embed themselves more deeply in our subconsciousness the more they are repeated, the most successful indoctrinations, for both good and bad ends, aim to influence both voices, repeatedly. The more aligned both voices are with the desired new learning, the more open one is to being indoctrinated.

In the end, though, it is only the one voice that truly matters. Because your inner voice is telling you your story *all the time*, you're rarely even conscious that you've been "telling" a story. Indeed, it's hard to imagine what it would feel like if suddenly you stopped telling yourself your story, or even just changed this one.

Therefore, if you control the quiet, internal, private voice, then you own the keys to the vault. At least that's how brainwashing experts have long proceeded in their sinister, and very successful, efforts to control and reform the minds of prisoners of war. Years of experience taught brainwashers that, once they gained control of a prisoner's private voice, his whole mind was theirs for the taking.

WHEN STORIES COLLIDE: THE TWO VOICES OF THE STORYTELLER

The public voice expresses the story we tell others. It is posture, and by that I don't mean *false* posture but rather presentation. It is our voice to the world outside ourselves. It may or may not reflect the truth.

The private voice expresses the story we tell ourselves. It can be the measured voice of reflection or the completely uncensored voice of cynicism. It can be our filter, our gut check, our crap detector, our relentless, brutal critic. It reflects our internal reality at the moment but may or may not reflect objective truth.

Both our public and private voices coexist throughout our life. Both voices help to form "realities" for us and, to a lesser extent, for those around us. Although the two voices move us forward in different ways, if they are to work effectively for us, they need to be *aligned*.

That's the ideal, of course: having both voices be as aligned* as much as possible. No, let me refine that. To be aligned is necessary but not sufficient; after all, you may privately believe that Joe in Accounting is skimming off the top, and you may even share that view publicly with colleagues—but if it's not true that Joe is doing that, then simply being aligned in your views means nothing. Or a man may feel, privately, that all women are to be mistrusted, and he may, publicly, tell joke after joke that betrays his misogynistic view, but merely having his voices in concert with one another doesn't necessarily reflect anything

---

* "Aligned" and "identical" are not the same. If one's public and private voices are identical, then one treats both voices without regard for the special, necessarily singular role each plays; whenever convicted mass-murderer Charles Manson has been interviewed from prison, he spoke as if no boundary existed between his private voice and the public expression of that voice. If one's public and private voices are aligned, then they support each other, each in their unique way, for one's greater benefit. An example of this might be Lance Armstrong, whose outward expression of his internally voiced desires lead him to achieve his goals.

positive or factual. The ideal, then, is to have both voices be aligned *and* to have each of them express a version of a story that is virtuous, productive, and realistic.

Unfortunately, that rarely happens. I estimate that in 80% to 90% of my clients the private and public voices are out of synch on one or more of their most important life stories, as well as dysfunctional—their stories around work, around family, around health, etc. In these cases, the two voices are not working toward the same goal, not operating from the same vantage.

Some examples, in minor and major affairs, that may feel familiar:

Public voice:	*Yes, if that's what you want me to do, I'm happy to do it.*
Private voice:	*Why can't I ever say no? I hate myself for being such a coward.*
Public voice:	*I know you didn't mean what you said the other day. You were just having a bad day.*
Private voice:	*That's the last time I'll trust you. You've crossed the line for good.*
Public voice:	*Sure, Betty, I'd love to get together for lunch sometime.*
Private voice:	*Not in a thousand years would I have a one-on-one lunch with you. Life's too short.*
Public voice:	*I'm sure I can do it. Let me give it a shot.*
Private voice:	*I've just set myself up for huge failure. Now everyone will find out how incompetent I really am.*

Examples like these must resonate. After all, how many times a day do we wish that our public voice expressed more accurately and explicitly what we want or need? For most of us, that would be a giant, probably welcome departure from our usual response, the one where we're reciting as if from a script, automatically and dispassionately, subverting our self-interest in favor of civility and etiquette. Which, sadly, is not really life but rather some watered-down simulation of life.

As the above examples and countless others show, our public and private voices can send very different messages that lead to entirely different stories, stories that may conflict or even cancel each other out. For example, Public Voice expresses regard for the short-term ("That was so much fun—let's definitely get back to Vegas before we break for the year!") but undermines what Private Voice needs for the long term ("I can't pass my MCATs unless I study all-out for the next two months"); or Public Voice puts professional well-being first ("If no one else is available, you can count on me to fly to Sydney to close the deal") while Private Voice recites a message more concerned with familial well-being ("Janice has been raising the children practically as if she's a single mother and I want to know who my kids are"). Each time this occurs—and it may occur dozens of times a day—our public voice becomes, in varying degrees, disingenuous, inauthentic, to ourselves and/or to others. *How we feel about our own credibility and trustworthiness, about our ability to see our missions through to completion, to see our life stories through to fulfilling ends, begins to erode.* In the best case, this "battle of voices" wastes precious energy. In the worst case, it thoroughly undermines our sense of well-being and inner peace. One client put it eloquently: "My public voice always says 'Can do!' My private voice always says, 'Can't do!'"

But wait. Must we really get these voices to align? And, if so, how can we possibly keep these two voices in check? Don't the demands of our world—the masked ball that is polite society—often obligate us to say and do things that we may not want or believe in, while privately we feel quite differently?

To get our story right, I believe, our private and public voices must each get the message right and true, working hand-in-glove. And to help facilitate this, most of us need exactly what it sounds like we'd need: voice lessons.

Voice lessons allow you to control both voices, and in so doing to control your story. *Specifically, if you can't get your inner voice right, you can't get your stories right.* The irrefutability of that simple statement has become clear to me after years at this. Say what you want outwardly, but it is your inner voice that is the master storyteller, the one that carries the greatest power and influence over your destiny, over who you become and where you end up. When you get your private storytelling voice right, and then align your public voice with that voice, your power will be breathtaking and nuclear. Proper "voice lessons"—which we can practice ourselves, once we know what we're going after—will finally allow both voices to recite from the same page. In this way, they will be authentic. In this way, your story will reflect the real world. In this way, your story will give you hope. In this way, your story will be consistent with your core values and beliefs. And in this way, you will take yourself where you want to go.

With the proper self-training, controlling both voices is indeed possible. There are three basic steps to gaining voice control:

1. acknowledge the existence of your private voice;
2. turn up the volume on it;
3. listen to it.

Listen to what your inner voice is saying. Is it a relentless, second-person critic? (*You're so stupid! You never do anything right. You'll never amount to anything in this world.*) A first-person complainer/whiner? (*I hate this job. I always get dumped on to do things nobody else wants. Why do I put up with all this crap?*) The supportive, encouraging "coach" voice? (*Hang in there. Take a deep breath and finish what you started. You can do this.*)

Listen to the stories your voice tells. By being fully aware of your silent story, you will unearth, perhaps for the first time, the private voice which is, in the end, the voice of greatest power. You may find your private voice to be surprisingly wise, confident and encouraging—an absolutely brilliant storyteller. At other times, perhaps more frequently, your inner voice may sound unjustifiably harsh, impatient, irrational, critical. By amping up the volume and listening carefully to the story being told, you begin the voice-training process. Once you genuinely hear the voice and the message it's carrying, you can determine whether the story is true, whether it can take you where you want to go in life, and whether it inspires you, finally, to hope-filled action.

VOICE LESSONS: TEN INNER VOICE SKILLS

The voice training that follows is designed to help you to discover, and eventually equip you to access easily, the many inner voices you have at your disposal. These private voices are powerful, virtuous, and useful—but useless if you don't know that they exist (most people seem not to), don't realize how powerful they can be, don't know that they can help you to achieve your ultimate mission, and don't know how to summon them.

The first step in accessing the various private voices you possess is simply by believing that they can be cultivated inside you. After that, you "merely" need to learn how to draw them forth, and to do so regularly so that you can invest energy in them and, by doing so, strengthen them, like muscles.

I realize there are many types of voices below. I don't expect you to memorize them, or cultivate them all at once.

1. *Quiet Your Inner Voice.* Shut down the internal chatter by immersing yourself in an activity that engages you fully. Complete absorption quiets the inner voice; in fact, it may be the first time your private voice—often so critical and negative—has had nothing to say to you in a very long time, and the silence may be deafeningly profound. Meditation, deep breathing, and yoga are especially effective ways to reach this tranquility but it may also be achieved by playing sports, building models or sand castles, riding a horse, painting, following a dung beetle, or any of a thousand activities. While everyone should develop this quieting skill, it's particularly beneficial to those in high-stress situations, such as medicine, sports, and law enforcement. Developing the ability to methodically quiet your inner voice better equips you, conversely, to clear away the ambient inner noise when it's time to perform and you need to access all your skills. In short, quieting your inner voice helps you to focus better.

2. *Summon Your Inner Voice of Conscience.* Spend energy exploring, clarifying, and understanding your values and ethics—your ideas and thoughts about integrity, honesty, and character. Ask yourself questions like, "What's really the right thing to do here?" or "What do I really believe should be done here?" Sometimes reflecting on how a deeply admired parent, friend, business leader, pastor, or military

leader would respond in this situation will help summon this voice. The more you draw this voice forward, the more available it will be.

3. *Summon Your Inner Voice of Reason and Wisdom.* Inside us all is the voice of sanity, of reason—yes, even of great wisdom. But far too many people, sadly, fail to cultivate this capacity. This voice represents your ability to rise above all the noise, the clutter, the distractions, the cloud of emotions, and to see the situation for what it really is and make judgments and decisions accordingly. The ability to see clearly in the storm is neither inherited nor something that develops with age. It comes from lots of hard, focused mental lifting. To nurture this voice, try this: The next time a difficult situation erupts and you feel the irrational, childish, "the sky is falling" voice bubbling inside you, sit down immediately, take a deep breath and (a) write down the facts of what is happening or has just happened (no emotion, please; just facts); and (b) write a brief story around the facts that reflects both wisdom and perspective and will make you proud when you read it six months or a year from now. Carry the paper with you always. Every time you start thinking or acting irrationally, stop and re-read this story.

4. *Summon Your Inner Voice of Support and Encouragement.* What would you say to your best friend or beloved family member if he or she were facing the predicament you're now facing (for example, made a foolish mistake or failed to get a promotion that was clearly deserved)? Whatever message you would send to those you most care about, whatever tone of voice you would use, send it to yourself. Use it on yourself. Again—as with the voice of conscience, the voice of reason, or any other dimension of your inner voice—each time you call on this voice, you strengthen it and further improve access to it. For many people I've worked with, this voice is particularly difficult to train. For some, unfortunately, what rises up is not encouragement but rather a hideously unmerciful critic. In some cases, this self-deprecating voice can be so contemptuous and toxic that bystanders are shocked when the voice is made public. "I'm the biggest

loser the world has ever known!" or "I hate myself for who I am" or "I'd be better off dead!" To kill off this highly destructive voice—the flip side of the supportive, encouraging voice—you must deprive it of energy. Don't feed it. Instead, redirect your energy toward your supportive, constructive voice.

5. *Summon Your Inner Voice of Toughness.* I call this your "fighting voice" and it's one of the most important voices we possess; after all, to complete our ultimate mission in life, we must be great fighters, and without access to this voice we're too easily victimized by the world around us. To draw it forth, visualize what a person who inspires you would say. For example, perhaps your parent was a great fighter in life, or perhaps you watched a friend courageously battle a terrible disease. (This exercise, as with exercises for so many other aspects of your inner voice, parallels what many Christians do when measuring possible responses to situations by considering "W.W.J.D.?"—"What would Jesus do?") If Tiger Woods, Christopher Reeve, or Mother Teresa inspires you, use your voice to mimic *their* legendary fighting spirit, courage, or resilience. Connect the difficulties now confronting you with a *purpose* or someone you deeply care about. For example: You are training for a marathon to win the respect of your son; you have committed to coming home at 5:30 three nights a week for the happiness and psychological well-being of your family; you are drawing a line in the sand about downsizing your division, telling your superior you won't dismiss your people until you've helped them find other work; you are eating more organic foods not just for your health but also to do your small part in helping the environment, the planet your grandkids will need to live on. Such articulated motivation helps you to be tough and stay tough on yourself when the situation calls for it. You become the hard-assed coach who, beneath the gruff exterior, has your best interest at heart. Eventually, you, the coach, simply won't tolerate whining, complaining, scapegoating, self-pitying, giving up, not going all out; this

voice will be there always, to bolster you, push you, implore you to fight courageously, no matter what.

As with all other voices, the more you visit it, the stronger and more available it is.

6. *Summon Your "I Don't Buy It" Inner Voice.* This is what I have also called the crap detector. If this voice is underdeveloped, you risk becoming tragically gullible. You may be easily indoctrinated, possibly for sinister purposes. But getting this voice pitched just right is difficult, because we all have natural tendencies: Some of us tend to be overly trustful and open; others, overly distrustful and cynical. That's why you must also work on the *opposite* of the "I Don't Buy It" Voice . . .

7. *Learn to Suspend Your "I Don't Buy It" Inner Voice.* Okay, you're a doubting Thomas about people and the world. That's smart—but only up to a point, because new learning and input (a.k.a. indoctrination) are not only good for you but may be necessary for your success, even survival. Tough as it is to suspend your suspicious, questioning voice, you must, because this is how the door to personal change opens. If your story around work, money, family, or health is dysfunctional, then you don't want to block out everything; after all, "everything" includes all that is new and functional, too. Since we're constantly required to make course corrections for our lives and businesses to succeed, then it is only through skillfully letting in selected forces of indoctrination that we can acquire the new learning and adaptation required for success.

Teach yourself to suspend your cynical, crap-detecting voice simply by saying to yourself—every time this voice clears its jaded throat—"Stop. This is good for me." Stop the cynicism dead. And once you say "stop," immediately focus again on whatever new lesson you are learning.

8. *Summon Your Inner Voice of Compassion.* Think of emotions such as kindness, empathy, and sympathy as if they were muscles that grow and expand in response to the energy we invest in them: Just as your bicep grows as a consequence of

the energy you invest in it when weight-lifting, so your compassion as a human being grows as a consequence of the repeated energy you invest in it. Every time you stimulate feelings of compassion within yourself, you increase that capacity; the greater the capacity, the more accessible the voice. Anything or anyone that stimulates feelings of compassion in you is valuable in your voice training. Feelings of compassion might be stimulated by reading, by listening to people's stories, by visualizing and imagining how you would feel if this difficulty or that predicament were happening to a family member. Volunteering for work in hospitals, nursing homes, and soup kitchens might be the moral equivalent of heavy-duty weight-lifting sessions. I've heard so many stories of self-confessed cold-hearts who made the effort, if begrudgingly, to do this kind of volunteer work, and every time the result has been nearly identical: a newfound appreciation for the plight of one's fellow man, which of course deepens one's appreciation for life's blessings.

9. *Summon Your Voice of Sincerity.* One of the most crucial voices we possess, first and last because it validates all the other voices. That is, it signals for us and for others that the stories we tell are authentic, that they represent what we truly think and feel and that we can be trusted. Those who let this voice atrophy suffer painful, even tragic consequences. We all know people whose sincerity quotient is extremely low, even nonexistent. We perceive them as being phony, shallow, manipulative, calculating, inauthentic. When we're with people whose voice of sincerity is weak or nonexistent, we get the impression that their head and heart are not connected, that they do not act in concert with each other.

When your public voice resonates with sincerity, people perceive you to be real, grounded, genuine. To get the public voice right, however, you must get the private voice right. One's public voice cannot reflect what it cannot read or detect. The voice of sincerity begins by listening to and acknowledging one's private voice, then finding an appropriate and honorable way of expressing it when speaking publicly to others. Do it enough and the merging of the two voices becomes habitual. *People start believing that what you say is really who you are.*

10. *Summon Your Voice of Intuition.* This is the voice of your gut, a voice of intuitive intelligence that doesn't follow the standard pathways of conscious logic and reason. It represents a somewhat mystical way of knowing and, as a consequence, is often devalued, perhaps intentionally repressed. But training this voice, listening to and respecting this voice, can pay enormous dividends in just about every dimension of life. In relationships and in parenting, in work and in investing, when playing golf or sitting in a classroom, the voice of intuition can prove invaluable. Simply asking the question, "So what's my gut saying here?" can summon the voice. Your gut response may be right—or not! you may want to do the "wrong" thing!—but it's a voice that very much merits a listen.

Six

THE THREE RULES OF STORYTELLING

I COULDN'T BE HAPPIER

In 1971, a landmark study by Philip Brickman and Donald Campbell introduced the concept of the "hedonic treadmill," which suggested that people's emotional reactions to life events worked much like sensory adaptation—your eyes adjusting to the dark, say—so that "good and bad events temporarily affect happiness, but people quickly adapt back to hedonic neutrality." The study also suggested that each of us possesses a more or less fixed happiness "set point." Memorably, further study posited that lottery winners, once the novelty and excitement of their financial windfall had worn off, were no happier than nonwinners; alternatively, the recently paraplegic, once the newness of their misfortune had faded, were not substantially less happy than those who could walk. People continue to pursue happiness, the study concluded, because we believe, *incorrectly*, that greater happiness lies just around the corner—in the next goal accomplished, the next social relationship obtained, the next problem solved. *Forget it*, admonished the unsettling new theory: In the long run, your efforts are futile.

If the hedonic treadmill model really was correct, then almost no change in life circumstance should ever lead to a lasting change in happiness or sadness. (Some events, particularly the loss of a longtime spouse, *are* associated with a marked, often permanent changing of the set point.) If true, then there was no way, through our own efforts, to raise our happiness set point, which seemed substantially, if not predominantly, a heritable gift or curse. Ashes to ashes, dust to dust: No matter how high or low you got, you would always return roughly to your set emotional level/mood.

In 2006, thirty-five years after this initial study, researchers Ed Diener, Richard Lucas, and Christie Scollon published a survey called "Beyond the Hedonic Treadmill." While acknowledging that their studies were in the initial stages, their work contradicted the idea of an unchangeable happiness set point and put forth the notion that, with work, one might be able to elevate it. "Happiness can and does change," claimed the authors. At least it did for some people surveyed—and if it did for some, then there was hope for at least some of the rest of us.

So what did those people do to raise it? When faced with tough times or disappointments, they tended to use reappraisal strategies (such as reordering priorities or creating new stories to explain events to themselves). Faced with the complications and difficulties of aging, older people whose set points rose, or at least didn't fall as much as the norm, made adjustments: They were more likely than the rest of the elderly population to use coping styles such as humor, information seeking, and "keeping going." Others who evidenced an increase in happiness set point included those who frequently changed activities and those who performed random acts of kindness each week.

If this newer survey is true—and everything about my professional experience supports the idea that one's set point *can* be elevated markedly—then we constantly need to infuse our story with new thinking, new energy. To do so can bring about shifts in happiness, excitement, enthusiasm, joy, inspiration that are not temporary but sustained. And to come back to one's now more fluid set point, it is (to paraphrase Dickens) a far, far better place one returns to than one had ever known before.

But one needs to work at this, continuously. If not, then one almost certainly retreats to previous, lower levels of happiness and engagement.

Perhaps the best way to raise the level, a method used particularly by spiritually inclined clients, is to *consciously increase thoughts of gratitude in one's daily life.* Whether I knew it or not, that's what I was doing when I committed to calling my sons at eight P.M. every night I was out of town—reappreciating and reconnecting on a regular basis with the greatest blessings in my life. One hardworking client felt terribly guilty that she couldn't be at her dying mother's bedside all day; by committing to calling her every morning, visiting her every lunchtime, and calling her every night after work, she could feel her mother responding (she now had a dose of love and attention she could count on) and the client herself felt her guilt giving way to pride that she was doing something tangible for her mother, something both of them could feel. Another client, a hard-charging, frequent-traveling VP who was always out of the house before his daughters woke for school, decided he'd put little notes to them in their lunchbags every morning before leaving for work. They said nothing about it; still, he continued to do it, feeling good about the gesture. One day, sitting in the airport terminal as he waited to board for yet another business trip, he opened his briefcase to find a love note from each of his daughters.

Building a sense of deeper gratitude into our stories may help to prevent that adaptation that brings with it complacency. Since it is eminently possible to identify the beautiful things in our lives, we must appreciate and reappreciate them.

The inevitably exciting conclusion of this later study by Diener, Lucas, and Scollon is that, were the workplace made more engaging and interesting, it could "provide an optimistic foundation for the various fields of applied psychology"; that is, what is implemented and learned there might eventually be applicable to society at large. The study's authors, who were also interested in the dynamics of organizations, called for a "system of national accounts of well-being in which people's happiness, meaning, and engagement are assessed over time and in various situations." In short, when we discover what makes people feel better—consistently and on a daily basis—then instituting changes to transform the corporate culture could meaningfully raise the set point of many employees.

This is exactly what we've done when we work with entire business units or whole companies. While ultimately it comes down to each individual's commitment to bettering himself or herself, we try to show management the importance of creating an environment that fosters respect—and then actually supports the idea, putting its money where its mouth is by providing useful programs and tools (making healthier snacks available, mandating exercise, mandating time off, monitoring balance in its employees' lives). Theoretically, this can only be positive for everyone in the organization, top to bottom.

And in actuality, it's true, too. Just ask Procter & Gamble. Or Nordstrom. Or GlaxoSmithKline. Or PepsiCo. Or Janus. Or Qualcomm. Or other giant corporations and mid-sized companies alike, all of whom have been through our program and are now far along on the road to reconceiving their organizations into ones that understand that you achieve long-term productivity and profitability not by the time your people clock in but by the energy they invest. That you're better equipped to plan and meet bigger-picture goals not by single-mindedness but by balance. That nothing compels employees to be loyal and hard-working more than a belief in the story—the good story—their company tells about itself.

REWRITING: TURNING POINTS

So positive change really is possible; great. How does one identify the right time to initiate the change?

All good stories, says Herminia Ibarra, professor of organizational behavior at INSEAD, hinge on dramatic moments, truth . . . and turning points. All life stories have turning points. Turning points can be positive: wedding day, the dawn of a relationship, leaving for college, a job promotion, buying a home, becoming pregnant or giving birth, getting a driver's license, committing to train for your first marathon or completing it, getting your first A in math, making the commitment in various ways to quit drinking, smoking, overeating. Turning points can be negative: death of a spouse, loss of a marriage, a heart attack, being passed over for partnership, taking a physical that reveals dangerously unhealthy blood chemistry; the failure of a business, getting disturbing feedback from direct reports on 360 evaluations, hearing that a close friend, a lifelong smoker, has lung cancer. It should be said, also, that one person's negative turning point is another one's positive; after the fact, many people have described a traumatic experience as "the best thing that ever happened to me."

A turning point is simply an event or circumstance that precipitates a significant change in the story, a change in how we think or feel about something important in our lives. Turning points can alter, suddenly, our day-to-day circumstances, our self-confidence, our perception, even our values and beliefs. Turning points usually entail powerful emotion. They can force us to face the truth as nothing else can. F. Scott Fitzgerald provocatively—and in my opinion wrongly—said, "There are no second acts in American lives." Maybe so—but only if one chooses to ignore the profound opportunities for transformation represented by the plentiful turning points in every life.

Here's the thing about turning points, though: They're not always obvious. (Nor must big events—a wedding or a new job, say—necessitate profound changes in how we live.) Many turning points are subtle, recognizable only in hindsight; they "tend to be much more obvious in the telling than in the living," write Ibarra and Kent Lineback in their article "What's Your Story?" in the *Harvard Business Review*. A turning point can be the tail-end of something gradual and cumulative—more accurately described as a tipping point than a turning point. "During our life we often experience periods when we seem to lose our sense of meaning and purpose," writes Robert Quinn in his book, *Change the World*. "There is no longer a feeling of alignment between our inner values and our tasks in the external world. We find ourselves working harder and harder and receiving less satisfaction from our efforts. We struggle through every day, lacking the vitality, commitment, and initiative we used to have. After much inner reflection and contemplation, we begin to realize that we need a new focus, a new vision, but it is difficult to uncover."

Hardly your typical *Aha!* moment he's describing—and yet the need for change as described here is so oppressive, one's skin almost crawls with it.

How, then, does a person this aimless and dissatisfied find the will to reassert control over life, to rediscover purpose, to tell a story that restores energy, fulfillment, and productivity where before there were fatigue, boredom, and despair?

By taking control over your story. You must be ready, if necessary, to rewrite it and rewrite it and rewrite it. (Norman Mailer once said that virtually all writing is really rewriting.) You may need, at least at first—before you get the hang of it, before you have "ritualized" new habits until you can stop thinking about them—to do it every day, even several times a day, if your story is to engage you every day. Perhaps this sounds curiously like plain old positive thinking; perhaps it sounds like making lemonades from lemons. What it really is, though, is treating your life, this vital and organic thing, as a story, this similarly vital and organic thing. Woody Allen once said that a relationship is like a shark: to stay alive, it has to keep moving forward. ("And I think what we got on our hands," he says morosely to his soon-to-be-ex in *Annie Hall*, "is a dead shark.") *Your story has to move.* It has to move you, and it has to move, period. In 2006, when Michelle Wie played in the Men's Sony Open tournament in Hawaii, her goal had been to make the 36-hole cut and become the first woman to do so in a PGA event in 60 years. But after shooting a brutal 79, eight over par, on the opening day, her chance of making the cut was pretty much gone. That evening, she called me, terribly disappointed, to talk about the round. Even Michelle—she of the fine-tuned ultimate mission at the wise age of fourteen—needed reminding that, rather than portray this to herself as a failure, she could use it as a boomerang to something positive indeed. If you're inclined, after all, a turning point is always just around the bend.

"More important than what happened today," I told Michelle, "is the story you tell yourself about the whole tournament after it's over. You control it. Tomorrow, on the first tee, I want you to imagine you're the leader. To win the tournament you'll have to shoot in the sixties."

The following day, Michelle dug deep and turned in a 3-under-par 68. Although she missed the cut, her fine second round had her bubbling with excitement. To her, it felt like a success; amazingly, her experience at this tournament from which she'd just been eliminated put her on an upswing.

We must learn how to turn our life story into a living thing, something we know how to grow, repair, and maintain.

THE THREE RULES OF STORYTELLING

Purpose, truth, action.

When writers really want to emphasize something, they put it in a one-sentence paragraph. If they suspect even *that* isn't emphasis enough, then they go to Plan B: break things up into still more melodramatic, one-word paragraphs.

Purpose.

Truth.

Action.

There are many parts to this life-as-story metaphor—the idea of the private voice versus the public voice; the idea that we're often bogged down by faulty assumptions; etc. These and other ideas I have yet to elaborate on need to be understood if you're to make the kind of profound life improvements that drew you to this book in the first place.

But if you take just one idea away from this book, *an idea that transcends and serves as foundation for all the others*, it is those three words, as one:

Purpose—Truth—Action.

All good storytelling coheres around those three ideas. They are the three criteria, taken together, by which we judge the workability and ultimate success of our story. With those three principles in your pocket, you can summon your deepest intelligence and wisdom to protect yourself from all forms of sinister indoctrination and faulty storytelling, bad influences from without and within; armed with those three principles, you are virtually guaranteed to keep your story vital, moving, productive, fulfilling.

Let's review them:

Purpose: What is my ultimate purpose? What am I living for? What principle, what goal, what end? For my whole life, and every single day? Why do I do what I do? For what? What is the thing that would get me, say, to walk across a narrow plank 175 feet above the concrete, and to be sure and at peace that it's the right decision, the necessary one, the only one? What is the thing I'm driving toward—or should be—with every action I take? Have I articulated to myself my deepest values and beliefs, which are the bedrock of who I am and which must be inextricably tied to my purpose (and vice versa)? Who do I want to be at the end? What legacy do I want to leave? What epitaph about myself could I "live with"? When all is said and done, how do I want to be remembered? What is non-negotiable in my life? What do I believe must happen for me to have lived a successful life? Is my story taking me where I want to go? Is it "on-purpose"? Consistently? And why am I telling this story? What is my real motive? Is my purpose noble or ignoble?

Truth: Is the story I'm telling true? Does it conform to known facts? Is it grounded in objective reality as fully as possible; that is, does it coincide with some generally agreed-upon portrayal of the world? Or is it true only if I'm living in a dreamland? Is it a lie I tell myself when I think, "This is the way the world is"—my own, probably biased evaluation of things, one that's dubiously defensible, and which I repeat to myself because it provides false comfort for the way my life has turned out? Have I cooked my own books? Where has my crap detector failed me? Do I sidestep the parts of my story that are obviously untrue because they're just too painful to confront? Is my story something I still believe when I really dig down, when I listen to my most candid, private voice, when I do my best to shut out other influences and hear instead what *I* genuinely think and feel? Which is the truer statement: *My story is honest and authentic* or *My story is made up*? Is my story closer to a documentary or a work of fantasy? What myths am I perpetuating that could potentially seal my fate in areas of my life that really matter?

Action: A good story is premised on action . . . is mine? With my purpose firmly in mind, along with a confidence about what is really true, what actions will I now take to make things better, so that my ultimate purpose and my day-to-day life are better aligned? What habits do I need to eliminate? What new ones do I need to breed? Is more of my life spent participating or observing? Are my actions filled with hope—hope that I will succeed, hope that the change I seek is realistically within my grasp? Or is my "action-taking" really more accurately portrayed as "going through the motions"? Do I believe to my core that, in the end, my willingness to follow through with action will determine the success of my life? Do I believe that if I act with commitment and consistency I will end up where I want to be, where I have always felt I am capable of being? Does the story I tell myself move me to action? Does it inspire hope and determination in me? Am I confident that I can make any necessary course correction, no matter what stage of life I'm in, no matter how many times I may have failed at it in the past? Do I proceed in the belief that I will never surrender in this effort because my success as a human being is what's at stake?

Purpose and truth, which have been dissected in previous chapters, are the first two planks of your storytelling. Action—which gets its own chapter in Part II—is necessarily the third and final plank.

The central point we try to convey is that one must hold one's story up as if against a three-part checklist: Your story must have purpose (can you name it?), your story must be true (is it?), your story must lead to hope-filled action (does it? what is it?). If you can't answer those three questions affirmatively, clearly, certainly, then your story will fail.

When a client achieves a breakthrough, it is always—*always*—because he or she has come to a fundamental understanding of the interlocked nature of all three rules of storytelling. It's not good enough to satisfy one or even two of the three rules and content yourself that your story has now improved; it won't leave you 33% better off or 67% better off. More likely, you may have fulfilled one or even two of the three rules but because all three rules are not followed, your story remains dysfunctional.

While one needs to understand deeply each of the three rules of storytelling, not all rules are created equally. Truth and action probably give people more trouble than purpose. For example, what about those people who have purpose nailed . . . but not action? This is probably the most common of the permutations, and in some ways the most tragic. In this group you find the novelists who have yet to set pen to paper, lovers who are single and celibate, entrepreneurs who don't know the first thing about how to procure a small-business loan.

What about those for whom truth is the toughest part? Some live in another universe altogether, of course—people whose biases are as prominent as their minds are narrow—and it's hard to imagine getting through to them.

What if you think you've got all three rules covered? Congratulations . . . but do you really? Francesca believed she was fully engaged with her fifteen-year-old daughter, Maggie. Apart from her responsibilities as COO, Francesca was consumed by her devotion to Maggie. Francesca was certain that her Ultimate Mission (purpose) on earth was to be an extraordinary mother to Maggie; unlike Francesca's relationship with her alcoholic father—who alternated between being emotionally abusive and unavailable, then died early of alcoholism, thereby submarining any chance for Francesca or her siblings to make peace with him—she and her child would have frequent meals and vacations together, she vowed to herself, and she would always speak and act lovingly toward her daughter. Francesca believed that she had assessed her past and her present pretty much the way they were (truth). And in her mind, she was now doing all she could to align her behavior with her purpose (action). Yet soon after coming to us Francesca revealed, on evaluation forms, that the time she spent with her daughter was rushed and distracted, because she felt so much pressure at work. She acknowledged, too, that her overweight and poor eating and sleeping habits made her jittery and disengaged. She was increasingly away on business, leaving her daughter alone. (Francesca and her husband had divorced when Maggie was five, and he was barely involved in the girl's life.) Francesca admitted that she didn't get much pleasure from her work, though she derived some satisfaction from the sense of accomplishment she felt, and from the power, and from having people under her; her father's career, such as it was, had been so riddled by inconsistency, instability, and failure that she was driven to be his exact opposite. Francesca grew emotional realizing that, as well-intentioned as she was, her relationship with her daughter might not, in truth, be the ideal she had aimed for it to be. The night following the first day of the workshop, she called her daughter to ask her some frank questions about how she, Maggie, felt about Francesca and their life together. Without hesitating, Maggie said she wished her mother were around more. When Francesca pointed out that she needed to travel for her job, and that a high-paying job such as hers paid the tuition for Maggie's private school, Maggie responded that if the trade-off for having her mother around more was for Maggie to go to public school, she'd do it in a second. (Francesca didn't bother to point out that being at the private school would probably give Maggie a better chance to get into an Ivy League school; she realized that this desire, too, was hers, not Maggie's.) Maggie also said she was constantly concerned for her mom's health—a fear Maggie said she expressed frequently to her mother but which Francesca either ignored, dismissed, or explained away—and Maggie said she had frequent bad dreams that her mother would suddenly have a heart attack and die, leaving Maggie alone.

In the end, then, what did Francesca have? Let's see.

For starters, her story wasn't true. She had *believed* its truth but a little examination showed that she was wrong. She *thought* she was giving her daughter what she wanted and what she, Francesca, never had; she was wrong about that. She *thought* she could justify eating and sleeping badly because her work demanded it; she now saw she was wrong about that, too, and that these habits served not only to make her unhealthy but, in doing so, made her daughter anxious, even giving her nightmares. In distancing herself from the person her father was, Francesca aimed to make sure she was a more available parent—and she was wrong about that as well. Her travel made her unavailable for long stretches; when she was with her daughter she was not really engaged; and her lousy health significantly increased the possibility that she would die prematurely—a command performance of what her father had been to her, albeit in somewhat gentler form. While it was true that Francesca didn't touch alcohol, it was untrue that her fate—at least her life span—was destined to depart radically from her father's.

What about purpose—did Francesca at least have that? Well, yes—her daughter was undeniably the most important element in her life. But her larger purpose—finally to be part of a parent-child relationship that was deep and engaging, and to make family life happily predictable, and therefore a source of security and comfort—was not close to being achieved. One might say Francesca had purpose, but what did it matter if this purpose was so obviously misaligned with the way her life actually proceeded?

What about action—was Francesca taking that? Well, sure—she was certainly busy all the time working, succeeding, and providing. But not only was she frequently disengaged with her activities both at work and at home, she wasn't close to getting joy from them; furthermore, she was spending her time being busy with many things while she should have been doing other things—and mostly those things—that supported her ultimate purpose.

Purpose, truth, action. That triad is at the core of everything in this book, everything in stories, everything, frankly, that makes for a successful life.

Let's see how the three rules might be applied to a company's story.

When a small Midwest insurance company sent its entire sales force to us, it was for the same reason most companies send their employees: because they believed we'd make their people more engaged, less likely to change jobs, and more productive, and thus make the company more productive and profitable. But even though we enjoyed a successful workshop, with an amazingly committed-to-change group, what we and they did went only so far in changing the company's culture for the better because the people at the very top didn't support it. (It happens more than you might think: Mid-level manager has budget for our program, the top people think it's just another offsite/trust-building/rope-course boondoggle . . . and when their employees return charged up about taking more responsibility for their physical well-being and start wondering why there can't be healthier options in the cafeteria, etc. . . . well, there's an impasse.) Unlike many of the companies we work with, who *have* changed their culture to an impressive degree—Procter & Gamble, Citigroup, Glaxo-SmithKline, Texas-based grocery store chain HEB, to name a few—this insurance company continues, to this day, to tell a bad story, one that does not fulfill any of the three rules of good storytelling.

For example, ostensibly the culture says it's important for their employees to lead balanced lives, that it's fine to leave early to attend their child's basketball game, say—yet everyone knows it's still frowned upon, and that such an early weekday departure would be seen as a lack of commitment. So that part of their story isn't true.

What's more, the company claims that it is now all about people, and that its success is determined only by the quality of its people. Yet the long-standing gulf between upper management and the rest of the company, as well as the impersonal and penny-pinching way they handled a recent round of layoffs, shows not only that the story isn't true, but that they really are devoid of a transcendent purpose.

Clearly, the company is not aligned with its stated values. There has long been talk there of adding features like a childcare center, a gym, water and snack stations, all of which would not only make their employees happier but also more engaged, more alert, more likely to perform better and likelier to stay with the company longer. But that's all it has remained, talk. No real action. The company's tentacles extend their reach all the way into the employee's home—no one on the sales team feels they can turn off their cell phone at home, engendering resentment toward the company—yet, on the flip side, the company doesn't want their workers' home or family life to extend into the office, engendering still more resentment. The company tells its people it wants results . . . yet doesn't do anything to create the more balanced environment that is needed precisely to help one to produce those amazing results. So there's little hope-filled action, either.

That's one faulty company story. And several of their sales team have since left for two competitor companies who tell better stories, stories that *are* full of purpose and truth and characterized by action, not talk.

Years of experience with storytelling at HPI have helped us to formulate these three rules. We've also discovered that successful stories happen only when you take charge. So whether you believe in your company or not, it's up to you, no one else, to be vigilant about telling only stories that fulfill the three rules of storytelling.

WRITE YOUR NEW STORY

NEXT STEP: Write your New Story, making sure that it fulfills the criteria for good storytelling.

Crafting a new story is liberating. Also challenging, scary, and painful. It *should* be painful. After all, it will be more clear-eyed than your Old Story was in defining what you really want from life; it hacks away at the excuses and rationalizations that appeared in your Old Story; and it demands real change, something your Old Story was probably not that interested in. In short, it is more purposeful, truer, and more action-oriented than your Old Story.

In other words, it's got all the ingredients of a really good story.

That doesn't mean that all new stories have the same feel to them. Just because it's called your "New Story" doesn't mean it's all sweetness and light. For some people, their New Story is characterized by an uplifting, cheerleading tone, while still satisfying, the three rules of storytelling (*The doors of the world are open to me, yet I keep tiptoeing in through the back. No more. I'm walking in through the front door.*). For others, their New Story sounds more like a bracing rebuke of what their life will be if they don't change, and change fast, although it still satisfies, the three rules of storytelling (*I am good at blaming others. The fact that I have little time and energy to fully engage is a lame excuse and I know it deep down. I've always been an overachiever without time, but somehow I still need to "create" time to be with my friends and family.*). For still others, their new story is part uplift (about the future), part sobriety (about leaving the negative parts of one's current life behind). In short, the tone of your new story should be whatever it needs to be—just so long as it meets the three criteria for good storytelling, the only recipe that can possibly work.

To accept seriously the challenge of writing your new story, you must write it while *fully conscious*. No sleepwalking through the process; no mailing it in. To craft your new story, you'll need to confront the truth of your old story. You'll need to hold tight to your ultimate purpose. You'll need to suggest an urgency for finding a better way. You'll need to dig deep. As Herminia Ibarra says in her book, *Working Identity*, making progress in storytelling means "listening more to inner, rather than outer, voices."

So you need to *actually write your story*. Why does this work so well? As Edward Hunter says in *Brain-Washing in Red China*, "Insincerity stands out in a diary; practically no one can successfully fake his true opinions over a prolonged period of time. The tone just doesn't ring true, and any experienced [Party] man entrusted with reading it can soon detect the falsity in the notes jotted down . . ."

It is here, in this written story, that you will discover (or, more likely, rediscover) your voice, the true and private voice, the intuitive voice. You will not only know it, but you'll find a way to turn up the volume and become a master storyteller.

Your new story is your blueprint for the future. It exists for you to chart new pathways for energy to flow in all those areas of your life you want to change. Your new story is a map of how you will change the dynamics of the energy you give to things. In this way, your new story helps to chart your destiny.

We always have clients begin their new story with these three words:

The truth is . . .

Indeed, the majority of sentences in the new story begin with that phrase. This forces the writer always to confront Storytelling Rule 2: It must be truthful. Beginning your new story with these words commits you to strip away denial, rationalization, or mythical thinking and to confront the truth about where your Old Story has led you and continues to mislead you. You're forced to connect the dots, to project, to get specific and clear-eyed about the brutal truth of what might happen if you continue on with the same story—taking poor care of yourself, disengaging from your family, going through the motions at work, cheating occasionally on your spouse, following "slightly" unethical business practices "occasionally."

In your New Story, describe how you'd likely feel if, say, you died young or, because of your disengagement, were divorced and lost your family. Confront whether the price you might pay is acceptable. Expose details you left out in your Old Story, or things you made up to support the faulty subplots you wrote there. Magnify the conflicts your Old Story very well might have created—diabetes and loss of vision, stroke and loss of speech, loss of self-respect and sense of personal integrity, maybe even unemployment or jail time from cooking the books—until you clearly see them and feel them. In your New Story, bring all the facts and evidence you can to support the conclusion that *your Old Story does not represent the truth*, that it's faulty, that it will not work. That it simply cannot take you where you ultimately want to go.

But that's not all that goes into your New Story. It's not just about exposing and breaking down what does not work. It's very much about articulating what *will* work. Your New Story must suggest a general plan of action. (The *specific* plan of action is reserved for the Training Mission, which will be discussed in Part Two.) Your New Story must therefore articulate a belief about where you want to go; that is, it must be *consumed by purpose*.

Let's look at some fragments from New Stories that our clients have written.

The truth is, my old sick story is causing me to hurt those I care about most. I present myself as an open, honest, caring person but this is only partly true. I can show more compassion and caring to those I don't care that much about than those I care most about. My relationships with family, friends, and co-workers are dying because I'm either choking them or starving them. I'm hurting them and I'm hurting me. From now on, I'm going to trust my co-workers with my feelings. I am committed to spending more of my time with my wife and daughters. I will stop cutting them off, cutting them down, holding them at arm's length. I will protect and honor them and their feelings. I will use my best energy to engage more on an emotional level . . .

I don't have kids or a spouse or really any responsibilities at home, as so many of my colleagues do, so I've allowed my work to become my family. I have no existence or identity apart from my work . . . I go in early, stay late, there's nothing to stop me, so there are no boundaries in my personal and professional life. As a consequence I often feel I'm being taken advantage of—but the truth is that it's my fault for never drawing boundaries.

The truth is that work is not the problem; I am. I've ignored health and exercise for the past 3 yrs thinking I'm still young enough not to worry.

My job is not who I am and it is not my highest priority. My family loves me and wants me—my time—not the money I earn. I am underachieving at my job because I have not been taking care of myself and because I forgot what I was working for. I need to create more energy, and focus that energy on improving my relationship with my family and friends. This new focus will make me more effective at work.

The truth is, no one has forced me to work the hours I do . . . I can accomplish as much if I only engage. Same with my workout regimen. From this day forward, my workouts will have more intensity. My meals will be better planned and I will show my wife, children, and direct reports how much I care. Sarcasm is out. Genuine praise will be substituted.

The luckiest day of my life was the day I met Nancy. She's been a great lover, partner in everything I do, gave me and helped raise 2 of the greatest sons in the world. These are just a few of the things that she's given me that I want to once again feel like I deserve. She's my best friend, my business partner, and my soulmate. I will make the time so that together we can enjoy the life that we always talked about could be ours, and still can be.

While I've had a role in leading the business, truth be told, if I had trusted my people more and stepped back, provided better coaching and let people run the business, I'd be better off. So would the folks I work with. So would the business. If I don't change the pace I've been going, NOW, I'll be dead at 60.

Who am I trying to be perfect for? Despite the hours I spend at work, I must be more engaged with my family when home. After all, why am I working? I will keep weekends free whenever possible to spend time with them. Alex will only be here one more year before leaving for col-

lege so I'd better not wait to implement my changes . . . what more of a wakeup call do I need?

I'm a controlling person. What I may view as control for the good of those I care for is really counterproductive . . . Control assumes my way is the right way. That isn't true. I need to let others have a say and be open to other ideas. Compassion doesn't mean taking care of people the way YOU see fit. Listen, with a desire to understand!! Stop kidding yourself!! Don't suffocate others!

I continue to think the reason I haven't advanced as expected is that I'm a woman in a male-dominated environment. The truth is, however, that I haven't produced on several projects, and on one project particularly important for my advancement, I just dropped the ball. Then I found myself thinking that if it had happened to one of my male counterparts it would have been okay. But when I really face the truth, that's probably my own wishful thinking, not reality.

The truth is, I'm in too much of a hurry to get nowhere . . . The truth is, I blame everyone else for me being too busy, too tired, too overwhelmed. I ask for help, yet when offered, I don't take it.

The truth is, I am not immortal or invincible. If I do not learn to maintain my physical being, my life will probably be significantly shorter and out of balance again. I treat myself with less respect than I do my car or my tools. I will develop a training program and change my eating habits to make the most of my life and maximize my time on earth. I owe it to my family and myself.

Time to take a shot at writing your New Story:

New Story

The truth is _____

_____

_____

_____

_____

_____

_____

_____

_____

_____

_____

_____

_____

After your New Story is written, ask yourself the following questions:

1. Does it take me where I want to go?
2. Is it grounded in reality?
3. Does it lead to action that stimulates genuine hope?

If the answer to all three questions is yes, then you're ready to move on to the second and final part of the program, which discusses the most vital life force of all, the one without which our stories and very lives do not happen, a force which we spectacularly ignore, misdirect, and downright abuse.

Physical energy.

Part Two

New Stories

History will be kind to me for I intend to write it.

—Winston Churchill

Seven

IT'S NOT ABOUT TIME

WHAT MR. ROGERS TEACHES US

In the workshops I often show a celebrated clip from an episode of *Mister Rogers' Neighborhood*, the great public television children's show from years ago, created by and starring Fred Rogers. Even in the late 1960s, when the show first appeared and American culture, for all its upheaval, seemed far quieter, slower-paced, less media-saturated, and less immediate-gratification-oriented than it would become, Mr. Rogers stood apart for his quiet, soothing manner and soulfulness, entertaining young children while at the same time teaching them about qualities like self-confidence, overcoming, belonging, and feeling special. Given our present-day warp-speed youth culture of quick camera cuts, fast food, and instant messages, it's hard to imagine a show like *Mr. Rogers' Neighborhood* (which ceased production in 2001) or a man like Fred Rogers (who died in 2003) appealing to today's kids.

Or might he just be the perfect balm for all of us?

The segment I play for the workshop is from the mid-70s. Rogers, who often had guests on the show, hosted Jeff Erlanger, a wheelchair-bound ten-year-old, whose disability resulted from the removal of a tumor from his spinal column in infancy. Rogers converses with Jeff about his "fancy chair," focusing on him with compassion and gentleness. But, while admirable, his compassion is not what makes the segment special; after all, most people, one hopes, would exhibit such compassion. No, what makes the segment extraordinary—and the reason I show it—is the stunning, laser-like quality of Mr. Rogers' focused energy. He is interested intensely, singularly, in everything the little boy has to say, in what he's thinking and feeling, in who he is at his core.

Want to see a human being fully engaged in what he's doing? Just watch Mr. Rogers in this clip (or in countless others).

And it's just as obvious that Jeff feels and responds to this full engagement, too. (Young children tend naturally to be fully engaged in what they're doing—though, sadly, with the proliferation in their lives of new technologies, media, and extracurricular overscheduling, their focus is fragmenting at a younger and younger age.) Here is a boy who seems—as most any other child would—shy about being in front of unfamiliar people, and perhaps (or perhaps not) feels it more so because of his handicap. He looks nervous, unsure of himself. Yet thanks to Mr. Rogers' engagement—it's so immersive you could almost drown in it—the boy soon joins in with him to sing "It's You I Like." As they sing together, the boy's voice grows stronger, more confident. Finally, he can't help himself and a giant smile lights up his face.

Now I can't tell you what impact the segment had on kids who watched the show when it first aired. I *can* tell you that when the lights go up after I've shown it, at least three-quarters of the room—surprise—are a mess. I understand that a lot of that emotion has to do with the scene's poignancy, and yet I am convinced that the depth of the audience's response has less to do with the boy than it does with the man. That's right. I think Mr. Rogers' extraordinary gift for engagement—for how he can make the small space, the eighteen to twenty-four inches, between him and the little boy as sacred as a shrine—is what is most notable. You can practically see the area around them glowing. Watching the segment—even for me, and I've seen it a hundred times—is to watch living proof of the hypothesis that *If all you had to give was your total energy, you could accomplish historic things.*

Who in your life do you give that kind of attention to? At least some of the time? Who gets that eighteen inches of close-up intensity? What gets you to focus with that level of commitment, of reverence for the moment? Is there someone or something in your life so sacred that nothing and no one—not ringing phones, not errands, not ballgames in progress, not the news crawl at the bottom of the screen or the one always running through your head, not money or career concerns, not insignificant noises or images whizzing by—could possibly break your concentration? When I lecture and converse about the "power of full engagement," I mean listening, seeing, and feeling with full force, experiencing with full force, yet that's a kind of focus we so rarely give to

things now. Why is that? What's the story we tell ourselves that prevents this from happening? Is our lack of full engagement just a stage
in our life that will pass someday? Or is the story that life in the twenty-
first century is too complicated? Or has it always been like this? Do we
assert that technology is the culprit? Or do we blame the competitive-
ness of an increasingly global marketplace? Is our story that multi-
tasking is necessary as never before? Hey, time is money. Time is
slipping away. We're not getting any younger. Anyway, is our somewhat
diluted attention really all that big a deal? Are we really losing *that*
much by not engaging fully?

Absolutely. Because it's not about time. It never was and never is.

It's about energy.

Every year I see companies buy into this idea—that it's about
energy, not time—in the hope that it will increase performance and
productivity. Every year I see companies marvel at how the idea delivers
that and so much more—greater employee engagement, retention and
initiative, better health. Better morale. A better place to work. Perish
the thought: more excitement, even joy.

Let's for a moment look at our national pastime: multi-tasking.
The essence of multi-tasking is exactly the opposite of the essence of
Fred Rogers. With Rogers-like engagement, extraordinary depth is
achieved; with the one-foot-in, one-foot-out level of engagement characteristic of multi-tasking, a startling number of things, all relatively
inconsequential, get achieved in a short time. (It bears noting also that
one's memory of, and joy in, accomplishing the multiple tasks that
make up multi-tasking can never, cumulatively, compete with the
memory of and joy in fully engaging in one thing alone.) Here's the
dirty secret, though: The difference in depth between full engagement
and multi-tasking is not incremental. It's binary. Either you're fully
engaged or you're not. It's really that simple, yet we tell ourselves it's
otherwise to keep the painful truth at bay. If a tennis pro preparing to
return a 140-mph serve has two thoughts going, and one of them does
not have to do with returning that serve, do you know what his chances
are of returning it well? I do. *Zero.* Not 10%, not 5%. The same goes for
hitting a golf ball, or doing push-ups the right way, or enjoying a glass
of wine, or reading a good book. A distracted artist will not produce
anything of real worth. An entrepreneur with scattered thoughts will
not come up with solutions superior to the competition's. Indeed,

multi-taskers are fortunate even to rise to a modicum of competence. Can't you always tell when you're on the phone with someone who's simultaneously watching TV or answering e-mail? Does your interaction with that person ever come within a thousand miles of what you'd call a satisfying conversation?

Multi-tasking is the enemy of extraordinariness. Human beings, sorry to say, can focus fully on only one thing at a time. When employees multi-task, they are not fully engaged in anything, and partially disengaged in everything. The potential for profoundly positive impact is compromised. Multi-tasking would be okay—*is* okay—at certain times but very few people seem to know when that time is. If you must, then *multi-task when it doesn't matter*. Fully engage when it does.

Not long ago I suggested to a client, president of a large manufacturing company, that he stop multi-tasking—not merely because it brought him no joy or even a sense of accomplishment, but because he would actually get more done.

From his look, you'd think I'd just said that meeting his revenue projections wasn't the be-all, end-all.

But when he returned home, for some reason he tried an experiment. "We had always used a 5-4-3-2-1 scale for employees to rate their own performance, with 5 being the best and 1 the worst," he told me. "I was looking over the data and realized that we all mostly gave ourselves 4s and a few 2s. All the time 4s and some 2s. Fours and 2s are such noncommittal scores. I realized that no one was owning up to how they were doing. So I simplified the scale to 5-3-1. Five meant you exceeded your task, 3 that you met it, 1 that you missed it. Much simpler. And I noticed that now when I measured myself at the end of each day, I kept giving myself 3s. Finally I could confirm what I had long suspected: that I was doing everything in a mediocre way. Why? Because I was multi-tasking. I collected data from others and they, too, were always giving themselves 3s. It was all half-assed."

What did he do? He added a ritual to the start of the workday (or the night before): He would identify the three things he wanted to get finished that workday—never more than three. At the end of each day, he used his 5-3-1 scale to rate himself. "Now I was giving myself 5s all the time. I found that I actually got more accomplished, more completed—and at a higher level—than when I was doing lots of things. Which in turn created more elasticity in my day to take on more tasks—

only now, when a new task came before me, I was sensitive about being fully engaged by it. I had to be focused, present. I stopped multitasking at meetings and suddenly they became shorter, crisper. Our operating efficiency improved threefold. Plus, it's been more enjoyable getting there."

Learning to invest your full and best energy in whatever you're doing at that moment is what I call "full engagement," a paradigm we've developed over more than two decades, which posits at its core that life is enriched because of the commitment, passion, and focus we give it, not the time we give it. Two years ago, I did several off-site workshops with partners from KPMG, the Big Four accounting firm, and their spouses. I'd been invited by Gene O'Kelly, their chairman and CEO, who was intent on improving the firm's culture by achieving greater balance between his workforce's professional and personal lives. The workshops went well, Gene felt, and he and I were in contact in the months following as he told me enthusiastically how the "energy, not time" concept was flourishing at the firm, and about some of the specific changes the company had implemented: encouraging more nutritious eating (and making healthier foods more available); encouraging work breaks, including stretching and walking; encouraging periodic disengagement, better sleep, programming in more family time so that it didn't just disappear at the bottom of an endless to-do list. He talked about how the concept was starting to resonate in his own life, too—how he was trying to engage more fully in what he was working on at the moment, rather than always focusing on his six-month or twelve-month plan. Then, in the spring of 2005, tragedy slammed Gene and his family: He was diagnosed with inoperable brain cancer and given three to six months to live. At age fifty-three, he'd been happily married for more than twenty-five years and had two daughters, one of whom was only thirteen. One day he'd been at the top of the business world, with everything going his way; the next, he was given a death sentence. And yet, extraordinarily, by applying some of what he learned about energy and engagement, he discovered only in his final months that for years—for decades—he'd been living, in many ways, in the future, with his eye always trained on the next eighteen months, or the next month, or the next day; working to the top, he didn't have so much use for the present day. While there were other important influences working on him in his extraordinary final few months, his commitment to deeply engaging in the moment provided him a peace and even joy as he approached death that was breathtaking. As he took account of his last months, he claimed that his newly fully-engaged-in-the-present moments—dubbed "Perfect Moments," which could sometimes be strung together to make "Perfect Days"—allowed him "more Perfect Moments and Perfect Days in two weeks than I had in the last five years, or than I probably would have in the next five years, had my life continued the way it was going before my diagnosis."

Full engagement represents the greatest quantity, highest quality, most precise focus and greatest intensity of energy invested in whatever one is doing at the time. Even dying.

THE LIE OF TIME

There's a story we tell ourselves that says time is everything. We believe in this story so deeply that it has spawned an industry—the "time management" industry. Time management has helped us in significant ways: It has allowed us (to name just a few benefits) to allocate time and other resources more strategically in the service of our objectives; to plan more intelligently; to be more precise; to avoid being late or missing critical events.

But despite all the good things time management has meant in our lives, it makes a promise—a tragic promise—that it can't deliver on. Ever. And every one of us who believes in this promise (almost all of us, at one time or another) is victimized by it. Past and present and—if we continue to believe it—future, too.

The promise we believe in, the one that is simply not true and can never be true, goes like this:

All time is sacred. Because we have so little time here on this planet, we must make every second count. To find meaning and harmony and to make sense of our life, we need to decide what has real value for us; must distinguish what matters from what doesn't. Once we determine true value in our lives, then we can invest time, very deliberately, in that which we care about most. And if we do this—just this—then we've virtually guaranteed our lives will have meaning and dimension, and the relationships and activities we invest our time in will "grow." Our lives will be fundamentally aligned with what we care about most.

So goes the promise, which is absolutely, unequivocally, 100% false.

Why? Because simply investing time in something is meaningless. It has zero value. The pervasive notion that simply by being there for the dinner, or the get-together, or the meeting, or any other activity earns you some "positive return" for your mere physical presence . . . how can that be anything but nonsense? If you're there but you're consumed by anger, distractions, fatigue—really, what does it mean?

Suppose your son has asked you repeatedly to attend one of his soccer games. For almost his whole season you've just been swamped, and now one game remains, the final, pivotal game. If they win, they make the playoffs. Your son begs you to come to this one, and you decide, yes: It's important for you to be there.

So you block out four hours in the middle of a workday. Your goal is to let your son see that you really care about him and his activities. You arrive at the game five minutes early, spend the whole time at the game—every last minute—then the two of you drive home together. Is that not devotion? Is that not full of meaning and love?

Well, let's see about that. Suppose a video camera were trained on you for the afternoon. What might the videotape show?

For starters, you spend fully three-quarters of the time nervously walking up and down the field, talking on the cell phone. Most of the time you're on the phone—all business-related calls, naturally— you take in the action on the field only dimly; when you look out, you aren't (indeed, can't be) concentrating fully. Whenever your son looks your way he sees a man only marginally interested in what he's looking at.

On two occasions, you grow animated because the referee doesn't know what he's doing; once a high school soccer star yourself, you know a thing or two. On the first instance, the ref misses a serious infraction and you just light into him from the sideline. It soon becomes clear to everyone that you know more about soccer than anyone there. Do you consider that you may have humiliated the ref? No, you don't, and then, there he goes and goofs again, this time on a rule interpretation, one that threatens to cost your son's team the game (in the end, it does not).

With two minutes left to go, your son has a wide-open chance to score—and he spaces. The opportunity is gone in an instant. You are dumbfounded, at first, then go a little berserk on the sideline, then calm yourself a bit.

The final whistle blows. Your son and his teammates walk off the field. They will not be going to the playoffs.

Looking at the videotape, one would see that you tap your son on the back of the neck.

"Nice game," you say.

"I really screwed up," he says. "I should have scored."

"How could you space out like that?" you say, unable to help yourself. "You gotta concentrate at all times!"

Your son shakes his head, distraught. You shake your head and give him one more tap. "Hop in the car," you say, and he does, and you do, and you both drive off.

Later, when you think about it, you tell yourself that you took off an entire afternoon from work (four hours!), got there before the game started, and stayed to the end. Your mission? To let your son know how much you cared about him.

Instead, you have just succeeded in moving the needle backward.

In my years doing what I do now, and my years as coach, I have personally witnessed or heard about this scene, and others in precisely the same spirit, too many hundreds of times to count.

It couldn't happen unless we continued to carry flawed, tragic assumptions about time. If you're going to show up in name only, time has zero value.

A DIFFERENT KIND OF ENERGY PROBLEM

Are we almost out of fuel to run the world?

For years we've been asking this question about our petroleum supply. It's an important, frightening question. But I'm at least as interested in a slight variation on it: Are we almost out of *human* fuel to run the world?

After all, for years business demands have only increased. Employees have had to adapt to the pressure of increasing shareholder value and improving profitability. We now consume "human" energy at unprecedented levels. Yet for far too many of us, the human energy well has run dangerously dry. Is it ironic that so much of the working population is failing, or close to failing, at developing and harnessing the very resource—energy—that makes it possible for them to be productive and constructive? Or is it just plain scary—for them individually, as well as for their companies and the country?

Since March 2003, 100,000 people from all over the world have provided us at HPI with important (and frightening) insights into their individual energy crises as well as our collective one, by answering our personal energy management questionnaire. From the data we've collected, the broad answer to my question is yes: At least half of us are running dangerously low on human fuel. The number of survey respondents who say, for example, that they are "fully engaged"—in that positive, balanced state of physical, mental, emotional, and spiritual energy—is 4%. *Four* percent? In polling terms, that's in the category of "statistically irrelevant." At the other end of the energy scale, 4% of respondents say they are "toxically disengaged," impoverished in every key realm of life. (The 360 evaluations of the participants by their colleagues, friends, and family paint a somewhat different picture: According to them, 18% of our clientele, not 4%, is toxically disengaged.) This segment lacks vision and purpose (they report), their emotions are stunted, they never feel fully rested, they feel they don't have the resources to improve their lot. In many cases, they've simply given up. In their poignant, alarmingly telling write-in comments, many of them confess that their daily lives are ruled by two emotional states: anger and frustration.

Count 51% of the total among the "disengaged." This group feels challenged in many of the ways the really down-and-out 4% do, but they at least feel some hope for their situations. That's the good news. The bad news is that they claim to have no clue about how to put their hope to work.

The final 42% consider themselves "engaged." While they score themselves as fairly balanced, half of them feel significantly disengaged in the physical realm—eating, exercising, sleeping, recovering. Now, it's great that they feel adequately fulfilled about their emotional, mental, and spiritual energy—I'm not at all belittling that—but physical energy, as we'll see in a few pages, is the *foundational source* for all of our energy. Too much more physical disengagement for people in this category and who knows which other realms of their life will begin to crumble.

In my travels around America to giant multinational corporations and mid-sized organizations, I've met far, far too many "dead people walking"—forty-year-olds, even thirty-year-olds, whose bodies, theoretically, still enjoy the capacity to repair themselves quickly with minimal care, feeding, and recovery, yet whose lives, particularly jobs, make more and more demands on them until, finally, they've started to break down physically, the light slowly leaving them. In sport, this condition is called overtraining. No amount of youthful vigor can alter this basic equation: *You cannot expend more energy than you create.* Ask any physicist. I don't care what kind of "stud" or "tough guy" or "animal" or "winner" you are, the kind of employee willing always to put in more hours than anyone else. You can't change that truth, which holds for *all* energy, including human. You simply can't. It's an impossibility. And it's not just a math equation that doesn't work. It's a story that doesn't work.

To answer my own question again: Yes, there is a human energy crisis. Yes, I'm worried about our collective ability to survive and thrive in the world. Each individual energy crisis robs that person of the ability to participate, and participate well, in his or her own life, in the workplace, in society.

A staggering number of comments from our survey tell us that people *want* to take better care of themselves—and yet feel blocked from those practices that would nurture them physically at work, at home, and in the community. They mostly eat and sleep badly, and exercise intermittently and ineffectively, if they can.

The most precious resource we have as human beings is our energy. Most of us, however, give little attention to responsibly managing this finite resource. We are quick to acknowledge the importance of skillfully managing time and money but, for whatever reason, fail to apply the same logic and sense of urgency to managing our energy. We consume energy with little or no regard for where it comes from or how it is produced. When the demands of life require more energy, we simply expect our bodies to ante up more of it. When the additional energy isn't there, we're mystified and frustrated.

One metaphor I use in our workshop is that of the "smart bomb." The military uses the term to mean a bomb that can make course corrections, after it's been launched, to hit its target: To make such corrections, the bomb must always be able to identify two clear coordinates, both of which are computed via precise GPS calculations.

Where it is at the moment. Where it's meant to end up.

If a smart bomb could identify neither of these coordinates, or only one, then it wouldn't—it couldn't—hit its target. It would be incapable of making the in-air course corrections necessary to succeed at its mission. It would not be inaccurate to call such a projectile a "dumb bomb."

You have been launched, long ago. You are following a trajectory, one whose route and velocity have been greatly determined by your parents and others. Are you content to continue in the direction you're going? Do you know both your position right now and your destiny? (Even the staunchest pacifists in our workshop tend to appreciate the analogy.) Do you have the ability to recognize where you are at any moment on your flight path? Do you have a clear sense of the target you wish to reach? If you don't, then how can you possibly make course corrections, in the midst of life, necessary to achieve your desired goal? Does your business—which, like each human, has a trajectory—have a clear sense of what it is and where it wants to go?

Individuals and businesses capable of making informed course corrections do well. Those who can't, fail. If you simply accept the trajectory you're on, you probably won't end up anywhere near where you want to go.

Here's the thing, though: While course corrections are made mainly through storytelling—that is, you must continually articulate, even write out, where you are and where you're going, if you're to embed these coordinates in your guidance system—*even good storytelling will leave you nowhere if you don't properly manage your energy.* Because even with both coordinates magnificently calculated, if you run out of energy before the journey is completed, guess what? You'll fall out of the sky. You'll fall short, probably way short, of the mark you meant to hit. And it wasn't that you lacked clarity; you lacked energy.

If you mind that your life trajectory is being compared to a bomb's, here's one meaningful way in which they depart: a bomb has a single target. You have multiple targets. To hit all of them, or most, you need to be extraordinary at managing your energy.

We must create a plan of action to rewrite this story, the one in which so many of us lack the energy to hit our targets. Before we can do that, though, there's another question to answer: How did the Old Story get started? And who's to blame for it?

The business world is, I believe, the biggest culprit.

In many ways, the business culture is responsible for this human energy crisis (and, by extension, for a good deal of our nation's health care crisis but, again, that's for a whole other book). Business leaders pay lip service, if that, to the notion that workers should of course take care of themselves, but for the most part they don't consider it "business-relevant" for the company to help the worker in this endeavor. That's something you do on your own time.

But wait: Aren't business leaders looked to as role models? And, but for a few, mostly maverick exceptions (Malcolm Forbes, Ted Turner, Warren Buffett, Bill Gates after he turned into a public philanthropist), isn't the primary behavior being modeled called "workaholism"?

At a recent leadership meeting I attended for a Fortune 100 company, a C-level executive said, "You only have twenty-four hours in the day. There are three things you must be concerned with. Your job, your family, and yourself. For me, it has always been about my job and my family. I have always put 'me' on the back burner."

The next day, I got an e-mail from someone else at the same company. "Why is guilt so rampant in the business world and how do you coach people to deal with it?" he wrote. One of the main sources of guilt, we have learned over the years—from speaking with clients and from the surveys we've done—is the idea that taking care of oneself is frivolous, indulgent, off message. Employees feel guilty when they are not working; then, when the hours at work start to run particularly long, they feel guilty that they aren't home. They feel guilty about exercising, feel guilty about reading a book. They feel guilty about taking a real lunchtime, so instead they eat on the run in an attempt to be more productive.

Now here's the math I *really* don't get: If the rising cost of health care is almost single-handedly making profitability difficult for many, if not most, businesses—and it is—then wouldn't everyone up and down the chain, including shareholders, approve of a culture that places greater value on the physical health and well-being of its workforce? Of course they would. And wouldn't our culture, and the individuals who comprise it, benefit up and down by creating environments that replaced the sense of *guilt* workers now feel for taking care of themselves with a sense of *obligation*—that it is one's individual, familial, communal, professional *imperative* always to be at one's best possible physical self?

I believe that *energy management* is the answer to most individual health problems, which for most people requires a change in their story about physical energy. With that change will come an understanding that physical energy is actually one of *four dimensions of human energy*, and that if the physical dimension fails, the other three fail, too; if the physical dimension flourishes, so can the other three.

Only by recruiting all four dimensions of human energy can you hope to fulfill your ultimate mission in life.

THE ENERGY PYRAMID

You are—tiresome as the cliché may be—what you eat. You are also how, and how often, you exercise. You are how well you sleep and recover. In short, you are how you take care of yourself. It's hard to imagine a legitimate counterargument.

Energy is at the heart of everything. As much as I believe in the "power of full engagement," it's an empty theory, a meaningless collection of words, if you lack physical energy. To live fully engaged for even just a week, or a month, or a year, and certainly for an entire lifetime, requires a reliance on daily, renewable, *physical* energy. To maximize and corral that energy requires eating right, exercising regularly, getting proper sleep, and allowing your body frequent opportunities to recharge. It's not a complicated equation (though I'll provide some specifics later).

By doing these good things for your body, you of course increase your chance to fend off all kinds of illnesses, maintain strength, and perhaps live longer. But there's more to it than that. When you take care of yourself physically, you have a bounce in your step both literally and metaphorically; your mood is likely to be sunnier, your thoughts sharper, your mission more realizable. You exhibit calm, confidence, resolve. Conversely, when you lack physical energy, then the other "energies" in your life also fail—your emotional energy, your mental energy, your spiritual energy. The great majority of the time, there is a correlation between what you have in your physical "bank account," on one hand, and what you have in your heart, mind, and spirit, on the other.

These four distinct yet related types of energy can be portrayed hierarchically:

As modeled above, it's apparent that the greater and better your physical energy, the more fully engaged you will be on an emotional, mental, and spiritual level, too, and the likelier it is that your stories will work for you. To be blunt, a lousy breakfast (i.e., what fuels your physical tank) does more than just make your stomach grumble. It can actually topple the whole energy pyramid—and, unless you're the exception, it likely does precisely that for you, on some level, every day.

Physical energy, then, is the first, largest, and foundational component, the energy we need for survival. All human energy originates in the physical body and begins in the union of glucose and oxygen. Without it, we are, quite literally, dead. Conversely, it stands to reason that the more of it we have, the more alive we are. Without sufficient physical energy, all emotional energy, mental energy, and spiritual energy eventually cease. One might say that this type of energy defines *that* we are.

Emotional energy is the energy associated with feelings, emotions, mood. This energy influences the *quality* of our stories and the way in which we do things—intensely or indifferently, patiently or hyperactively, loudly or quietly. This energy may be said to define *how* we are.

Mental energy influences the focus of our stories, our precision in thinking, cognition and logic; the alertness, sharpness, fineness of our thoughts and ideas; our efficiency and self-awareness. This energy may be said to define *where* we are.

Spiritual energy influences the intensity of our stories. It is the energy of purpose, our values and beliefs. It compels us to go beyond ourselves in ways no other energy can, the force behind what we do. This energy defines *why* we are.

To take one example: An athlete lacking sufficient physical energy also lacks the emotional strength to manage the storms of competition (e.g., a tennis player unraveling after a bad line call). At crucial moments, she doesn't perform well mentally and makes bad strategic decisions. The final kicker to real competitive success—that deep hunger that makes you fight harder than your opponent—is also gone; bye-bye, spiritual energy. If you lack physical fuel, there will be a ripple effect on every story you tell and everything you do or attempt to do.

If we lack sufficient physical energy, then, we will individually face an energy crisis that rivals the one the world faces with petroleum-based energy: We continue to consume at unprecedented levels with little or no concern for the supply side of the equation.

Let's return to that lousy breakfast I mentioned, and how it does more than just make you feel bloated or depleted or jittery. It can *actually influence the core of your stories—your values and beliefs*, aspects of your character you would have thought free of the influence of such pedestrian concerns.

Richard runs out of the house at eight without eating breakfast, as usual. No matter: He gets his charge from two large cups of black coffee and the adrenaline rush of walking into the office. By ten o'clock, though, he's starting to flag. He's only dimly aware that this is also the time when his mood turns darker: He's reminded of all the work that's still to be done, how much he's behind on his weekly calls and reports, how he's done nothing this week to advance the rather ambitious initiative he's recently been tasked with, to overhaul the reporting system for his unit. He even snaps at his wife when she calls to tell him that tonight's dinner with old friends they haven't seen in ages had to get bumped to an hour earlier. (She's said more than once that she hates calling him around this time because of his grouchiness; he thinks she's imagining things.) He inhales three cookies which sit unattended by the office kitchenette, and this gives him the temporary high of a sugar boost, but it won't last long. His emotional energy is suffering.

He's also not using this time particularly well. He's suddenly in the midst of a frenzy of multi-tasking, to recharge himself, and he's working inefficiently; as it hits eleven o'clock, he realizes that he's reread the same e-mail three times because it's not making complete sense to him. Which is particularly galling since he wrote it. His focus is gone. His mental energy is depleted.

Spiritually? Often he relies on this little trick: closing his eyes and seeing his children's faces, to spur him to work harder, to remember why he works so damn hard. Yet that's not really doing it for him now. There is practically zero engagement in the job at which he's toiling and, God knows, certainly no pleasure in it, even though the organization he works for and the work they do—developing training and education programs for older people in the workforce—is something he usually takes great pride in! Depleted physically, he begins to question whether what he does is worth it. *Why am I doing this?* he asks himself. *Is this what I want from life?* He's losing his spiritual connection to his story because he's out of fuel.

To advocate better eating, exercising, and sleep habits, then, is not merely to improve one's physical existence, though of course that will happen. Our lives, our stories, are most deeply felt when we experience them in all ways—physically, emotionally, mentally, spiritually. It is at this point, and not before, that we are fully realized human beings.

FROM STORIES FLOWS ENERGY

Individual energy is the resource that creates—wealth, innovation, money, fulfillment—and yet *we're expected to create energy itself faster than we can replenish it.* That's a problem. Government won't fix the problem. Neither will industry as a whole. Your company? Unlikely, as I have said—but even if it did, it probably wouldn't make enough of an effort to solve the problem meaningfully. As with many large-scale social changes, this one may have to come from the bottom up—that is, one individual at a time.

Every day, both worker productivity and organizational profitability seem to demand increasing workforce engagement. You accomplish this through skillful storytelling and skillful energy management. The foundation of all energy management is good storytelling: Energy follows our stories; we give life (energy) to something with every story we tell. Some stories engage us deeply in our work while others have the opposite effect. As I said earlier, our experience at HPI has made it abundantly clear that managing energy, not time, is the most important key to success—by which I mean bottom-line productivity and profitability. It's not the time we invest in a mission or project that matters most, but the energy we bring to the time that we have. Investing time simply takes us from absenteeism to presenteeism. To get the return we want for the time we invest requires that we be engaged; full engagement, in turn, makes the time invested priceless. We've all experienced the consequences of setting time aside for things we care about but, because we failed to skillfully manage our energy—we were too tired, too frustrated and angry, too distracted and unfocused—the time invested actually worked *against* the mission. It was a waste. What we meant to accomplish wasn't, at least not well. And what's the point of doing something just to do it? The "failure" of a lunch with a valued direct report that's abbreviated and incomplete, of a long-awaited anniversary dinner where you feel distracted, of an all-too-rare weekend with the extended family where you're mostly exhausted, of an indifferent session on the treadmill—those aren't time management failures but energy management failures.

One of the exciting discoveries we've made is the almost perfect correlation between engagement, on one hand, and happiness, on the other. Engagement is an acquired skill that allows us to be in the present space; it's in that space where people feel happiest. (The happiness we feel about an upcoming event is really not future-oriented, but rather present-oriented happiness in the anticipation.) The more engaged we are in something, the more alive we tend to feel; the more alive we feel, the happier we feel. Becoming fully engaged in a mission that deeply matters brings a rich sense of meaning, depth, and dimension to our lives. Disengagement has the opposite effect. Disengagement pulls us from the core of life—characterized by intensity, passion, and meaning—to its boundaries, characterized by safety, protection, and disassociation. By being engaged, not disengaged, we experience true happiness and joy in our lives. We ignite our talents and skills. We are aware early and precisely of necessary course corrections we may need to make.

If you have a full supply of energy that you manage efficiently, are able to burn off robustly, and can replenish continually, you help not only yourself; there is a positive ripple effect for you and your company. This requires that you get your story straight about the dynamics of engagement, health, happiness, diet, and exercise. A study published in MIT's *Sloan Management Review* in 2003, which examined the effect of fully engaged workers—called "energizers"—on their colleagues as well as on the larger organization, found that energizers were not just the highest performers but also more likely to have their ideas considered and put into action; were better able to motivate others to act; and elicited more from those around them—that is, others tended to devote themselves more fully to interactions with an energizer (such as giving undivided attention in a meeting led by an energizer). Those around energizers were even found to be more likely to devote discretionary time to an energizer's concerns (they would, for example, spend their commuting time working on a problem put forth by an energizer, or would send an extra e-mail or two to find necessary information, or would go out of their way to introduce the energizer to a valued contact). Moreover, the reputation of energizers spread quickly throughout the organization, and people positioned themselves to work for these engaging colleagues.

"The desire to work for or with energizers seems to account for our last finding about energy and performance," said the study. "Not only are energizers better performers themselves, but people who are strongly connected to an energizer are also better performers . . . in short, we systematically found that energy is more than just a New Age concept. It has a substantial and predictable effect on performance and innovation in organizations."

It should be emphasized that to be an energizer does not necessarily mean to be entertaining, charismatic, or intense. It means bringing yourself fully to a given interaction, so that you can keep your attention on the people you are involved with at that moment. Is that not what our best salespeople do? Our best chief executives? People are energized in interactions, says the study, "when hope becomes part of the equation. Hope allows people to become energized when they begin to believe that the objective is worthy and can be attained. They get excited about the possibilities and stop looking for the pitfalls." Energizers, it goes on to say, are notable for two characteristics that influence others' willingness to hope: People feel as if they're getting the truth from energizers, even when it's not necessarily pleasant; people feel that there's integrity between what energizers say and do.

How does all this connect with the idea of storytelling?

Fatigue puts you into survival mode and colors every story you tell. Increased physical energy will play a huge and fundamental role in the creation of your New Story. So let's see how, with some vital but still relatively unobtrusive changes, you can eliminate your personal energy crisis.

Eight

DO YOU HAVE THE RESOURCES TO LIVE YOUR BEST STORY?

The car in front of you drifts, slides back into the lane, drifts again. You crane your neck to see what's up. Again the vehicle drifts . . . Of course. The driver is struggling to stay awake.

According to Charles Czeisler, a leading authority on sleep, 80,000 drivers fall asleep at the wheel every day, 10% of them will run off the road and, every two minutes, one of them crashes.

It's no way to drive. It's no way to live. If you're one of those 80,000 people per day, it's probably not a story you want to tell.

So many of us have hit our "engagement limit" and zoomed past it. Demands are made on us from multiple sides and we're expected to have energy for it all, as if the fuel supply were endless. But it isn't, and just because we sometimes treat it as if it is doesn't make it so.

If you have any hope of living out your best story, then you need to have a maximum amount of high-quality energy to spend, which means you need to *produce* that maximum amount of high-quality energy. And that simply can't be done without eating right, exercising regularly, and resting and recovering appropriately.

Yet way more than half the people we see do not. Here are some typical storylines that block exercise:

If I exercise when I get home, it takes time away from my kids.
If I exercise at work, it jeopardizes my standing.
If I exercise early in the morning, I won't get enough sleep.
If I exercise before I go to bed (as if I have any energy left then), it may lead to divorce.

172

Here are some storylines that have the opposite effect:

Exercising with my wife gives us valuable time together doing something important to both of us—and as exercise partners we make each other accountable.

Exercising for thirty minutes during lunch hour sets a great example for those who work for me.

By exercising in the early morning, I require less sleep due to my improved fitness, and have more energy for my kids when I get home.

Without proper exercise, nutrition, and rest, the body slowly begins to break. You're operating at a perpetual deficit. You're always exhausted. You're seriously disengaged. Your body is now in survival mode. Your stories change. To rationalize how and why this happened requires that, at some fork in the road, smart people must become suddenly stupid; pragmatists, illogical; straightshooters, gullible. There are other, totally defensible factors that bring us to this overtaxed point, of course—lots of responsibility, good intentions, aging, ambition, sudden change in circumstance—but they are almost never the only factors. You tell yourself things you can't possibly believe—for example: *Getting just a few hours of sleep night after night, year after year, is the best option or the only option for me to get everything done and to make it through.* Or this: *When others neglect their bodies, it shows, but for me it will be different.* Or: *I can overcome the tug of sleeplessness by sheer will.* Or: *My life is only marginally affected by my being out of condition.* Or: *I am not in fact what I eat.*

Come on. In an impoverished physical condition, how can you hope to live a good story? How can you hope to have the energy even to figure out what that story is?

OUR PHYSICAL STATE INFLUENCES THE STORIES WE TELL

Do you think the story you tell changes if one or more of the following conditions is true?

- You are tired or fatigued.
- You have low blood sugar.
- You have a headache.
- You are ill.
- You are in pain.

Of course it does! As we've seen, when your physical self changes—such as by a sudden drop in blood sugar—then your emotional self changes. Your mental self changes. Even your spiritual self changes. Your whole story changes. Josh Waitzkin, the chess prodigy who inspired the movie *Searching for Bobby Fischer* and who became an international master at sixteen, went through our program and found that incorporating our nutrition and fitness principles gave him not just greater physical stamina but greater mental stamina, too.

It is crucial to be aware that what seems like reality to you can completely change when your physical state changes. And in that instant, of course, your story's shape and color change, too. With more physical energy, you can engage more deeply on a physical level—that's obvious—but you can do so on a greater emotional, mental, and spiritual level, too. If you do not maximize your physical energy through proper nutrition, exercise, and rest, then you simply cannot maximize the other three types of energy. And there's a looping effect: If you're too tired to tap into, say, your spiritual energy, then your failure to do so may influence your physical energy, too, and a vicious circle is begun. Many of us know that losing weight on a traditional diet is terribly difficult. One reason for this is that the story most people are told or tell themselves—*Lose weight to feel and look better*—is, frankly, not exactly a narrative for the ages. As a life goal for far too many people, the objective of losing twenty or forty or even one hundred pounds simply to look better is just not compelling enough. Many who fail at losing weight that way *have* lost it when their motivation changes to something more urgent, powerful, and transcendent—lose weight to be around for your grandchildren; lose weight so you will not be wheelchair-bound the last portion of your life; lose weight to improve your chances of having a healthy and uncomplicated pregnancy. By finding motivation from a higher, spiritual source of energy, you can affect your physical energy, too.

The body we start out with is capable of wonderful things. But if we wish to achieve something truly extraordinary in our lives—be it athletic, intellectual, social, artistic, professional—we must build on this "standard-edition" body and invest it with extraordinary energy.

Obviously, human bodies are not all created equal. Some of us start with more than others, some less. Some bodies have unique flaws, some unique strengths. Even within one person, flaws and strengths vary from one stage of life to another. But *no one* has a physical specimen that, without work, will aid them in accomplishing everything they want, in getting their new story to work just so. Not Tiger Woods, not LeBron James, not Michelle Kwan, not you. That's the bad news.

You'll also consider it bad news—certainly not a thrilling reminder—that somewhere between ages twenty-five and thirty, the standard-edition body we were given begins to lose efficiency in its ability to expend and recover energy. For virtually every one of us, if we did very little and just let "nature take its course," we'd pretty much lose the ability to produce extraordinary energy by age forty.

But, yes, there's good news. Really. Our body is spectacularly adaptive, perfectly agreeable to being modified and improved. I've never encountered anyone incapable of improving dramatically on what they've been given, so long as they want it and work at it badly enough. One of the most extraordinary examples of the infinite adaptability of the human body is Erik Weihenmayer, a mountain climber who scaled all seven of the world's great summits, including Mount Everest, *after losing his eyesight as a teenager*. Erik—not only a world-class climber and a skier, but also an author and speaker—exemplifies many things to many people, but none more than this: With the right kind of training, there is almost nothing our standard-issue physical self can't achieve.

GETTING YOUR STORY STRAIGHT ABOUT EATING

When a new group of clients comes through HPI, my team of fitness and nutrition coaches and I hear their stories of perpetual fatigue and wavering ability to focus, then about their dietary habits, and the first thing that often comes to our minds is: diabetes.

Not that our clientele is diabetic, mind you. In fact, almost none of them is—yet. But the way they eat—or, rather, overeat, or eat horribly—

throughout the typical workday, from a range of high glycemic foods such as bagels, chips, sodas, and sports drinks, triggers an insulin response that can increase the risk for insulin resistance and eventually lead to diabetes, as well as increase triglycerides, promote fat storage, and cause a subsequent energy crash. When blood gets overrun by glucose, insulin is called in, cavalry-like, to clear the system of the excess glucose, a process that takes about two hours. During this time one is considerably more sluggish and less engaged than if one were to avoid foods and portion sizes that cause such glucose spikes and crashes.

On average, individuals who attend our executive course in Florida arrive with excess body fat, some as high as 48% (the healthy range for most men is 5 to 20%; for most women, 15 to 30%). The attendees achieve an average score of only 51% on our nutrition index. (On our scale, 85–100% = "fully engaged," 70–84% = "engaged," 51–69% = "disengaged," and 50% and below = "seriously disengaged."). In other words, even now, in 2007, with readily available, nutritionally dense foods and a generally heightened awareness about nutritious eating, too many otherwise informed people have yet to straighten out their story around food. Over and again, their stories are convoluted and self-destructive, and do not meet the Purpose-Truth-Action template.

For example, an unusually large number of respondents are flabbergasted when they learn that their *energy demands increase dramatically twice a day*:

1. after waking up, and
2. when exercising.

You'd think our nutritionists had just pointed out that the earth was in fact flat. At both these junctures during the day, your need for adequate fuel is critical. This fuel must come in the form of food, the right food. Yet in their survey responses, fewer than half of our clients treat these special periods as special at all. Indeed, we hear all kinds of faulty proclamations: *I'm not hungry in the morning, so why should I eat? . . . I hate the taste of food in the morning . . . If I eat something before I run I'll get an upset stomach.*

Because of my experience in athletics, both as competitor and coach, I understand that we often make deals with our body—*Go all-out for me another thirty seconds and I'll give you the next ninety seconds off.* But some things are non-negotiable. You can't function now on fuel you promise to provide later. All the willpower in the world won't overcome cells starving for glucose; the body, if you will, has a mind of its own. Because so many people eat with little sense of nutritional balance, though, all kinds of strange math invade one's thinking.

> *I worked out earlier so I can have a big piece of pie later, since I already burned off those calories.*
> *I overate at lunch, I'm disgusted with myself, so for the rest of the afternoon I won't consume a single calorie.*
> *I skipped lunch today so I can have a much bigger dinner than usual.*

It simply doesn't work like that.

The better and more balanced our diet, the more engaged we can be, the better we'll perform. Ergo, to perform exceptionally requires a considerable investment. Whether it's your bank account or your body, you can't withdraw what you haven't put in.

- Always eat within an hour of waking up.
- Eat a meal or snack rich in carbohydrates within two hours before exercising *and* after exercising.*

What you eat and when will either enhance or hinder your performance. You can't get around this fact.

Once upon a time, we all had our food story straight. We ate only when hungry, only until we felt satisfied, and then no more. Our body's need for fuel was our lone guide. When was this intuitive Golden Age? When we were infants. By the time we hit adulthood and enter the work world, though, a lot of that primal, fundamental connection with our bodies has been shrouded by other complications, many of which start early. For example, there's the Clean Plate Club (*My overeating will help starving children*), which teaches one to eat past the point of satiety. There's eating as a way to gain a parent's love and

---

* You won't spike before working out because you're about to consume an extraordinary number of calories; you won't spike after working out because you have a glycemic debt and you're ready to absorb carbs quickly.

approval. There's the pressure we feel to eat or overeat in social situations. Some people—for religious or allegedly health-related reasons—fast regularly.

As we age, our lives, particularly at work, often prevent us from responding quickly, much less immediately, to our body's various needs (for fuel or rest); we start to change; what is unnatural begins, finally, to seem natural. Our appetite starts to fail—that is, we get stupendously hungry, or hungry at the "wrong" time. We start eating when there's food before us or go too long without eating, simply because we neglect our needs, rather than eating when our body requires it. Repeat these patterns often enough and our bodies become confused and finally indoctrinated anew, unnaturally, so that we actually start responding to food in a different way; just like that, our story around food becomes corrupted. We start taking in too much fuel. Or bad fuel. Or fuel at the wrong time. Or we're always eating on the run, chewing and swallowing so fast we don't even know how much fuel we require. (Forget the whole notion of actually *enjoying* the food.) To give an example of how a change in circumstance can make the body trick itself: Suppose you found yourself stranded on a desert island. After a few hours you'd feel hungry. But as you adjusted to the fact that there was no easily available food, your brain would start sending out signals that you were *not* hungry, which in turn would allow you to become more focused, so that you could devote your energy (which your body creates by starting to burn glycogen, protein, and fat reserves) to one of two survivalistic activities: finding food or figuring a way off the island. Indeed, while you're hacking through the jungle or fashioning a fishing rod, you might experience that physical exuberance sometimes called an "anorexic high."

This can only go on for so long, of course; the body, while miraculous in many ways, cannot turn illusion into fuel; and burning fat becomes, after a time, dangerous, and eventually lethal. The point, though, is that, as conditions change, so do our physical responses. In a sense, as notions like "survive" and "thrive" begin to change meaning, the body starts smartly to tell itself a new story.

With the marooned-on-an-island example, however, at least the body is doing all it can to survive, to live another day. But the adaptations that our body and mind have made for the way many of us live now—to crave salt and sugar; to want to stuff ourselves; sometimes to deprive ourselves for dubious reasons—is not for our greater good. All it does is work to kill us faster.

We must change our story *back* to the way it was when we were young, so that we reconnect again with what food does for us. To get our story straight around food, *we must learn to eat strategically.*

That's not always easy. Practically every American restaurant serves individual portions large enough for three people. Or the waiter or waitress frowns to see you've left food, not knowing that you're trying to eat smart; believing that your half-eaten meal will translate into a smaller tip, she compensates by slipping you a free dessert, hoping for that bigger tip. Or you often eat with people who have food issues, from allergies to eating disorders. (Our experience and countless surveys show how prevalent "food issues" are, so it's pretty much a lock that you're very often eating with such people.) Or you rarely have time to prepare meals the way you'd like.

Strategic, balanced eating *is* possible. But you have to get your story straight. That's precisely what our nutritional staff does with our clients, week after week. Here's a very brief summary about eating (more extensive nutritional guidelines and explanations may be found at our website, www.humanperformanceinstitute.com) from our master storyteller and chief nutritionist, Raquel Malo:

"Re-Authoring" When to Eat, and Why

If you go too long without eating, or you eat too many high glycemic foods (which include candy, soda, certain sports drinks, and almost anything white—bread, pasta, rice, rice cakes), you will experience those glucose/insulin spikes that make your energy waver dramatically. Once you pass four hours without food, you're depleted of sufficient energy, no matter how many calories you took in at your last meal.

Survival-Based Eating

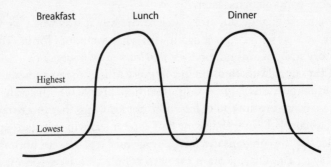

As you can see above, at the end of the day you're set for a deep crash; eating in this way will render you incapable of engaging with your family when you get home. While you didn't mean for your story to play out this way, that's how it's written; that's how your family experiences it. You need a new story around eating.

You *must* eat every two to four hours except when sleeping. You should drink water every thirty minutes to one hour. Snacking between meals helps to maintain energy and never allows your blood sugar level to get too low—thus enabling you to engage better all the way through to the end of the day. (Healthy snacks include fruit, low-fat yogurt, cottage cheese, nuts, sunflower and pumpkin seeds, trail mix, nutrition bars, and peanut butter.) If you do this, you will maintain energy throughout the day, right up until you're ready to go to bed; see the chart below.

Opportunity-Based Eating

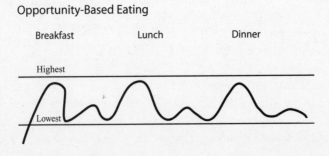

Feeling Satisfied vs. Feeling Full

After a meal, you want to feel satisfied, not full, and certainly not verging on a food coma. What are some smart habits to help you achieve this?

1. *Eat slowly*. Put utensils down between bites. Stop periodically and assess your satisfaction. Eat particularly slowly when consuming calorie-rich foods and other food high in fat content, because less is needed to make you feel satisfied or full.
2. *Eat light and often.* This not only stabilizes blood glucose levels but
   - improves metabolism
   - improves energy levels, brain function, and mood
   - controls cravings
   - decreases the likelihood of overeating
   - maintains muscle mass
   - prevents excessive fat storage
3. *Do not multi-task while eating.* Focus on what you're doing. Engage.
4. *Eat only what you need for the next two to three hours of your day.* Practice eating less food to assess how long the meal lasts.

Our best stories are full of great feeling and thinking. Our lives are most deeply felt when we experience them emotionally, mentally, spiritually. But none of that is fully possible unless, first, we are physically whole. And that is not possible without the right fuel—namely, healthy food. *What you eat, how much, and when will either enhance or hinder your performance.*

GETTING YOUR STORY STRAIGHT ABOUT EXERCISE AND MOVEMENT

Most of us work and recover from work in sedentary settings. Cubicles, cramped spaces, chairs, couches. We sit before computers. Traveling to and from this sedentary life we sit in a car, in traffic. Over time, as the traffic has thickened, the cars have gotten more comfortable. CD players, digital radio, three hundred cup holders. Gradually, remaining motionless for large chunks of our waking life has stopped seeming abnormal and actually become sort of, well, okay. Pleasant.

We need to move at regular intervals. We're built to move, not to sit. Movement makes the blood flow better. The more we move, the better we feel. The more mentally alert we are. The better we function cognitively. The less muscular tension and discomfort we experience. The more hormones get released, prolonging the salutary effects. Physical movement serves to enhance engagement by improving oxygen transport to cells. Lack of movement for extended periods of time (more than ninety minutes) makes it hard—impossible, actually—to be fully engaged. And the longer you don't move, the harder it is to be engaged. Why are we wiped out after a long meeting or flight? No, it's not *all* from the boring agenda items you're reviewing on your laptop or the dry airplane air. It's because we've been physically inactive for hours. Our blood hasn't circulated but instead has pooled, along with oxygen, in our now swollen feet. (A bit of advice: Never make big decisions while your feet are swollen.) When sitting, you're stifling blood flow to your largest muscle group, your behind. (And literally causing yourself—sorry—a pain in the ass.) *Lack of movement = lack of energy.* To rest, after all, don't we lie still so that we'll lose energy so that we'll fall asleep? The more inert we are during the day, therefore, the more we resemble the walking dead. In our survey, the average respondent achieves only 56% on physical fitness, the lower end of the "disengaged" range.

The more you move, conversely, the more energy you create, the better you perform. *To perform better, you need to move more.* You simply can't *not* feel the positive effect of movement. (Better still is to move when outdoors: Sunlight elevates your serotonin level, further increasing your energy.) Movement almost instantly makes you more alert. One hopes that air-traffic controllers, when on duty, at least pace.

As Chris Jordan, our chief exercise physiologist and master exercise/movement storyteller, says week after week: *Movement is the most powerful stimulant the body experiences.* It needn't even be extended or rigorous movement. Just movement, plain and simple, provides a surprisingly good bang for the buck, particularly when it's breaking up extended periods of inactivity such as mid-afternoon meetings. For instance, standing up—nothing more, just standing up from a sitting position—doubles your metabolic rate! Go for even a short walk and you've more than doubled the burn rate again. To prevent the mental and emotional disengagement that inevitably follow when you don't move, even small movements of the hands, feet, and arms should be made every thirty to forty-five minutes, and large movements such as walking, climbing stairs, or full-body stretching should be practiced every ninety minutes to two hours. The bigger the range of motion, the better; flexing hand muscles won't stimulate you as much as flexing arm muscles, and so on. Movement facilitates oxygen transport to the cells. Every time you move a limb, you improve blood circulation to that limb *and* to the brain, which controls that movement, thus increasing alertness, focus, engagement. When sitting for long periods, don't remain statue-like; instead, rock back and forth. (I realize that might not always be socially acceptable—say, if you're sitting in a chapel or at a funeral or a board meeting.) Uncross your legs—having them crossed constricts blood flow—or at least switch legs often. As with food intake—where eating light and often is recommended—so, too, moving little and especially often (during the workday, at least) is beneficial.

Exercise may be defined simply as *any movement that is challenging to the body*. What do I mean by that? I mean making a movement that falls outside one's "comfort zone." *When exercising, you should not feel comfortable*. The phenomenon known as the "postman's roll"—that ten to twenty-pound spare tire that some mailmen carry around, and oddly never lose, despite the fact that many of them walk several miles every day—is easily explainable: During their habitual rounds they're almost never exerting themselves.

Exercise means exerting yourself. Fortunately, we all have an innate sense of whether we're pushing ourselves. On the other hand, when working out you should not experience pain; if you do, then you're exerting yourself too much. One rule of thumb is that if you can't hold a conversation while running, or can't perform at least eight repetitions of any given weightlifting exercise, then you're past the discomfort zone and into the pain zone. If that's the case, then pull back. Discomfort, not pain, is what you want to feel.

Comfort: bad. Pain: bad. Discomfort: perfect.

Once you've come up with your preferred exercise(s), then there are really only three requirements:

- do it outside the comfort zone
- do it on a regular basis
- be engaged when doing it

At the institute, how do we define "regular"? For aerobic exercise, our experience shows that to make a real difference, you must do it at least three times a week (if you can do more, great, but it's not required), thirty minutes a session (ditto), with no more than two days of rest in between workouts. For resistance training, we recommend twice a week, on non-consecutive days, one to two sets per exercise, eight to twelve repetitions, with no more than three days of rest in between. Finally, with flexibility training—which people often skip, though it expands range of motion, and offsets the muscle contracting that occurs from resistance training—we recommend three to five days per week, after each exercise session, for at least five to ten minutes, two to five reps per stretch. More extensive exercise guidelines and explanations may be found at our website:

www.humanperformanceinstitute.com

The time commitment is hardly excessive. For a mere thirty minutes a day per week—and one or even two days off with no formal exercise—*we guarantee you will see and feel noticeable, significant improvement in your cardiovascular fitness, muscle tone, and flexibility.* Do anything less than the recommended regimen and we can't make that guarantee.

The reason we can guarantee an impact with so little time commitment goes to the third point: *When exercising, engage.* Remember, it's not about the time you give to something, but the energy. The passion, the commitment, the engagement. When you exercise, you needn't give it two hours, ever; but you *must* give it your focus for the brief time you're exercising. There's a staggering amount of waste created every day in gyms across America as seemingly dedicated patrons run on treadmills or climb StairMasters while watching CNBC or ESPN or listening to their iPods, not at all connecting with the physical activity they're supposedly "engaged" in. While I don't discount the other benefits of such an activity—clearing the mind and socializing, to name two—if these lunchtime warriors really wish to condition themselves, they can do so, in far less time, so long as it's concentrated, *intense* time.

We guarantee results so long as you do *not* multi-task during your workout, not even in your head. Working out with intensity, with engagement, is the only way to exercise correctly. "I ran three days a week for eight years and my fitness was never all that great," said one client, "but I just kept doing it because it was better than nothing." After coming through our program, he realized that, so long as he was engaged when exercising, he could verify more palpable results *in less time*. "I can really feel how the interval approach helps my heart and my stamina and my muscle tone so much more," he said. His story is repeated over and over. Chris Jordan's message is clear: *Come to your workout to work out, to improve yourself physically—not to (literally) go through the motions*. As I said earlier, if a world-class tennis player awaits his opponent's 140 mile-per-hour serve with two thoughts in his head, one of which does not concern how to return a 140-mph serve, his chance of returning that serve successfully is 0%.

In the meantime, when you're not working out, take the stairs, not the elevator. Take a walk after lunch. Walk to another department rather than e-mailing. Take a shower, not a bath. Take the stairs two by two. Avoid drive-through facilities. These are a few small but meaningful changes you can make during the workday, or just before and after it, to help you boost your energy levels and get to the next level of conditioning, on your way to a fitter, stronger body. Of course, the benefits of exercise go beyond just enjoying more muscle tone or not having to stop at the third-floor landing to catch your breath on your way to the fifth. A study published in the January 2006 issue of *Fitness Matters* showed that employees who worked out not only performed better than those who didn't but got significantly higher marks for their "intercollegial behavior"—respect for their co-workers, a sense of perspective, and generally helping to create a better working atmosphere. More proof, once again, that good health is good business—even though far fewer than half of all major U.S. companies actively encourage exercise among their workforce.

GETTING YOUR STORY STRAIGHT ABOUT RECOVERY (REST AND SLEEP)

We're addicted to speed and accomplishment. And each year the addiction appears to grip us more: We seem ever to be moving faster, demanding more, accomplishing more—or trying to. While numerous forces are responsible for this development, the number one culprit has to be Thomas Edison. After more than 100,000 years of human existence in which our levels of activity and engagement were determined almost exclusively by the answer to one question—Is the sun out or not?—the advent of electric light helped us to chuck our diurnal tendency. Spend forty-eight hours in Las Vegas and you'd hardly know that humans were *ever* creatures who treated the day for tending to vital business, and the night for replenishing one's physical resources. I find it interesting that a considerable percentage of our clients will say, "I'm just a night owl; I'd like to change but I can't"—as if a mere century or so of technological innovation could trump hundreds of millennia and more of primate hard-wiring.

We've become expert at moving horizontally—that is, crisscrossing our cities and our planet to check off the endless items on our life to-do list, one thing after another after another. But we've become far less skilled at going *vertically*—that is, moving cyclically, particularly in going from activity periods to refractory periods and back, from full engagement to full disengagement and back.

Yet to accomplish all we want, in ways that fulfill us deeply, we must learn better how to slow down, how to stop, how to disengage. If you really want your life to turn on, then you must first learn how to turn it off.

Now I realize that as you write, or rewrite, your story, it's hard to include in it long stretches of inactivity. Good stories, after all, are characterized by action and verifiable change, not by extended silence and stillness. But, as unnatural as it has become for modern man and woman to pause even for a moment, I believe *downtime is productive time*. It is vital to include sufficient sleep and rest (recovery) in your story. Without it, not even the most nutritious diet and the most obediently followed exercise regimen can ever fill your tank with the energy you need to achieve maximum performance. Given the Type A, "alpha" personality of so many business executives, planning sufficient recovery into one's life may be just about the biggest physical challenge they face.

A delicate balance must be struck between energy out (stress) and energy in (recovery). Spend too much energy without sufficient periods of recovery and the system will fail (as stated before, in sport this is called overtraining). On the other hand, too much rest and not enough exertion and the system also fails; that's undertraining.

The rhythmic interactions of stress and recovery create the pulse of life; the oscillation of engagement and disengagement optimizes energy management.

In our surveys, the average respondent scores a mere 51% on recovery ("disengaged") and 47% on the sleep score ("seriously disengaged"). Even those who are "fully engaged" at work and in life score a very mediocre 70% on recovery. No other health index testifies to more regular abuse. While what constitutes optimal sleep varies by individual, to merit a great score, most adults would need to honor sleep for what it is—the mechanism by which we fully recover each day—and that would mean going to bed the same time every night for about seven and a half to eight hours of deep sleep, and take a thirty- to sixty-minute nap each mid-afternoon, Of course, almost no one who comes through our program gets that. And even if they're regular about the time they go to bed and wake up, the sleep is usually not high quality (more about that in a moment).

Breaks—either short naps or periods of disengagement during the busy workday—are also vitally important. We recommend that they be taken far more often, roughly one every ninety minutes, than is typical for most people. After all, world-caliber athletes, whose performance can be judged more precisely and unambiguously perhaps than in any other field of endeavor, build numerous, regular, "intense" breaks into their training because they know that, without them, maximum effort and high-quality execution are impossible.

Cycles of full engagement can best be sustained with brief intervals of recovery (five to fifteen minutes) approximately every ninety minutes. The fitter one is physically, emotionally, mentally, and spiritually, the shorter the required interval of recovery that's needed. Speed of recovery is usually an accurate measure of fitness.

Once again, though, very few people take breaks. The primary gripe? *My company would frown on it.*

Bad story! There are numerous ways to deal with that problem. Some rituals that people have used to help build in breaks during the workday: One client sets his watch to go off on the hour, at which point he stands, drinks water, and keeps working for five minutes *while standing*; another client always takes a short walk down the hall after finishing one type of work (e-mailing, say) and before starting another; another client has built in (at least) three five-minute breaks during the day—at 10:30, 1:30, and 4:30—to meet a colleague in front of the office and bask briefly in sunlight.

Because we generally don't give the concept of recovery its proper due, when people actually do it, they do it poorly. For example, how often has this happened: After a ridiculously busy day at work you're dead tired, you lie down in bed . . . and you can't sleep.

Odd. Why would that be? Just when you need recovery *most*, the mechanism controlling it suddenly doesn't work? One explanation is that, as anyone who regularly exercises knows, the physically fitter you are, the deeper and better you tend to sleep (called "delta sleep"); thus, the quality of recovery—disengagement—is directly linked to the quality of one's physical exercise—engagement. *In short, the beneficial effects of exercise continue even after you stop, even while you're asleep!* On the other hand, for those who are not so fit and, more crucially, who rarely engage fully in what they're doing, it's simply harder to switch completely off, because they're never switched completely on.

Second, and just as important: It's difficult to switch off, period. After such a consuming day at work, it's tough not to still be thinking about all you just did and all that remains to be done; it's hard to compartmentalize the work part of life and keep it separate from the recovery part. You have not fully disengaged, no matter how engaged you've been, no matter how tired you are now. Almost everyone multi-tasks these days, and maybe at times it's necessary; but we must acknowledge that by doing so—by developing this habit of *not* being fully engaged by any one thing but fragmenting our attention across many things—we are likely compromising our very capacity to disengage, too. And with it comes a cost.

The most obvious cost is in how lack of proper sleep destroys performance, not to mention mood, at work and home. Shift workers—those who simply can't get the kind of high-quality sleep that all human beings need—are at higher risk for all kinds of accidents, injuries, and maladies. Indeed, the consequences of insufficient recovery can be tragic—if, say, the overworked person is employed in a life-saving job. Every year, approximately 100,000 Americans lose their lives due to medical errors. At a critical point in the majority of these cases, a wrong decision was made that could have been prevented. Certainly a healthy percentage of these decisions resulted because the practitioner was not fully replenished and engaged; in many cases, he or she had a seriously depleted energy bank account. If we read such a statistic in the newspaper—*100,000 Americans dead by accident!*—it would be enough to make us shake our heads, maybe even feel rage, disgust, sympathy. But what if a loved one were lost to one of these errors, an error that was absolutely preventable? It would be incomprehensibly tragic and pointless to us. Because someone's story did not include in it a need to recover, it had tragic, permanent consequences for us and our loved ones.

A few other examples of how the lack of recovery—insufficient sleep—leads to tragic consequences:

- Interns who work twenty-four-hour shifts increase the chance of stabbing themselves with a needle or cutting themselves with a scalpel by 61%.
- The risk of crashing a vehicle following a twenty-four-hour shift increases 168%. The risk of a near-miss increases 460%.

Those who believe that they simply can't take time out to rejuvenate—and that they'll somehow still manage to get things done, and done well, on insufficient rest—are kidding themselves. To maintain optimal efficiency, the average man or woman must be turned off (in sleep mode) approximately one-third of every twenty-four hours. Highly fit individuals require fewer than eight hours. And, as stated before, going to bed early and waking up early, as well as going to bed and getting up consistently at the same time, will give you more energy than, respectively, going to bed and waking up late, or sleeping at inconsistently-set intervals.

Finally, while I'm not advocating that "night owls" should change their tendencies overnight (if you will), it's important to remember that no one is locked into being this way, and walking around in a permanent haze of fatigue. (It's a virtual guarantee that night owls don't get a proper amount of sleep.) We have repeatedly shown at the institute that many people can permanently transform from "night person" to "morning person" in as little as thirty days, and thus to be aligned, once again, with their diurnal/nocturnal nature, those cycles that Edison and his cronies unwittingly made many of us ignore.

To live your new story, a simple but profound truth must be embraced: If you want to really turn your life on, then you'll have to find some time to turn it off.

Nine

INDOCTRINATE YOURSELF

A large mass of ice floats in the ocean but only a meager percentage—5% or less—is visible at the surface.

Now suppose, as Freud did, that the complete iceberg represents our complete mind; the visible surface of the iceberg our conscious world; the vast, subsurface mass our subconscious world.

Freud was a smart guy. It turns out that the analogy is startlingly accurate: According to two studies on brain function (Baumeister and Sommer; Bargh and Chartrand), 5% or less of the mind should be classified as the "conscious part"—controlled by self-regulatory, willful acts—while an astonishing 95% is nonconscious, automatic, instinctive.

Let's break down this iceberg mind. You're mostly, if intermittently, aware of the material that's just at the surface (sometimes above, sometimes below), stuff you retrieve instantly as it becomes necessary—your allergy symptoms, the deadline you're scuttling to meet, the growing hunger in your belly, the dinner you and your spouse will be having that night to celebrate your twelfth wedding anniversary. Close to the surface but just below the waterline are data and experiences to which you have ready access, though at the moment you're not aware of them: the stuff which, once an association to it is triggered, you can and will consciously call up. These are not things you're thinking of, for instance, while reading this sentence—you *can't* be, if you're fully engaged in reading—but as soon as I mention them, you can summon them in detail. The voice of a close friend talking about the progress he's making in his fight against cancer; who you played tennis with last week; the moments surrounding your daughter's birth; the traffic accident you were in five years ago; the high school math teacher who gave you your only failing grade. As soon as your mind is directed to such events and concerns, they instantly blossom into full consciousness.

But so much more affects our stories than what percolates above or just below the surface of our awareness. Unquestionably, our subconscious needs, conflicts, and childhood traumas can play havoc with our thinking, emotions, and perceptions. For example:

- You become so preoccupied with the project you're working on that you forget to eat lunch. By 3:30 in the afternoon, your attitude has turned decidedly negative. You display less patience with others and a greater sense of pessimism. Beyond the reach of your awareness is this simple fact: Your blood sugar level has dropped significantly because you haven't eaten anything since breakfast.

- No matter how often you hear others describe you as defensive and aloof, you're unable to counter the criticism. Your colleagues all agree that you're among the brightest, most talented contributors in the division, but your guarded, suspicious style with people has caused your bosses repeatedly to block your advancement in the firm. After working with an executive coach for nearly a year, you finally unearth what appears to be the source of your defensiveness: utter rejection by your father for the first seven years of your life. At age seven, your parents divorced and you never heard from him again. According to your mother, your father was convinced that you were not his child. His two modes of interaction with you— ignoring or being openly contemptuous—left a deep scar. From the time you were seven until now, age thirty-seven, you buried the painful memories. Because you've worked hard, you can now connect your past trauma with your trademark style with people—wary, closed. Your propensity for aloofness and defensiveness is a story that's beginning to make some sense.

As we go down deeper into the iceberg, it gets murkier, and it's more challenging for us to bring into consciousness the often mystical forces of the subconscious world. Residing here is most of the hidden matter that influences our stories—all the instinctual urges coded in genes (governing autonomic responses like fight-or-flight, for example), all the conditioning that took place during childhood, all the indoctrination that has occurred since the first day of life, all the trauma and conflicts festering beneath the surface, waging a constant battle between our wants and needs. It is this subconscious material that's hardest to retrieve and bring to the surface, to full awareness. Yet it's the mortar that goes a very long way in determining who we are and the shape our life story has taken.

Many people find it hard to accept that our lives are ruled by habits and routines and ossified memories, rather than moment-to-moment acts of conscious intent. They don't want to acknowledge that our stories might actually be so profoundly influenced by factors outside our normal state of awareness. After all, once we acknowledge the extent to which our behavior is governed by subconscious forces, how daunting—how futile!—is it to exercise full responsibility (whatever *that* means) for our life when but a paltry 5% of that life is really under our control?

Rather than being troubled by the percentages, and the perception they may give rise to, I see them as a glorious challenge. Forget that so much, percentage-wise, of what we do is out of control. *The part that matters—the part that makes the real difference—is the part we control.* It's this capacity that separates us from all other life forms. This evolutionary masterpiece is the only hope we have for making course corrections in our life story.

My experience in working with clients all over the world, and all over the map psychologically, long ago convinced me that our single greatest human asset is awareness, particularly self-awareness. This capacity to be reflective, to be conscious, is our most sacred capacity. (I don't suggest I'm alone or paradigm-busting in this; I believe René "Cogito ergo sum" Descartes would back me up.) The evolution of the species has, despite frequent missteps, moved progressively towards greater self-awareness; the more self-aware we are—that is, the greater our capacity for conscious, deliberate thought, for creating new stories—the better able we are to change directions, to adapt, to survive and thrive. While consciousness may represent a mere 5% of our complete mind, the influence this fraction exercises over the vector and tone of our life is far profounder than that. This precious one-twentieth resides in the cerebral cortex, and it might be likened to the steering wheel or the gas and brake pedals in a car—only a slight but very intentioned touch to each significantly redirects the several-tonned vehicle, turns it 10 degrees or 90 degrees or makes possible a complete U-turn, speeds it up or slows it down, starts or stops it altogether. While one might be able to make a decent guess at the parameters of our future by taking a snapshot of our subconscious 95% (were such a thing possible), it is our conscious 5% that allows us to make course corrections to that future, especially when the 95% has taken us off a desirable course. The conscious 5% is unquestionably the most important portion inside us. It is, in fact, what truly separates us from all other species. It is what creates the possibility for self-directed change.

Let's get back to the iceberg, the deepest part. Stored here is all the nonconscious material that clearly affects our beliefs, our attitudes, our view of the world, our story. Stored here are subconscious forces (wants, needs) that may be in direct conflict with conscious aspirations, intentions, values. Stored here are our most frightening and potentially destructive memories, such as severe childhood trauma. Suppose this trauma, to take one example, involved abuse: physical, emotional, mental, or sexual. Such abuse creates toxic memories that the individual, acting in survival mode, defends furiously from gaining consciousness; to allow such material to surface is perceived (subconsciously) to be overwhelming, maybe even deadly. The depth and concealment of this material, of these memories, does nothing to diminish their potential influence on our stories; indeed, there's likely to be a strong link between the stories we tell and the vast content stored below the waterline of our iceberg mind.

In devoting tremendous energy to keeping these traumatic events from being accessible, the individual's beliefs, attitudes, and stories get distorted. In fact, the ongoing power of these forces to distort might best be portrayed as having a boomerang effect: The individual's very defense *against* these "hidden stories"—a lifelong expression of extreme defensiveness, aggression, irrational anger, distrust, fear, rage—in turn betrays the existence of unresolved conflicts stored deep in the subconscious; indeed, don't we find people who "doth protest too much" most likely to be hiding something? Despite one's best, most public intentions to live a productive story, the hidden story may undermine any real chance for it. To any careful observer—and, one hopes, to the individual in question—great tension exists between the conscious and hidden stories.

Oh, no, you're saying. Please. I'm not getting on the couch. I don't have the time; that's not the way I work. Can't we just leave our hidden material alone? Must every effort be made to make what is unconscious conscious, what is unresolved resolved?

Well, no . . . and yes.

Fortunately, it is not a prerequisite of meaningful personal change that one connect one's current dysfunctional story with something specific from the past; even if that were possible, it's hardly a lock that one could undo the damage easily, if at all. Very often we can move forward and make positive changes with little or no clue as to how or why our convoluted story got formed that way.

Unfortunately, though, when a conflict exists between our conscious and subconscious worlds, the advantage clearly goes to the subconscious, precisely because the influencing factor is beyond our conscious knowledge of its being there. We often have no clue that there's distortion going on. However, when current dysfunctional stories *can* be linked to past dysfunctional stories and the accompanying faulty assumptions that arise from them—feelings of inadequacy, resentment, the injustice of it all—the insight can be liberating and invaluable. And can better equip us to create new stories that work.

For this reason we must recognize and appreciate how our current stories are formed and molded from much more than the material that is simply percolating at the surface. While not everyone experiences severe childhood trauma (most do not), we *all* experience various forms of indoctrination in our lives, we all possess instinctual urges, we all experience conflicts between wants and needs, we all struggle with misguided stories from our past. The more aware we are of hidden needs, conflicts, and past traumas, the better chance we have of crafting stories that meet the three criteria for storytelling (purpose, truth, hope-filled action). Once a memory of an important event or happening can be brought into consciousness, you can start to explore how that past material might be affecting your current story. To what extent, for example, is your current lack of confidence in math linked to the story you told yourself when you failed high school algebra?

While simply making the connection between the two stories will not immediately elevate your confidence in math, this may well be the point where a successful change begins.

DEEP DIVING

So how do we prevent these "hidden stories" from contaminating our current stories? We become courageous subconscious explorers. We learn to be skilled awareness divers. (If it seems I'm taking the iceberg metaphor a little far, we use it in our workshops to great effect.) To get our current stories right, we must be willing to dive into the world of our subconscious and explore the terrain. Every dive we make holds perceived risk and uncertainty. The deeper we go, the greater our fear that we won't return safely to the surface.

And yet every dive we make *increases* our confidence—confidence that we can explore and better understand this mysterious, uncharted world that plays such a powerful role in our storytelling and, thus, in our destiny. Each dive increases our confidence that we can do it safely. To map this vast cerebral space (known in neuroscience as neuronal space, site of frantic activity in some regions and inactivity in others) will likely necessitate countless dives throughout our lifetime.

> **Exercise:** Think back to a time when you did something or became involved in something that you now deeply regret. As you contemplate the event or series of events, perhaps you feel disgust, shame, even shock that you ever allowed yourself to veer so far off course. Try to reconstruct the thinking and logic (or lack of it) that allowed you, ultimately, to do what you did. What or who were the greatest influencing factors? What was the story you told yourself that opened the door for this to happen? By looking closely at your personal history in this way, you may gain valuable insight into the faulty dynamics of your storytelling, dynamics which, based on your history and if left unexamined, could have tragic consequences for your future.

• • •

Living fully conscious lives, which is the essence of full engagement, requires a genuine understanding of what lies beneath the surface. Full engagement in life requires a healthy co-existence between our conscious and subconscious worlds, one characterized by openness, frequent travel, accessibility, and courage.

Some questions to help you with future sub-surface probing:

1. What hidden influences might be behind some of your faulty thinking and beliefs that helped to create your current story?
2. Do you get very defensive about your faulty story? If you do, then what are you protecting? Specifically, in what parts of this story are you most fragile and vulnerable? What are you most afraid of here? If you follow the fear, where does it take you?
3. The story you currently tell yourself clearly hasn't inspired you to make a change. What's the logic and rationale you've used to keep this faulty story alive in your life for so long?
4. Is this really your story you're telling or someone else's? Whose voice is it?

FROM SUBCONSCIOUS TO CONSCIOUS AND BACK AGAIN

Connecting to the past may be helpful but it's neither necessary nor sufficient for effecting real change. What *is* necessary?

First: We must *consciously* face the truth that something in our story isn't working properly—our sleep habits, our lack of exercise, our lack of joy when we're with family and friends, our carelessness with money, our lack of engagement when we're with our aged parents. Then we must *consciously* identify any faulty assumptions, distortions, hidden conflicts, and prior indoctrinations. Getting these insights to surface may require a number of deep dives. To bring the story to full consciousness, it needs to be written down. This is what the Old Story is about.

Second: Once the manifestations and subconscious influences in our dysfunctional story are made conscious, in black and white, we can begin to craft a story no longer contaminated by the forces of hidden persuasion, one now more obviously aligned with our ultimate purpose. This is what the New Story is about.

Good. Fine. This is all positive effort and tough to do, very tough. One is to be commended for doing it.

But we can't stop there. There's another thing still to be done.

To gain real power in our lives, *our new story must become re-embedded into the world of the subconscious*. After all, we're creatures controlled by habit and routine, right? It's in that 95% force in our lives—automatic, instinctive, not conscious—where our new, functional story must find its permanent home, allowing us to keep the 5% conscious part uncluttered.

EMBEDDING

NEXT STEP: Embed your new story into your life by indoctrination.

How do you indoctrinate yourself? By investing energy repeatedly and for as long as it takes until the new story becomes "embedded"—that is, becomes instinctual and irreversible. For most people, ninety days appears to be the point-of-no-return, though significant momentum occurs in as little as three weeks.

The most effective way to embed a new story is by:

- writing it and rewriting it—including keeping a journal, even for just one day, to document all the energy investments you make—physically, emotionally, mentally, or spiritually
- re-reading it (for example, reviewing it every morning before leaving for work)
- thinking about it
- visualizing it
- talking about it, both publicly to others and privately to yourself (listening to others tell your story, and listening to your own voice telling it on tape, are two unusually persuasive methods, though some people are uncomfortable with them), and finally
- deliberately acting it out by your new behavior

I realize that the process I recommend here represents a significant departure from the belief, heralded by analytical psychologists, that real change cannot happen without an understanding of why and how one's dysfunctional stories and their underlying unconscious conflicts were formed in the first place. I disagree. I believe that, given how our brains work, the more we repeatedly go back to our old, dysfunctional stories, and the more energy we invest in them, the more we strengthen them. Unless we give them the opportunity to die or wither, they won't.

When we invest energy in new and constructive things, we give *those* things strength and life. New pathways open up. Energy flows through them, with increasing fluidity. New stories are given life. New perceptions occur, new meanings take hold, new behaviors become possible. For example, if your objective is to become more compassionate, then doing things like lowering your voice, listening more attentively, trying to mirror the expression of the person with whom you are conversing will all help to activate the "chemistry" behind compassion, and you actually start to experience how greater compassion feels; keep doing it, and it will feel more and more natural. Commit to putting continued energy into doing something new and right and it soon becomes part of your subconscious, that big, "beyond-our-reach" 95%.

The final act, then, involves fashioning highly specific rituals. Asking the waitress, each time you go to a restaurant, to remove the breadbasket as soon as it hits the table. Never turning on the TV without giving yourself the specific time by which it will be shut off. Turning off your cell phone at dinner so you're more engaged with your family. Exercising from 5:30 to 6:15 AM four days a week. Complimenting your direct reports at least once a week for something they did well. Repeat; create new pathways for energy; see them become habitual and eventually invisible to you. The gesture becomes "ritualized." Soon, many of your most familiar experiences become "embedded"— that is, automatic, instinctive, becoming so well-traveled that they require less, maybe even zero, conscious energy. Experts say that within thirty days, usually, you'll go from having to push yourself to do it to feeling pulled to do it; after sixty to ninety days, this pull becomes increasingly pronounced. The energy that went pointlessly and maddeningly to finding your once-again-misplaced house keys—which you can easily teach yourself never to misplace again—is now freed up and available for engaging in other, more important experiences. Your life energy is not being eaten up by the acts that belong in the subconscious 95%.

By courageously diving into the subconscious, we go from a conscious, but vague, awareness that something isn't right in our lives to facing the truth of it and linking it to our greater purpose in life. Only by creating and embedding a new story about what you *can* do—at work, on the golf course, as a parent, as a potential leader, as a spouse—will the trajectory of your life change in that area.

Now let's determine what it is, specifically, that we want to embed, and move to action.

Ten

TURNING STORY INTO ACTION: TRAINING MISSION AND RITUALS

If your Ultimate Mission is your life's Mission Statement, your Executive Summary, your View From 30,000 Feet, then your Training Mission is an important component of your overall reorganizational plan. And your Rituals—the actions you take to fulfill the aims set forth in your Training Mission—are your concrete measurables, evidence that you are correcting that component, so that you can correct the overall plan.

Inevitably, there are many changes you wish to make to turn your life into the story you want it to tell. It would be nice to think that all these changes could be made in one enthusiastic burst of self-transformation. But that doesn't happen. Pick a few changes and just make sure that each is

- important enough to you
- realistically fixable
- clearly defined
- supportable by behavioral changes (rituals) that will do the trick

A couple of examples of actual Training Missions and their supporting Rituals:

Training Mission 1:

To become more engaged with my wife at home and with my direct reports at work.

Rituals to Support My Training Mission

1. Every day find two things to compliment Sandy on
2. Date night with Sandy every other Saturday
3. Be more engaged in the time together with Sandy
4. Home for dinner at least 3 times per week and encourage direct reports to do the same
5. Listen more, talk less in time with direct reports
6. One-on-one lunch with direct reports every Thursday
7. Thank direct reports for their hard work and contributions at least once a week
8. Devote ten minutes of weekly meeting for direct reports to discuss matters affecting their work/life balance
9. Review training mission (and New Story) first thing every morning

Training Mission 2:

Find ways to engage more with family, especially given all the travel I do for work, and to be more engaged at work.

Rituals to Support My Training Mission

1. When home, bedtime stories every night at nine PM
2. Call home at eight PM every night out of town
3. Establish and meet a minimum number of days per month to be home for dinner
4. Make phone call to parents every Sunday evening at 8:30 PM
5. At least twice a day, instead of e-mailing colleagues with questions or information, walk to their office instead
6. Eat breakfast every day
7. Never go longer than four hours without food
8. Drink water regularly throughout day

Once you've succeeded at one Training Mission, you've not only improved *specifically* (in those few areas) but you've improved *generally*, showing yourself capable of meaningful change. This arms you with the confidence and track record to embark on another training mission, perhaps more ambitious than the last. Each time you "ritualize" a new, improved behavior and turn it into a largely unconscious habit, one that requires less and less energy as it becomes simply a part of your new way of being, you free up new conscious energy needed to change in other important ways. As long as you engage in the step-by-step, clearly defined program as set out by the Training Mission—*conscious, honest engagement*—you'll be amazed at how relatively quickly the power (and size) of your unconscious mind begins to take over, making your better behavior the norm.

Now write down yours:

My Training Mission

_____

_____

_____

_____

Five Rituals to Support My Training Mission

1. _____

2. _____

3. _____

4. _____

5. _____

THE TRAINING EFFECT, THE STORY EFFECT

The more curls you do with a dumbbell, the more your bicep grows. Increase the repetitions or the weight and the bicep increases in size and strength. It's not rocket science. It's the simple effect of training your bicep.

Whenever you invest energy in anything, there is a "training effect." The greater and more frequent the energy you give to that thing, the more life you give it, and the bigger and stronger it becomes. Its impact grows. The training effect is inescapable. It happens whether you intend it to or not. It happens whether its impact on your life is good or bad. It happens whether the repetition is an action or a thought. It affects you outwardly and inwardly, and likely affects others, too. If you repeat it at the same time of day, or in a predictable sequence, then you will train yourself eventually to act or feel or think a certain way at that time of day, or at a predictable juncture in the sequence. (Think Pavlov, who so famously conditioned dogs to salivate merely by ringing a bell—because they'd been trained, through repetition, to associate bell-ringing with feeding.) If you have eggs and cereal every morning with your kids, then there's a training effect in a variety of ways: the omega-3 in your blood will rise but so might your cholesterol (some say no); also, you're bonding with your children. There's a training effect on them, too: They see breakfast as a ritual and an important source of fuel. They see that you have time for them at the start of the day. The habituality pays dividends, sometimes bad, sometimes good, but it always pays. Often multiple training effects are happening at the same time, some positive and some negative. So many working mothers torture themselves because they feel guilty that they're not home more with their kids, and that their kids will take something negative away from that. Maybe yes, maybe no—but these women also need to honor themselves for making an impression on their children that doing work outside the home can be fulfilling, even joyful.

So long as you invest energy in anything, there will be a training effect. Don't expect to "outthink" your body or your brain, as if you can do something while also denying its impact. Perhaps the training effect is not exactly a euphemism for Newton's Third Law of Motion—for every action there is an equal and opposite reaction—but it's clear that if you do something, then *something* else happens. No one gets away with anything.

Now suppose that, rather than growing your biceps, you've long wanted to be more patient. How would you make your patience "grow"? You'd invest energy in it, of course; that is, you would seek regular occasions to build it, to develop it, in the same way you regularly go to the gym to work your bicep. Fortunately—or unfortunately—

there is no shortage of opportunities to grow patience: finding yourself in a traffic jam, being put on endless hold, trying to get out of the house in the morning as the kids dawdle putting on their coats, working with a new colleague who's trying hard but still not up to speed. Invest energy in patience and it will grow, like a muscle; conversely, if you invest energy in impatience, then *it* will grow. By giving something energy, you give it life.

The same is true with your job, your marriage, your relationship to your kids, your golf swing. Invest energy in each and it grows; stop investing energy and it stops growing, and eventually dies. Just as our bicep adapts and expands its capacity in response to the investment of energy in weight-lifting, so do patience, compassion, trust, mental focus, and integrity respond to energy investment. When we give something energy, we grow it; when we give something extraordinary energy, it grows extraordinarily.

There is a training effect for stories, too. With each repetition of a story you tell yourself, that story travels your neural pathways more easily. Tell yourself that story again and again and again and soon enough those pathways that were once unpaved roads, metaphorically speaking, have now become slick six-lane superhighways. Gradually, repetition reinforces the primacy and value of that story—not to mention pushing away or ignoring alternative stories undeserving of your energy, which then atrophy or die, and the pathways they once traveled now narrow again, growing less supple with disuse. You become indoctrinated by your current story. You are training yourself to believe it and to live it. Steve, the incredibly successful client who was dogged by the presence of his late father, commissioned himself to write a letter to his dad every Friday, saying things in it that he hadn't when his father was alive (such as gratitude he wished he'd expressed), as well as documenting what was going on right now with Steve, his family, and the family business. For thirteen Fridays in a row he did this—sometimes a page, sometimes five. After three months, he felt as if he understood his father better, as well as himself. That's not to say that everything was perfect because of a Friday letter, but his relationship to his father had changed, for the better.

Every story we tell has some effect. Stories move the needle every time we tell them. Because of this powerful "story effect," it's imperative that the story you tell be a constructive, and not destructive, one: The effect of training makes it hard to break the bonds that form. It's crucial, then, to be utterly conscious about who you are and what you're doing with your life—in other words, to be brutally truthful with yourself about your purpose—so that you are aware of your story and can assess whether and how it's helping or hurting you. Obliviousness is, as they say, not an option. Without this awareness, you can't take corrective action.

There's a problem, though. You may be thoroughly well-intentioned about examining your story, yet often it's difficult, if not impossible, to see the immediate consequences of your story on yourself or others. Your story's impact may not reveal itself for years. For example, who sees the consequences of eating one bad meal? Or not working out for one day or one week? Impossible. So we continue not to work out, and to eat bad meals. And the next day and the next. We "get away" with it. We don't see the consequence of our inactivity (*I'll get to it when things are not so crazy at work . . . when the weather is warm . . . when the kids go off to college*), and then one day we get a physical, our first in five years, and—shock of shocks!— our bloodwork and other health indicators are all at alarmingly unhealthy levels. One client, a banker who smoked and was considerably overweight, later had a heart attack and quadruple-bypass surgery. He told me that for years his doctor always labeled his bloodwork and other health indicators as "moderately" high. "That word 'moderately' totally let me off the hook," he said. "Every year I walked out of his office after a checkup, that word allowed me to do nothing." And then one day he had a heart attack. How did his story come to such a pass? Again, as the character says in *The Sun Also Rises*, when asked how he went bankrupt: "Two ways. Gradually and then suddenly."

I don't mean to suggest that the training effect is more a negative than positive development. Far from it. Indeed, when you are pursuing your New Story and trying to fulfill your Training Mission, you *want* to be at the mercy of the training effect: This is where the power of your unconsciousness is delightfully beneficial, working *for* you. Thanks to the training effect, once you've finished an initial period of training, you'll gradually be required to spend less and less of your conscious energy toward making that positive change.

RITUALIZING

The first time Jack B., vice president at a consumer products company, pulled into his driveway after work and intentionally left his cell phone in his car, he had to pretend to himself that he'd done so mistakenly; without indulging that little lie, he couldn't quite close the car door behind him, his diabolical electronic lifeline perched in its holder, beckoning him. But he made it inside his house and, astonishingly, the world didn't fall apart. He didn't get fired the next day. The following night, he again left his phone in the car, only this time he didn't feel the need to concoct a story for himself about why. The world continued spinning on its axis; he still had a job the following day. Within three weeks, his "change experiment" had become a habit. His cell phone would not cross the threshold of his home. His initial reasons for leaving it behind were so he could be more attentive to his kids and wife; so he could feel a boost when he saw them, not that on-edge, work-never-ends feeling; so he could actually relax more. But he discovered that he now enjoyed at least one more benefit, too, a change he would have considered counterintuitive had he not experienced it himself: He became *more* productive. At the office he concentrated better because he was aware that that was the time when all things had to get handled, no two ways about it—and his team knew it, too. His direct reports could no longer treat him as if he were their trouble-shooting ATM, available no matter the time of night or day. Six months later, Jack's world was still standing and his "radical" change still had not put him in jeopardy of getting fired. The idea of it made him laugh, in fact. Thanks to this one small but crucial new restriction on his home life, he was so much more energetic at work (at home, too) that he felt more indispensable to his firm than ever.

That's certainly one way to develop and embed a "ritual," the term I use for a new way of doing or thinking that transforms into an advantageous habit: Make up a story to tell yourself. But lying to yourself is hardly a prerequisite for getting a profound change to take hold. In fact, the more honest, open, and explicit you can be about it, the better.

Let's explore more closely the connection between a more formal Training Mission and turning it into action. The Training Mission might be, say, to expand your horizons; the ritual, to read a book for

twenty minutes on the train ride in before you turn your attention to
The Wall Street Journal. The training mission might be to charge, rather
than shuffle, through those periods of the day when your drop in
blood-sugar level renders your ideas worthless, your concentration
non-existent, your energy quasi-catatonic; the ritual, in response,
might be to set your wristwatch alarm to go off at eighty-minute intervals, which is your signal to stand, stretch, stride down the hall, and
step outside for five minutes of recharging with a granola bar, fresh air,
and the serotonin spike of actual sunlight. The Training Mission
might be to improve communication with your direct reports; the ritual, to sit down with each of them individually for twenty minutes
every Wednesday morning. The training mission might be to reconnect with your spouse; the ritual, ten consecutive Tuesday nights of
ballroom-dancing classes.

Once you've enjoyed success at making these modest but vital
changes, and you see for yourself just how swiftly constructive rituals
can be cultivated and integrated into your life, you'll develop the confidence to take on more, and more ambitious, rituals, in the service of
fulfilling your Ultimate Mission.

Now probably you think I'm making ritualizing sound too easy,
unrealistically so. Real change requires more than desire, more than a
good intention, which is a necessary condition for change but not a
sufficient one. After all, come New Year's Eve, many of us, stocked for
winter with good intentions, resolve finally to change our stories—
seriously this time, no kidding, cross our hearts. Yet sadly, rare is the
resolution that's still in play by Valentine's Day.

Don't shy away from rituals that, by themselves, seem simplistic or
trivial, given the magnitude and scope of the life change you are target-
ing. We've learned something very important at the institute: Never
underestimate the power of a single ritual to effect significant change.
Jack B., the VP who trained himself to keep his cell phone out of his
house at night because it trivialized his family life and threatened actually to endanger his marriage, still had work left over from the day that
needed to be done. So besides just leaving his cell phone in the car—a
clear signal to his wife and daughters that he had rediscovered his
respect and even love for them and for the sanctity of their family—he
instituted another ritual. In his words, he "got permission from my
wife to do one hour of work in the evening after the kids have gone to

sleep, but then she and I spend an hour winding down together in bed—talking, watching a movie, reading next to each other." Although Jack was sure it would be a hard change to stick to—just as he'd feared with the cell phone—he found that it was in fact surprisingly, satisfyingly easy. Precisely because it was just that one hour of work, and he was forbidden (or forbid himself) to let it bleed into the next, he was more engaged than he was used to being in his home office. More often than not, forty-five minutes was enough for him to accomplish what he needed, sometimes as little as twenty. The time with his wife was then undistracted and more enjoyable, energized by the fact that he'd gotten his work done and that he wasn't (as he used to do) "plotting in the back of my mind how I would slip out of bed later." Says Jack: "It's amazing what it's done for our relationship, and it's made me more efficient in my work, too."

I won't back away from the claim that rituals *are* relatively easy to inculcate—*so long as you work toward them with this checklist in mind*:

- Identify the story/stories that are causing you pain, agitation, unhappiness, frustration.
- Identify a few behaviors or habits you could improve to reduce or eliminate these negative feelings.
- Decide on an action, one consistent with your values and beliefs, which allows energy to flow in the new targeted direction, and make sure it is highly structured, reasonable, and not overtaxing to your present lifestyle.

Creative thinking is pretty much a necessity in this ritual creation process; after all, to get to a new way of being you'll probably have to be clever. Be open to enlisting others. For example, if the story that needs changing is the one around your health, and the action you need to take is to carve out several times a week to exercise, then the question is, How? Your mornings are filled with a long commute, your nights consumed by family. Perhaps you make lunchtime Monday, Wednesday, and Friday your inviolate workout session, get a colleague to cover for you during those three slots with the proviso that he call through only in emergencies (which happen much less frequently than we tend to think), and you return the favor by covering for him or her another three hours during the week. Or maybe you decide that the change you need to make is to eat healthier, especially those Thursday staff lunches when your dining choices are not yours to make. E-mail those who attend the meetings that you'd like to order from a variety of healthy places and then have an assistant, or each of you, on a rotating basis that taxes no one, make sure to order from those menus. Before you know it, you're looking forward to the food at Thursday's gathering and wondering why you don't eat healthier the other four workdays. You shouldn't hesitate to include others in your rituals. So long as you're not coercive or obnoxious about it, chances are great that the positive change you want to make is something they're looking to make, too, but have so far just lacked the proper incentive, structure, or camaraderie to succeed.

One mid-level manager chose to be creative in this way: In an attempt to spend more time with his son, at the beginning of each quarter he found out all the key son-related events coming up—such as soccer games, piano recital, birthday, parent-teacher conferences—and then "encoded" them into his work calendar as "AMX." When those in the firm wanting to schedule time with him looked at his calendar, which was available on the company intranet, they saw the serious-sounding letters peppering his calendar. If someone called to make an appointment at one of those times, his assistant told them, "I'm sorry, but he'll be with AMX then." Everyone came to believe that AMX was an important client, which of course it was, his most important. Everyone came to treat those occasions as untouchable. The manager, meanwhile, had forever ritualized time with and for his son.

Another executive made the small but significant change of scheduling meetings only at 11:30 AM or 4:30 PM, knowing that attendees were more likely to be focused and wanting to get out quickly, thereby increasing the chance that *he* would get out quickly. The alteration became a ritual; the actual time spent in meetings was cut by half, with no loss in effectiveness. Another team leader who felt that her existence during traditional business hours had been reduced largely to putting out one fire after another, e-mailed everyone in her company, "I will not be reading e-mails between 3 PM and 5 PM." The result? She got far fewer e-mails, period, and "they know if they want to get hold of me between three and five, they have to call or walk to my office—and most of them don't." There was even an unexpected ancillary benefit: "It's amazing how many things that were problems before, simply because they could be rattled off in an e-mail, are no longer problems now," she said. "I don't know if they solved them by themselves or they really weren't problems to begin with, but now I get actual work done in the office, while I can feel my team's confidence has grown noticeably, since they're handling much more and don't need always to fall back on me for support." Instituting even the simplest, most obvious rituals—the low-hanging fruit, as it were—can yield profound results.

Another client, a professor, realized that her morning routine—her husband would drive her and their son to school, then drop her off at the university, then go off to his work—was deficient on several counts. The drive to school was too quick to allow for any meaningful conversation with her son; she got no exercise sitting in the car; she had no time to herself. What she did, then, was to tweak it. She and her son walked to his school, during which time they had fifteen or twenty minutes to talk and make up haikus for each other about what they had done the previous day *and* they were both getting exercise (and she relieved her guilt that her husband had to play chauffeur every morning); then, once she'd dropped off her son, she took the bus to her office, instituting a rule that her bus reading could only be books she wanted to read for pure pleasure, not work-related material. Compared to how she used to feel when she set foot inside her office each morning, now she felt more physically, emotionally, mentally—and spiritually—alive.

If some of these rituals were so simple and obvious, everyone would be doing them already. Indeed, the moderately creative innovations documented above are, I think, even more than that. I would venture so far as to call them "counterculture," something that gets done almost subversively.

Counterculture? Subversive? Isn't that a tad melodramatic for describing relatively modest changes to our work lives? I don't think so. I use such provocative language not so much to overpraise those who have the nerve and fortitude to do things differently, but to acknowledge that creating rituals anywhere—inside the office and out—really *isn't* as easy as perhaps I've made it sound. Indeed, it is *you* who have to figure a way to rise above the typically staid, status quo nature of corporate culture. *You* have to exhibit the steadfastness and strength to change within a work environment that is unlikely to change, at least not in any dramatic way. Almost all of these rituals—

which are premised, as is everything in this book, on the belief that it is the energy we give things that really matters, not the time—flouts that verse in the corporate bible that says "time is everything." That bureaucratic belief doesn't evaporate just because you've finally resolved to change. Your micromanaging boss is not suddenly going to disappear. He or she will never come to you in the morning to point out that it would be wise for you to eat a better breakfast so you'll feel more energetic during the day. He or she will never tell you to change your work habits and look at the imbalance in your life because you're a walking heart attack. The HR person will not e-mail you that it's been eight months since you expressed to your wife that you love her.

So it's up to you.

Once you understand the importance of creating rituals, of repeating them with consistency until they become habits, you will soon enough be able to maintain them easily—that is, without much conscious investment of energy. And the energy you were unwittingly depriving yourself of all this time will once again be yours.

Beware: The new levels of engagement, wakefulness, and enthusiasm you experience may actually shock you.

Let's revisit the group to which I referred way back in Chapter 1—that staggeringly smart gathering of engineers employed by a giant telecom company. To refresh your memory: They complained of being stuck in a culture where—it felt to most of them—they could make no meaningful improvements to their three primary stories (which are almost everyone's three primary stories): the story around family, the story around health, the story around work. Everything in the vast organization was entrenched, futile, impossible. *The typical business day is so full of surprises and chaos, I couldn't structure it if I wanted to . . . Exercising during the workday sends a bad message . . . My family just has to understand that this is what's expected of me and everyone.* The signature sentiment, as one person put it: *It is what it is.* Remarkably, almost none of these brilliant, accomplished people could at first see the extent to which their three stories were interconnected, or that their family story and their health story were influenced by their work story—*not* the other way around. They accepted, if not embraced, their situation even as its effect on their life was potentially devastating. Of the thirty-two engineers in the room, only four were "counterculture" enough to have instituted rituals to bring balance to each of their three stories, and balance to the three stories together.

After getting mostly shoulder shrugs and the occasional protestation of paralysis from them, I asked the room what would happen if their boss walked in and tasked them to reinvent the corporate culture so that (a) it would remain as profitable—or more so—while (b) also allowing for more balance, connection, fulfillment. Did they think they could do that? I asked. Every arm shot up.

They broke into groups and for the next thirty minutes I could practically hear brains humming. Suddenly, after the better part of a morning session in which I'd been frustrated at trying to draw anything out of this group of fine minds characterized mostly by cynicism and resignation, I couldn't shut them up. It was a breathtaking display of solution thinking.

To the problem "How do we make our lives healthier?" here are some rituals they came up with:

- ✓ Incorporate exercise into off-site meetings (7 AM walk/run as a group, tai chi class, etc.).
- ✓ Have more outdoor meetings, to be in the sun and raise serotonin levels.
- ✓ Have VPs who attended the program share nutrition and fitness information with admin assistants.
- ✓ Offer healthier food in vending machines.
- ✓ Offer fruit, nuts, or nutrition bars next to candy.
- ✓ Try to avoid lunchtime meetings so people can work out, have planned lunch away from the office.
- ✓ Encourage bicycles for transportation between buildings.
- ✓ Encourage more face-to-face meetings instead of e-mail (promotes movement and small "recovery breaks" throughout the day).
- ✓ Order fruit and protein instead of (or in addition to) cookies for afternoon snacks.

To the question "How do we engage people better during meetings?" here are some of the rituals they came up with:

✓ For all meetings, provide clear statement of agenda/goals/objectives.
✓ Start meetings at fifteen minutes after the hour so everyone is present.
✓ Make all hour meetings a half hour to ensure participants stay focused.
✓ "No laptop / no cell phone" rule at meetings.
✓ Offer healthier lunches and snacks during meetings (using nutritional guidelines set out by HPI).
✓ If agenda is complete, end meetings early.
✓ Hold "standing meetings"—where people literally stand during the meeting.

To the problem "How can we promote greater efficiency in communication and work?":

✓ Create "meeting-free" time zones (best suggested time: Fridays, one PM to five PM) to allow people to focus.
✓ Ask VPs and participants in the HPI program to e-mail their organizations about changes they will be making; e-mail direct reports, to encourage key principles—face-to-face meetings, meeting guidelines, nutritional and fitness guidelines.
✓ Talk to direct reports about the need for mental and physical breaks.
✓ Demonstrate "top-down commitment"—senior management must model the changes in their own lives.
✓ Offer e-mail etiquette training to keep messages productive.
✓ Encourage more breaks (whole wheat pizza and non-alcoholic beer sponsored by a department and its customers).
✓ Offer senior management roundtable and random invites.
✓ Ask VPs to provide nutritional guidelines to secretaries.
✓ Schedule regular meetings with direct reports.

These somewhat revolutionary (at least for the corporate world) rituals had the effect not only of producing greater harmony and engagement in the engineers' various stories (health, family, work) but also encouraging them *generally* from becoming victimized by rote thinking, from feeling that it's "the system," unyielding and eternal, that is responsible for their poor health or attitude. No more victimhood or martyrdom; by ritualizing positive behaviors, the individual takes control, evades corporate rules and mind-set, yet still keeps his or her job and usually thrives at it like never before. Inventive men and women, like those who came up with the insights just catalogued, have shown us that ritualizing even the most minor-seeming changes have a major impact. They score consistently higher than average on survey questions about happiness and engagement. Those who return to us after having been with us once, then making changes in their work and home life, invariably show marked improvement in their level of engagement. Why not? What they're doing is writing a different story for themselves.

So, did these rituals stick? Did individuals and departments and entire companies undergo real transformation?

Absolutely. In about 80% of cases, clients make meaningful headway in one or more of their major stories, personally and professionally. For approximately one-third of our clientele, the changes are profound across the board.

Certainly, nothing delights me more than seeing entire organizations make top-down reforms, whereby the institution implements rituals designed to help *all* of its workers, or at least those willing to take advantage. This is thanks, in part, to chief executives who have been through our program and understand that engagement is guaranteed to *spur* profitability, whereas simply increasing the time demands on employees guarantees nothing. A. G. Lafley, CEO of Procter & Gamble, is one who realizes that organizing his company's story around health can improve corporate morale *and* profitability. At his urging, they've begun to provide more nutritional food in their cafeteria, bottled water and healthy snacks for more frequent breaks, encourage "walking meetings," discourage multi-tasking at meetings. For his company and others that have followed this path, numerous indices of success—including employee retention, lower absenteeism and lower "presenteeism"—are all improved. We've worked with many institutions sufficiently excited by the notion of improving employee engagement (and one of its trusty counterparts, greater corporate profitability) that they have made a systemic realignment. The CEO and board of San Juan (New Mexico) Regional Medical Center confronted the fact that they could not reasonably be the best caregivers possible if they violated their principles with their own workers (what kind of story is *that*?), so they changed the way they care for their staff and run their hospitals. After more than a hundred employees came through our program (more than 10% of their total workforce), they established an in-house program to simulate the Orlando course, so all their workers could benefit. Their trainers aren't necessarily HR people but nurses, ER workers, department heads. They've enjoyed greater employee retention and morale, and the increased attention to energy and balance has translated into exceptional performance by the medical staff. (Can you name a corporate transformation that could have a more palpable, positive impact on its clientele?) Hospital employees who routinely worked twelve-hour shifts with no lunch, much less breakfast, now understand the imperative of smart eating, both for themselves and their patients. The hospital created its own state-of-the-art fitness and training facility—even bought their own BodPod, the next-generation body-fat measurement device—and opened it not just to staff but to the entire community. Because of the shocking rise in the incidence of childhood obesity and diabetes, New Mexico passed a law mandating better education for kids about nutrition and exercise; the medical center is footing the bill to send a dozen local teachers to Orlando to learn from our experience, and to help develop a fitness and nutrition program suitable for children and teenagers.

At GlaxoSmithKline's main training facility in North Carolina, all 1,200 members of its recent recruiting class are being trained in our basic principles of physical energy—eating, exercising, resting and recovering. At PepsiCo, recently departed CEO Steve Reinemund made energy management and storytelling core elements in their leadership program.

At a five-hundred-person Southwest-based textile company we've worked with, the president, a dynamic leader and former college athlete now sixty pounds overweight, realized that two of his three most important stories—the one regarding his family ("I want to be a role model for my four sons and an extraordinary companion to my wife") and the one regarding his work ("I want to ensure that over the next generation, we innovate and perform better than our company ever has")—were guaranteed to fail because his third important story, the one regarding his health, would likely culminate in a premature heart attack or some other life-crippling condition. So he put on his executive calendar—"where everyone can see it"—the three-times-a-week aerobic workout he would be doing at the company gym. Not only did doing so make him accountable to himself but "it's good for everyone else to see the role that exercise should have and can have—and maybe some of them will start to put it on *their* weekly schedules." When he works out at home, it's almost always with one of his sons.

Whether it's the individual or the company instituting rituals to improve their story, it's advisable not to make fifty major changes at once; minor change is difficult enough. It's often helpful just to start by adopting one small ritual and sticking to it. Take flossing, for example—yes, flossing. It's got everything one wants from a life change: It's targeted, manageable, and of course beneficial. Tell yourself that you will be religious about flossing for thirty to sixty days—the amount of time needed by most people before an activity becomes habitualized. Or take the habit, to some, of automatically putting one's keys away when one walks in the door. In almost every workshop I'll ask the room, "Who here never has trouble finding their keys?" Roughly half the group raise their hands. When I ask them how they've achieved this, the answer is always the same: They put their keys in exactly the same place, every single time. There is no sense of uncertainty surrounding their keys; when they need them later, there is no confusion, chaos, or lost time or energy. It's something they long ago stopped thinking about at all. It's automatic. If you're in the half who are *not* in that habit, then choose a hook or dish or corner of a countertop to put your keys and make yourself do it every single time you walk in the house for three weeks. You'll never again have to worry about lost keys. The energy and time that now disappears down a sinkhole while looking for them can then be used for something far more interesting and important.

Of course, this is a very small example. But take the energy wasted on a bigger task, or multiply the time wasted by many such small examples, and you'll free up phenomenal amounts of energy (and time) each day.

By instituting rituals and following them, you satisfy the third and final rule of good storytelling: taking hope-filled action. Slowly, you disengage from faulty stories that don't work, and begin investing energy in stories that do.

Eleven

MORE THAN MERE WORDS: FINISHING THE STORY, COMPLETING THE MISSION

This book is all about the metaphor of story, an abundantly powerful and rich one, so I'd be unwise to dilute it with a whole new metaphor. However, for the longest time—since my business partner, Jack Groppel, and I began our work as coaches and advisors to world-class athletes—we have used the concepts of "Ultimate Mission" and "Training Mission," and have integrated them, as you've already seen here, into our work. In our workshops, we often extend this "mission" idea to include "Mission Critical," "Mission Success," and "Mission Failure," terms more likely to evoke thoughts of NASA than of narrative.

Convinced though I am that no metaphor compels and stays with us quite like the story metaphor, the "mission" idea has also served us and our clients well, and no contingent more than the athletes and business leaders with whom we've worked. After all, athletes and executives (to take two constituencies) are intensely goal-oriented creatures and so the NASA-tinged concepts of Mission Critical, Mission Success, and Mission Failure compel them. Just as the people in the space program have a mission—to conceive a plan, build the vehicle necessary to carry out the plan, launch it, have it accomplish what it's supposed to (orbit, research, stay aloft for x days, repair a space station), and return safely—so, too, does an athlete (to come up with an ambitious but reachable goal, condition herself, train, compete, win), and so, too, must the business leader (to conceive of a discrete, ambitious, reachable plan within a timeframe, to gather the team, resources,

218

and data needed to give herself the best chance to accomplish that goal, inspire the team, execute the plan). For anyone in the space program or for an individual athlete or business leader, mission success is non-negotiable. Nothing short of that suffices. Not accomplishing your mission means one thing only: You have failed.

So after reading all the words and concepts in my book, and then examining your own reservoir of good intention, will all this mean anything if you don't do something about it, and *now*?

No. It will mean only mission failure. End of story.

If you do not work to unearth your deepest purpose and write your Ultimate Mission; if you do not actually write your Old Story; if you do not find the courage to seek the truth and write your New Story; if you do not commit to writing your Training Mission and investing the energy to follow the rituals laid out there until they embed themselves into your life . . . then you will have failed. You'll be living the same old story. Nothing significant and positive about this interaction will have transpired. This book will have been a waste of your money, time, and what warmed-over energy you gave to it. Sorry to be so harsh.

But presuming that that is *not* the outcome you seek, what will it take for you to commit to commit? How do you ensure Mission Success?

One useful exercise I do with clients is to get them to "touch the white fence," no matter what.

What do I mean by the white fence? What white fence? Well, with some groups that come to Orlando to work with us—pro athletes, those from law enforcement and the military—I tell them on the first day that I expect them each to accomplish at least this goal: Follow a modest little obstacle course we have out back, jog this way and that way through the woods surrounding our handsome little nine-acre campus, touch the white fence that perimeters the grounds, then return to the main building. Agreed?

Everyone shrugs as if it's nothing—and it is, except for the sometimes unbearable midday Florida heat and humidity, which I talk about briefly, as well as the nastiness of the occasional water moccasin, which I also describe for them. But probably that won't pose a problem. Are we good?

Everyone shrugs. Of *course* we're good. No problem.

Then I tell them about the poisonous snakes and alligators that are indigenous to this part of Florida. They've been known to grab a leg or two, if you're not alert.

There's a little less nonchalance in their shrugs now—and a *lot* less after I mention the three, maybe four wild boars who live near the edge of the grounds and who, when they feel threatened, may attack.

So now almost no one is ready to go touch the fence—no one, that is, except for one group of people, every single one of whom is as ready to touch the white fence after hearing about all the potential intervening dangers as they were when I first described it as a piece-of-cake exercise. In fact, they're *more* psyched. Who are they?

The crimefighters: Special Forces, SWAT guys, elite anti-terrorist FBI units, cops.

While every other group visibly withdraws when I tell them about the snakes and twelve-foot alligators, the military and law enforcement members can hardly keep their seats. "Cool," said one Special Forces member, enthusiastically, when the challenge had suddenly become more precarious at my mention of the possibility of wild boars. "Can I bring my piece?"

"Absolutely not," I replied.

Okay. So we send everyone off to touch the white fence. Very few of them are willing to say they're too scared to go; bad way to start off a workshop. So they go.

On more than one occasion, we have surreptitiously filmed groups going off into the woods. One was a foursome of NFL linemen—fearsome-looking individuals, each weighing roughly 280 pounds, strong as bulls, been through all kinds of on-field violence, used to brutal conditions and conditioning. In the footage of their journey into the woods, they're seen running through low brush toward the fence . . . when one of our staff members, hidden in a blind, makes the sound of a wild boar.

You've never seen four people move faster in your life. They raced back to the main building as if they were doing forty-yard sprints at the NFL scouting combine.

I was standing just outside the building when they raced toward me. They were winded. Although I hadn't yet seen the video footage, I knew exactly what had happened. We always get the same response from athletes.

I greeted them and, innocently, asked them how it felt to complete the mission and touch the white fence.

We didn't, they said.

Why not? I asked.

Didn't get that far, they said.

You guys? I said. *Come on. You're studs.*

Wild boar, they said, still gulping for breaths.

You saw wild boar? How many were there?

We don't know.

Well, what did the one you saw look like?

Well . . . we didn't actually see it.

You didn't see it?

No, they said. *But we heard it.*

Was it near the path?

No, in the woods.

You're sure the wild boar was there? I asked.

Oh, yes, they said, but only after a moment's hesitation.

I told them that there had been no wild boar, that the noise had been produced by a staff member. After apologizing for scaring them, I explained that we did it to make a point, namely: Don't expect it to be easy to touch the white fence. You're going to have to work at it. You're going to have to fight through doubt, fear, inertia, and temptation on the path to getting there. You may have people around you who are unsupportive or indifferent to your noble intentions and struggles. If you don't have *the right story* to help you past all this—if, instead, you have no story or a faulty story—then you let even imagined wild boars (and real ones) block your path. You start believing there are valid reasons for giving up or taking shortcuts or making up rules that suit you better—flimsy reasons like *Maybe other people need to touch the fence but I don't* or *Things were fine before I ever heard there was a fence* or—saddest of all—*There is no fence.* Do that and you pretty much have no shot to ever touch it, and to get to the next level after that.

And yet, *with the right story supporting you*, a story that gives meaning and purpose to all the chaos you will experience and the risks you will need to take, *it's doable*. Absolutely. Because it's then and only then that your courage and inner strength will surface.

I recount this episode not to elevate law enforcers and the military above everyone else (nor to suggest that pro football players or pro athletes in general are wimpier than others). I do it to point out that when the crimestoppers have a task to complete, they do it, unbendingly. *Every time.* Mission Success to them means accomplishing the goal; anything else is Mission Failure. *Every time.* Now some people may have issues with the mind-set that's required to achieve that kind of non-negotiable attitude, but you can't deny them this uncommon virtue: They achieve what they set out to achieve. *Without fail.* They are accountable to themselves.

Why?

In most cases, I believe it's because they are fully indoctrinated by a story which says that, in effect, they do what they do for a purpose higher than just themselves. (With athletes and executives—two obviously goal-oriented bunches—their professional purpose, though often well-defined, is rarely *that* lofty.) The crimestoppers and law-enforcers do it to protect their families, their communities, their country. They are fighting terrorists or murderers or bad guys and if they don't do their job *even once*, then their loved ones could be in greater jeopardy.

In short, they've got purpose locked down. It's there, with them, all the time. Remember the first rule of storytelling? *Purpose.*

And because of this "higher" purpose, they know they simply must be clear-eyed about what's before them, see danger for what it is, see the enemy for who they are. There's your second rule of storytelling: *Truth.*

Having satisfied the first two rules of storytelling, purpose and truth, nothing at this point can interfere with the third and final rule—*hope-filled action.* Get the job done. Just do it. Make it happen. Touch the white fence.

ACCOUNTABILITY (ABOUT WORK)

No matter how many of the real or perceived problems in your current story are caused by work, I doubt you'll tender your resignation the next morning you show up there, or completely renounce your career choice (nor is that what I've been recommending here, necessarily). But if you're serious about writing a new, better story—about *completing the mission*—then you undoubtedly need to make sure your relationship to your work, particularly if you work within any kind of bureaucratic structure, is, to put it plainly, workable. Mutually productive; not in contradiction.

The checklist below enunciates key areas where your needs and your employer's must be aligned, or are heading toward alignment, in some reasonable timeframe.

Corporate Story	Your Story
• The corporation needs your energy, time, talent, skill, and wisdom to complete its mission.	• You need the money the corporation is willing to pay so you can complete your mission with your family and loved ones.
• The corporation determines how much it is willing to pay and what you must do and not do in return for the money.	• You must determine if the money the corporation is willing to pay is sufficient, and what you're willing to do and not do in return for the money.
• The corporation needs your heart, spirit, mind, and body fully engaged in the corporate mission. It will take as much as you're willing to give.	• You need your heart, spirit, mind, and body fully engaged in your own mission and you must determine how much you can give before it begins to compromise your personal mission.
• The corporation needs you to become fully aligned with its core values and rules of operating and to be fully committed to achieving its mission. This is an important part of what they pay for.	• You must determine whether your values, rules of operating, and personal mission can be sufficiently aligned with those of the company for the relationship to work.
• The corporation must understand and respect your story or the relationship won't work. The story must work for both!	• You must understand and respect the corporate story or the relationship won't work. The story must work for both!

ACCOUNTABILITY
(ABOUT EVERYTHING ELSE)

So let's be clear: Just writing your New Story isn't enough for making meaningful, lasting change to your life. Same goes for "heightened self-awareness." As they say in New York City: That and a token will get you on the subway. If the ideas in this book are to have any real usefulness, then it isn't enough merely to consider them, or even to reflect on them, or even to articulate where it is you've always wanted to get. Granted: If you've gotten all the way to this point in the book and decide to ditch it here, and not go through the whole story process, chances are very good that you can never completely go back to your old ways again, because you must realize how many unacceptable stories you're telling yourself right now. But if you're serious about defining your own destiny, then you must do more than just agree that you need a new story.

Confrontation and accountability and brutal honesty are frightening. We abdicate responsibility for our own lives, according to psychologist Joost Merloo, because we fear life's built-in contradictions. Because we're forced to live with doubt and inconsistency, and yet we desire certainty and absolutes, we often start to embrace convictions we don't really believe. Because we can't bear ambiguity, many of us simply conform and even join rigid-thinking organizations.

You must figure out what you're required to do to reach that new place, then make the necessary changes for that to happen. To follow through:

- Write your Ultimate Mission. You may want to share it with someone.
- Write your Old Story. Compare it to your Ultimate Mission to see where they diverge. Again, you may find it helpful to read it to someone and possibly to solicit his or her opinion of it.
- Write your New Story, and read it once a day, same as above.
- Write your Training Mission, same as above.
- Write your Rituals that support the Training Mission and start implementing them. To follow them with regularity, you may need to write out a schedule.

- Continue reading your New Story each day until you know it by heart.

We encourage those who come to our workshops to attend our "Webinars" on exercise, nutrition, and storytelling. We also send them e-mail checkups at thirty, sixty and ninety days out from their visit. After thirty days, we also mail them a note that they wrote in the workshop, to themselves, which lists their Training Mission rituals; it asks if they are well on the way to integrating these changes into their life. You can't overestimate the power of being reminded of something, in your own handwriting, from an earlier version of yourself.

Be accountable to yourself, starting now. Right now. After all, you've been telling yourself this current story, the most important story you will ever tell and the one that's not really working, for . . . how many years now? How much more time do you need before making the change? You can't put it off for one more day; every day you don't do it, you prolong and deepen its hold on you. Every second of life is another opportunity to get your story right. Your story—be it the one you have now or the one you'd like it to become—is not something you lease or rent. You *own* it. Your story is your destiny.

Identify your purpose for being here.

Be truthful with yourself about what you're doing or not doing to honor that purpose.

Take the necessary actions to align what you need and want with how you actually live, and do it energetically and confidently.

Now there's a story you can live with. The rest is just words.

Twelve

STORYBOARDING THE TRANSFORMATION PROCESS IN EIGHT STEPS

Now that you're familiar with the major concepts from our workshop program—how our stories are our destinies; how everything we do, with or without our conscious knowledge, helps to shape our stories; how stories either take us where we want to go or they don't; and the three fundamental criteria of all good storytelling—you may want it in short form. Story in a Box, as it were.

Here it is, in eight steps.

- The most important story you will ever tell is your own life story.

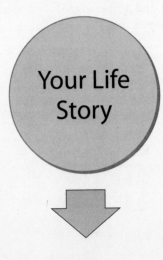

- The center of your life story is purpose.

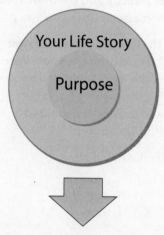

Step 1: Identify Purpose (Ultimate Mission)
Questions to help in the process:

- How do you want to be remembered?
- What is the legacy you most want to leave for others?
- How would you most like to hear people eulogize you at your funeral?
- What is worth dying for?
- What makes your life really worth living?
- In what areas of your life must you truly be extraordinary to fulfill your destiny?

Purpose_____

_____

_____

_____

_____

Step 2: Facing the Truth

Here you must identify and confront your dysfunctional current stories. Some questions to get you going:

- In which of the following area(s) of your life is your story not working? If your behavior is not aligned with your core purpose, then this story cannot take you where you want to go.
- In which areas do you need or want to be more engaged to fulfill your Ultimate Mission?

❑ Work / Job / Boss
❑ Family
❑ Health
❑ Happiness
❑ Friendship
❑ Money
❑ Self-indulgence
❑ Fame/Power
❑ Death (constructive awareness of)
❑ Sex / Intimacy
❑ Trust / Integrity
❑ Parents
❑ Religion
❑ Spirituality
❑ Love
❑ Food / Diet
❑ Exercise
❑ Children
❑ Spouse / Partner
❑ Other

Step 3: Select a Story to Work on First

Because almost all the core stories in our lives need at least some editing, here are some questions to help you with the selection process:

- Which of the stories above causes you the most concern and grief?
- Which of these stories causes the most disruption in your life?
- Which of these stories creates the greatest misalignment with your ultimate mission in life?
- Which of these stories would you most like to work on right now?

My Choice of Story to Edit:

_____

The story you've chosen to edit is your Training Mission. If you're to enjoy genuine transformation, then you must commit to work on this story for the next ninety days.

Step 4: Write the story you've been telling yourself that has allowed the misalignment to occur; this means including the faulty thinking and strange logic that helped to form the story you now wish to edit. Write in as much detail and with as much specificity as you can. Your task is to unearth completely your current dysfunctional story.

Some writing suggestions:

- Don't worry about grammar, spelling, or how it sounds. Just start writing.
- Capture both the content of your dysfunctional story as well as the tone of the private voice you use when telling this story to yourself (such as frustrated, cynical, unrealistic).

- Also capture the public voice you use to tell this story.
- Exaggerate the emotion in your story, to help get it going.
- Bring as much color and texture to your story as you can.
- Identify any faulty assumptions in your story. To help you articulate the faulty story you've created, ask yourself the following questions:

  1. In what way(s) does the story you tell yourself allow you to ignore that it's not taking you where you ultimately want to go in life—is not on purpose?
  2. What logic do you use in the story to justify that your story does not reflect the truth?
  3. In what way(s) does the story not inspire you to take action to make this part of your life better?

Before you finish your Old Story, take a few dives into your subconscious world. Ask yourself these questions:

  1. What hidden influences might be behind some of your faulty thinking and beliefs that helped to create your current story?
  2. Do you get very defensive about your faulty story? If you do, then what are you protecting? Specifically, in what parts of this story are you most fragile and vulnerable? What are you most afraid of here? If you follow the fear, where does it take you?
  3. The story you currently tell yourself that you wish to edit clearly hasn't inspired you to make a change. What's the logic and rationale you've used to keep this faulty story alive in your life for so long?
  4. Is this really your story you're telling or someone else's? Whose voice is it?

Okay: You're ready to prepare the final draft of your current story that isn't working. From here on, we'll refer to this current story as your "old" story. This may be your second draft of the story or your tenth. When you're ready, write your final draft in the space below.

Old Dysfunctional Story_____

_____

_____

_____

_____

_____

_____

_____

_____

_____

_____

_____

_____

_____

Step 5: Sit back and read your Old Story. How does it make you feel? Sick? Stupid? Dumb? Embarrassed? Does it stir powerful feelings of disgust? Can you see and *feel* the story's dysfunctionality?

Step 6: Write a new story that

- is fully aligned with your ultimate purpose
- reflects the truth
- inspires you to take hope-filled action

To help you articulate your new story, some suggestions:

1. Start with the words "The truth is . . ." Describe as vividly as possible what will likely happen if you continue with the Old Story you've got. Face reality head on by connecting the dots.
2. Don't labor over every word. You'll edit it later. Just get your initial thoughts on paper, quickly.
3. Because your New Story packs a cannonshot of reality, it will necessarily stir negative emotion (the more powerful, the better).
4. Your New Story should clearly reflect and connect with your Ultimate Mission in life. Anyone reading your New Story should have no trouble connecting it with what you care most about.
5. Your New Story should be inspirational for you when you read it. It must move you powerfully: move you emotionally and move you to take action.
6. Your New Story should contain a strong message of optimism and hope that the change you seek will indeed happen if you remain dedicated and persistent.
7. Make sure that this is your story, no one else's! Be sure this is what *you* really want.
8. If possible, craft your New Story in the context of a major turning point in your life. This change you seek should be characterized as a breakthrough.
9. Work hard to summon your voice of sincerity. Your inner voice must be able to express the message, con-

tent, and direction of your New Story completely and unambivalently.

10. In your writing, aim to bring forward your best voice of reason, of wisdom, of intelligence. These voices can't come forward without your encouraging them.

As with your Old Story, getting your New Story right will likely take several drafts. Once you feel you've finally got your story straight, write it here:

New Story _____

_____

_____

_____

_____

_____

_____

_____

_____

_____

_____

_____

_____

_____

_____

_____

Step 7: Design explicit rituals that ensure your New Story becomes reality.

- Rituals are consciously acquired habits of behavior that enhance energy management in service of a mission.
- Rituals represent the vehicle by which your New Story receives the investment of life-giving energy.

A few suggestions as you think about creating your new rituals:

1. Link the ritual to one or more values (since the ritual by itself is largely meaningless, connect it to deeper reasons; one executive who vowed to take physical breaks every ninety minutes walked the hallway, poking her head in offices to say hi and see if she could help; in being so public about taking care of herself, she also felt as if she served as a good example for her workaholic direct reports).
2. Invest energy in it for thirty to ninety days.
3. Be precise in the timing and other details surrounding the ritual (exercise at the same time for the same number of days a week; when you walk in the door, put your house keys in exactly the same place each time; etc.).
4. Acquire no more than a few rituals at a time.
5. Focus on where you're going, not where you came from (for example, rather than focusing on the cigarette you can't smoke, focus on the LifeSaver you're sucking on, the wallet photo of your kids you pull out, the brisk walk around the block you're taking to clear your head).
6. Create a supportive environment (for example, recruit a buddy or colleague or spouse to work out

with you; have your kids give you a report card each evening to see if you did what you said you would).

7. A particularly valuable ritual is to begin every day of your ninety-day mission by reading your New Story.

Rituals

1. _____

2. _____

3. _____

4. _____

5. _____

Step 8: Establish a daily accountability system for the rituals you've committed to.

Almost every successful athlete we've worked with has used a daily training log. It helps to ensure that they do what they've committed to doing, at the time and with the focus that they committed to doing it.

Some suggestions:

1. Make your accountability system easy to complete and accessible. It could be a sheet of paper on your bedstand or, if you love technology, a spreadsheet on your computer. The point is that you must fill it out daily to keep the transformation process alive.

2. Think of your daily accountability form as both a time management system and an energy management system. Did you do what you said you would at the time you committed to (time accountability)? Did you invest the right quantity, quality, focus, and force

of energy (energy management)? You can use a scale of 1 to 5 or A through F to reflect your energy investment success. An example:

Daily Training Log

Sample

MY MISSION: *To be more energized and engaged in the afternoon at work and with my family at home.*

May 22–28

Rituals	Sun.	Mon.	Tue.	Wed.	Thu.	Fri.	Sat.	Notes
Daily mental preparation 5:45 AM	5	1	5	5	1	1	5	
Eat breakfast	1	1	5	5	1	5	3	
Eat until satisfied, not full	1	1	3	3	5	1	5	
Break every 90 to 120 minutes	3	3	5	5	4	-	-	
Exercise	1	1	5	1	5	5	1	
Exercise intensity	-	-	3	-	3	3	-	
Drink water—carry water bottle	5	5	5	5	5	2	2	
Small portions during lunch/dinner	2	2	3	3	5	1	5	
Snack every 3 to 4 hours	5	5	1	5	5	-	-	
To bed by 11:30 PM	5	4	5	5	1	1	5	
Quality of sleep	2	2	4	5	4	2	2	
No multi-tasking with direct reports	5	2	2	5	5	2	5	
No multi-tasking with family	5	5	5	5	5	5	5	
Cell phone off during dinner	5	5	2	5	5	-	-	
Fully engaged—30 min. at home	3	2	3	5	5	-	-	
Afternoon engagement	3	3	4	5	5	2	2	
Evening engagement with family	3	2	3	4	5	-	-	
Afternoon productivity	3	1	5	2	1	5	3	

1 = not successful   5 = very successful

(The entries listed under Rituals are not all major rituals, per se: Most are modest rituals, components of a larger ritual—e.g., "eat breakfast," "eat until satisfied, not full," and "small portions during lunch/dinner" are a few of the component rituals to eating better; other entries are not even rituals at all but rather are there to help you assess the *quality* of your progress—e.g., "exercise intensity" and "afternoon engagement.")

Daily Training Log

MY MISSION: _____

_____

Date: _____

Rituals	Sun.	Mon.	Tue.	Wed.	Thu.	Fri.	Sat.	Notes

1 = not successful   5 = very successful

3. Consider reviewing your accountability log with someone you respect (spouse, colleague, friend). Ask that person to serve as your coach during the ninety-day mission.

4. Be obsessive about your record-keeping and compliance during the ninety days. Eat, drink, and sleep your mission.

5. If your enthusiasm about the change you're making starts to wane, or if you start getting bored reading your New Story (this will likely happen at some point), go through the entire process again but in a

much shorter time frame. Rewrite your story to reignite your excitement and commitment to change.

For help and guidance through the transformation, please go to our website, www.humanperformanceinstitute.com, where we present the process step-by-step.

What do you do after your ninety-day mission is complete?

Select another faulty story that's not taking you where you ultimately want to go; edit it and begin the process again.

If our stories are our destiny, then to achieve a destiny of our own design, rather than one that's merely a default, requires commitment, honesty, and energy. It means editing our stories for as long as we're alive.

The Final Chapter

RAYMOND'S STORY

In October 2003, Raymond, a forty-one-year-old executive at Procter & Gamble in China, came through our program with seventeen of his colleagues, as part of a P&G pilot group. While he was himself signed up for the two-and-a-half-day seminar, Raymond saw his mission more as one of due diligence—to assess whether the program might benefit other P&G executives. Anyway, he'd already been through numerous "health-wellness" programs that spelled out various constructive, common-sense strategies: regular physical and spiritual renewal, especially meditation; drinking lots of water; and other behavior modifications, small and large. But while Raymond remembered some of the ingredients of these programs, he was never able to put them all together in a sustainable manner. He found that the ideas were presented "in a hodge podge," and that no mechanism really compelled him to stick with the whole system—if there was such a mechanism to begin with.

As with everyone who came through our program, Raymond spent the first hour of the first morning getting BodPod and blood chemistry evaluations. His results put numbers, unequivocal and alarming, to various health indices of which he was aware but hadn't felt like confronting. Despite his being on Lipitor, the cholesterol-lowering medication, Raymond's blood lipids and specifically his triglycerides were in the "dangerous" range. His body fat was 37%, and for his body frame he was sixty pounds overweight. Yet for the past eight years he had spent an hour a day, five days a week, pedaling a stationary bike! Raymond admitted that no one would guess he was even related to his relatively fit brother—his *identical twin* brother.

Although Raymond had long been aware of these health "red flags," at any given time he could tell himself one of three stories to justify why he'd done little to confront and reduce the jeopardy in which he was now in: It was "just too hard" to make the necessary changes; he was working like crazy and didn't have the time; a better time would eventually come around and he would fix the problem *then*. (Raymond would later dub this story "New Year's resolution syndrome.")

For Raymond—or anyone—an obstacle perhaps more daunting even than the *timing* of making changes, or the *difficulty* of accomplishing them all, was unearthing *the very mechanism* of change—that is, the trigger that could persuade you, once and for all, that to change was to gain your life, and that not to change was slowly and inexorably to let your life slip away, to die slowly. The toughest part was finding incentive sufficiently powerful that you embraced and stuck with the program long after the initial thrill of measurable self-improvement had passed.

A rational, intelligent, high-energy, and passionate man, Raymond had believed that data and discipline alone would rescue him. If he just kept riding his bike, if he just kept drinking lots of water, if he just kept succeeding at work, then his problems—stress, wild dips in energy, his gut, his blood work scores, the disconnection he often felt from his family, his perpetual lack of time and balance—would go away. "When I rode the bike," said Raymond, "I perspired like crazy, yet I always failed my stress test. It really wasn't helping me." And yet he didn't change his routine. He kept riding at a speed that allowed him to concentrate on what he was reading or watch a movie on DVD. Worse, he exercised as soon as he woke up without taking any breakfast. He didn't realize that he was burning his muscles, not fat. He just believed that his overweight and his other physical problems would go away. Or at least subside significantly. Somehow.

Of course, the problems didn't subside. Data and discipline could not save Raymond. What would?

Story. Just as he had subconsciously leaned on stories to explain himself to himself—those reasons why he simply couldn't change—so, too, it would be a story—a new, better, *conscious* one—that would compel him to see why he absolutely *had* to change.

By the middle of the first day of the workshop, the P&G executives began sharing their stories—stories that rivaled so many others we'd heard over the years: life trajectories that failed the individual and, in the long run, didn't really work for the company, either. Amazingly, so many of these brilliant, analytical, successful types had never recognized this until they told their stories aloud and began to examine them.

As the day unwound, Raymond revealed a poignant, tragic fact to the group: his father had died of cancer without getting to see his grandchildren, who were now eight, six, and three. Expressing this aloud got to Raymond, deeply.

"I was in a bad place," he would say later. "I wasn't behaving in accordance with my values. I'd started taking Lipitor three years before, at thirty-eight, and now I realized, as if for the first time, 'At the rate I'm going, I might damage my liver.' My wife was worried. I said I loved my wife and children but what exactly did that mean?"

Raymond admitted that his old story was stagnant, shot full of blind spots. He knew deep down that important things in his life just weren't working; for heaven's sake, he barely resembled his much fitter identical twin. Wasn't that evidence enough that even a smart, capable person could get way off course?

Once Raymond rediscovered what mattered to him, he felt a huge burst of strength. He wanted to write and follow a new story, one that was purpose-driven, grounded in truth, and which empowered him to do things he had long ago stopped thinking he could do.

"I needed a new set of tools. In Florida, I learned the scientific reason behind interval training—how it was far more beneficial than simply pedaling a stationary bike for an hour five times a week, and also takes less time. I learned why I needed to exercise with the proper intensity—not so that I could be reading at the same time. I came to understand genuinely how nutrition affected health. But the tools weren't just technical. They weren't about weight loss. They were about giving me a comprehensive, detailed appreciation for the concept of energy. How nutrition affected energy levels, and thus how you could use nutrition to *manage your energy*. Same with exercise—how, if you did it properly, you could manage your energy better. It was surprisingly simple. Do you have enough gas in your tank? Is it good quality energy? Are you hopeful about things? If not, then how can the quality of your energy be good?"

Raymond told us that his goal was to live longer. To live to see his own grandchildren. To take care of himself so that he could continue to take care of others.

Acknowledging that his old story wasn't working, he vowed now to confront his values, which, over time, had slowly but profoundly become misaligned. Because he wanted desperately to be there as long and as vibrantly as possible for his family—his Ultimate Mission—he'd found the mechanism to compel him to make this a reality. And while this new story centered around his family, the impact of his renewed commitment had implications for those he worked with at P&G.

When the two-and-a-half-day program ended, Raymond told several of us, "Watch me in four to six months."

As much as Raymond believed he would have no trouble keeping his commitment, immediately upon his return to China he built outside accountability into what he was doing. He wrote frequent e-mails to Chris Jordan, our extraordinary fitness director and a member of our team with whom he'd really hit it off. "To keep my new story alive, I wanted to put more pressure on myself," said Raymond. "I relished it. I'd always been confident but now I consciously made myself into a role model." The periodic reports to Chris became increasingly positive "because what I was doing got easier and easier," said Raymond.

"I consciously spread positive news about the things I learned," he said. "I pushed our president to bring Jim to China to do a program with us."

Raymond was able to stick to his new routine because he began to ritualize it. "Monday is my rest day," he said. "On the other days, I wake up at 6:30. Breakfast at 7, exercise at 7:30, out the door by 8:15. One reason I didn't find the routine difficult was because it was really a return to basics. So many of those things we learned growing up— with our parents creating morning rituals, real regimentation to develop good habits in us—frankly, we kind of lose that as we get older and more scattered and more stressed." Raymond felt as if he was merely, and familiarly, returning to a way that had worked for him long ago.

Six weeks into his Training Mission at home, Raymond had achieved real results: His bloods lipids were back in the normal range and he stopped taking Lipitor for the first time in three years. He'd lost twenty pounds, down from 220 to 200.

He had no trouble extending his new discipline to work. In each management meeting he led back in China, he would insist on frequent breaks, and make available the kinds of healthful snacks we'd advocated in Orlando. Other P&Gers began to see the changes in Raymond. "I felt as if there was nothing I was not capable of doing, and I think people noticed. I couldn't be rattled. I wasn't getting wound up like I used to. Things weren't fazing me or scaring me."

Nor did anyone at work view these breaks during the day as a sign that Raymond had gone off to Florida and come back less committed and productive than before; just the opposite, actually. "People knew I was a really disciplined person, and now they saw that I used that discipline to take more frequent breaks, to drink water more regularly, and that I did it with more composure. And how I felt energetic throughout the day, without fading like I used to."

For all the benefit his colleagues got from watching his example at work, the people happiest at Raymond's transformation were his family. Said Raymond, "Following through on my commitment proved to them that I meant what I said when I said I loved them."

Why was Raymond able to write this new story—easily, even joyfully, and without falling back? *Because purpose fueled the change.*

Four months later—six months after going through our program—Raymond took a business trip to Cincinnati, where P&G is headquartered. Before heading back to China, he detoured to Florida to get tested again. His body fat—at 37% just a half year before—was now 21%! He'd lost fifty-five pounds; he was down to 165. He was still off Lipitor. His other indicators were all in the normal range. And "though I had thought I was always a high-energy person," he said, "I had never felt better in my life, never had so much energy." He felt as if his energy had increased "exponentially." Daily, he was experiencing a clarity of mind that outstripped what he was used to.

He also had a new appreciation for the quality of energy, not time, that one spends on any activity. "I learned better how to stay in the moment," he said. "People told me that I used to always say, 'Life is too short,' but back when I was saying that, I was still wasting lots of my life—on worry, on anger, on being stressed, on not being fully engaged in what I should have been doing or thinking about. Now, I was much, much better about not being angry about the past or worrying about the future. I really saw how useless it was. People around me marveled at the fact that a Type A personality like me could seem calm, under pressure or not. A lot of it had to do with being in better physical shape, which allowed me to get through things better."

At Raymond's next performance appraisal, his boss, the president of P&G for Greater China, commented that of all the many improvements Raymond had made, none stood out more than his "ability to handle stress." The president also commented on a remarkable uptick in Raymond's performance, as well his growth as a manager.

Just a few weeks later, Raymond found out that he had skin cancer. "The word 'cancer' is a horrible, stressful thing for anyone to hear; for someone who's Chinese, the phrase 'skin cancer' is close to a death sentence. And if I'd had the diagnosis a year before, I would have been unbelievably stressed. But when I heard it now, it wasn't nearly as terrible. Learning to live in the moment helped me to deal with it—not to be so stressed, to take things in their own time." From the time he was diagnosed with the skin cancer to the time he went to the States for treatment, it took around seventy-two hours. He focused on what he could control and stayed calm while sorting out his next steps. "Fortunately, it turned out that I had the mildest form of basal cell cancer," he said, "but the whole experience was dramatically different from what it would have been."

Once upon a time, when Raymond would get home from work all wound up, he wouldn't think about putting his children, particularly his youngest, his son, to sleep. Now he does it more regularly. He wants to talk with him about all kinds of things, and does. The conversations he and his wife have are more engaging. While he doesn't at all consider himself a finished product as father, husband, employee, or human being, Raymond is happier and, because of the rituals he has adopted—which he follows regularly, seamlessly, automatically—he feels more in control of that happiness.

Raymond's transformation is full-blown, evidenced in all four dimensions of the energy pyramid:

- physical: weight loss, improvements in cholesterol and other indices
- emotional: improved relations with his family, particularly his son
- mental: greater engagement and productivity at work, and energy and approach that have inspired colleagues
- spiritual: his ability to deal with his cancer scare by continuing to live in the moment

Recently, when I asked Raymond to name the most important lesson he learned from his experience with us, he said, "It doesn't take an extraordinary person to do this. I'm an ordinary person but any ordinary person can have extraordinary results. I'm leaving my post after twelve years and recently there was a gathering for me, and my colleagues were talking about what they would remember about me. So many of them said it was how extraordinarily energetic and alive I seemed. But I'm just an ordinary guy who had the benefit of doing this. And because of my progress, I have such tremendous confidence now. Being able to successfully ritualize what I learned made me trust myself even more."

It has been nearly four years since Raymond has been through the program. He has translated all he learned into habits, ways of being. What he learned has become a way of life for him. He believes that his chances of seeing and knowing his grandchildren have never been better.

Acknowledgments

First, to my parents, Mary and Con, for infusing my life story with love and meaning.

To my three sons, Mike, Pat, and Jeff, who continue to be my greatest teachers.

To Andy Postman, for contributing his brilliant writing skills, enthusiasm, and intelligence to this project. Andy, you've been a joy to work with and represent a consummate professional.

To Jack Groppel, my business partner, for your support, loyalty, and cherished friendship since the beginning.

To Chris Osorio, for your unwavering confidence and loyalty, for your friendship and for your uncommon wisdom and clear thinking through it all.

To Renate Gaisser, for your relentless pursuit of excellence and timeless contributions over the many years.

To Becky Hoholski, for your help with the manuscript, attention to detail, and brilliant ability to manage chaos.

To all the HPI staff of whom I am so proud—most especially Steve Page, Raquel Malo, Chris Jordan, and Lorenzo Beltrame.

To all the athletes who have touched my life and formed the basis of my thinking.

A special thanks to Tom Gullikson, for his cherished friendship and support since the beginning of my career.

To the countless great thought leaders and researchers who have inspired my thinking.

To the thousands of clients who have served as a living laboratory, whose stories of honesty, courage, insight, and compassion have taught me so much about the how and why of human energy. It has been my privilege and honor to have the opportunity to help you in some way to complete your most important mission.

A special thanks to Barbara Fredrickson, Bob Quinn, Kim Cameron, Sue Ashford, Jane Dutton, Gretchen Spreitzer and the entire staff of the University of Michigan's Ross School of Business.

To Stephen R. Covey, Marty Seligman, Stephen M.R. Covey, Fred Harburg, Will Marre, Admiral Ray Smith, Jodi Taylor, Leo Greenstone, and Paul and Kathy Connolly.

To my terrific agent, Loretta Fidel, and to Fred Hills and Dominick Anfuso at the Free Press for supporting and believing in this book from its original conception; and to Wylie O'Sullivan at Free Press for her generous efforts.

To my brother Tom and my sister Jane (Sister Mary Margaret Loehr), whose depth of character and compassion are constant sources of inspiration to me.

To special friends Jeff Balash, Randy Gerber, Paul Hancock, Tim Heckler, David Leadbetter, Peter Moore, Phebe Farrow Port, Tore and Eddy Resavage, Paul Roetert, Peter Scaturro, Jeff Sklar, and Dennis and Pat Van der Meer.

Finally to Vickie and Bob Zoellner and to Gordon Uehling for making the dream possible. I will never forget.

Endnotes

Introduction

PAGE

4 "The human brain, according to a recent . . .": Robin Marantz Henig, "Darwin's God," *The New York Times,* March 4, 2007.

11 "Kirk Perry, VP at Procter & Gamble . . .": Cait Murph, "The CEO Workout," *Fortune,* July 10, 2006.

One *That's* Your Story?

PAGE

20 "As corporate consultant Annette Simmons says in her book . . .": Simmons, *The Story Factor,* Basic Books, 2001, p. 54.

24–26 From "According to a *USA Today* survey . . ." through next many statistics:

Jerry Langdon, "Some Workers Not Using Their Vacation, Survey Says," *USA Today,* March 1, 2001; www.usatoday.com/careers/news/usa039.htm

The John Liner Review, Volume 11, Number 3, Fall 1997, Standard Publishing Corp., citing a 1990 study by Foster Higgins & Co., Princeton, NJ. Princeton Survey Research Associates

"Your Job May Be Killing You," a Q&A with James K. Harter, *Gallup Management Journal,* April 13, 2006

"Exercise Protects Against Cognitive Decline," presented at the Annual Meeting of the American Academy of Neurology and reported by Reuters Consumer Health Bulletin, May 9, 2001, and also reported in IHRSA Wellness Report, May 12, 2001

CCH Unscheduled Absence Survey (1999); www5.ncci.com/ncci/web/news/infostop/safework/sw08_2000_5a.htm

"Breakthrough Ideas for 2006," *Harvard Business Review,* February 2006

"Equating Health and Productivity," *Business & Health®* Archive, September 1997, quoting Kent Peterson, past-president of the American College of Occupational Medicine

Jones et al., 1988, and Barth, 1990; Lippe, 1990; and Neary, et al., 1992; referenced at agency.osha.eu.int/publications/reports/stress.php3?section+11

Paul Hemp, "Presenteeism: At Work—But Out of It," *Harvard Business Review,* October 2004, pp. 49–58

Reichheld and Sasser, "Zero Defection: Quality Comes to Services," *Harvard Business Review,* September–October, pp. 105–111.

27 "Yet as Michael O'Donnell, editor-in-chief . . .": Sarah Lunday, "A Place Where They Don't Dread Coming to Work." *The New York Times,* June 24, 2001.

32 "According to a Gallup poll, people who have a best friend at work . . .": Tom Rath, *Vital Friends: The People You Can't Afford to Live Without,* Gallup Press, 2006.

Two The Premise of Your Story, the Purpose of Your Life

PAGE

40 "A mother of four quoted in Dan McAdams's book . . .": McAdams, *The Redemptive Self: Stories Americans Live By*; as quoted in "Self-Portrait in a Skewed Mirror" by Carlin Flora, *Psychology Today*, January/February 2006, p. 64.

65 " 'To find integrity in life,' writes Dan McAdams . . .": Flora, ibid., p. 66.

66 "A December 2006 article in the *Harvard Business Review* . . .": *Extreme Jobs: The Dangerous Allure of the 70-Hour Work Week*, by Sylvia Ann Hewlett and Carolyn Bruce Lee; in *Harvard Business Review*, December 2006, about a research project initiated in 2004 by the Hidden Brain Drain Task Force chaired by Lee.

Three How Faithful a Narrator Are You?

PAGE

69 "While each life story is unique . . .": Flora, "Self-Portrait," p. 62.

81 "The benefit of worry . . .": Susan Mineka and Richard Zinbarg, "A Contemporary Learning Theory Perspective on the Etiology of Anxiety Disorders," *American Psychologist*, January 2006, p. 20.

81 "But those naturally given to feeling off balance . . .": ibid.

83 "One, identified by psychologists Michael Scheier and Charles Carver as 'dispositional optimism' . . .": Scheier and Carver, "Attention and Self-Regulation: A Control-Theory Approach to Human Behavior," Springer, 1981.

83 "A 1987 study by Neil Weinstein . . .": Weinstein, "Unrealistic Optimism About Susceptibility to Health Problems," *Journal of Behavioral Medicine* 481.

84 "Dr. John Gottman, one of the leading voices . . .": Gottman, *Why Marriages Succeed or Fail,* Simon & Schuster, 1995.

84 "Barbara Fredrickson from the University of North Carolina and Marcial Losada from Catholic University of Brazil . . .": Frederickson and Losada, "Positive Affect and the Complex Dynamics of Human Flourishing," *American Psychologist*, 60 (2005), pp. 678–686.

Four Is It Really *Your* Story You're Living?

PAGE

90 "We are, after all, easily indoctrinated, amazingly easily . . .": Edgar Schein uses the term "frozen" in his book *Process Consultation,* Volume 2, Addison-Wesley, 1987, pp. 92–93.

91 "If I, as a young woman, had had someone explain to me . . .": Deborah Layton, *Seductive Poison*, Anchor Books, 1998, p. 299.

94 "While some indoctrinations, according to psychologists Philip Zimbardo and Susan Andersen . . .": Zimbardo and Andersen, "Understanding Mind Control:

Exotic and Mundane Mental Manipulations," quoting study by Schwitzgebel & Schwitzgebel, 1973; Varela, 1971, Weinstein, 1990; in *Recovery From Cults: Help for Victims of Psychological and Spiritual Abuse*, edited by Michael Langone, p. 104.

95 "It has been pointed out that the opening salvo in Mark Antony's . . .": Zimbardo-Ebbesen, *Influencing Attitudes and Changing Behavior*, Addison-Wesley, 1970, p. 12.

95 "Of course, some organizations *do* use . . .": Robert Farley, "Scientologists' Policy Toward Outcasts Under Fire," *St. Petersburg Times*, June 26, 2006, p. B5.

95 " 'Disordered brain function is indeed easily reproduced . . .": Denise Winn, *The Manipulated Mind*, Malor Books, 2000, pp. 12–13, 15.

99 "I finally decided that religion was altogether bunk . . .": Edward Hunter, *Brain-Washing in Red China*, Vanguard Press, 1951.

106 " 'It is so easy to become our surroundings' . . .": Layton, *Seductive Poison*.

106 " 'Our brains are valuable forgers' . . .": Daniel Gilbert, *Stumbling on Happiness*, Knopf, 2006, p. 89.

Six The Three Rules of Storytelling

PAGE

133 "In 2006, thirty-five years after this initial study, researchers Ed Diener, Richard Lucas, and Christie Scollon . . .": Ed Diener, Richard E. Lucas, and Christie Napa Scollon, "Beyond the Hedonic Treadmill," *American Psychologist*, May–June 2006, p. 309.

134 "The inevitably exciting conclusion of this later study . . .": ibid., p. 312.

135 "All good stories, says Herminia Ibarra . . .": Ibarra, *Working Identity*, Harvard Business School Press, 2002, p. 17.

136 "Many turning points are subtle, recognizable only in hindsight; they 'tend to be much more obvious in the telling than in the living' . . .": Herminia Ibarra and Kent Lineback, "What's Your Story?" *Harvard Business Review*, January 2005, p. 68.

136 "During our life we often experience periods when we seem to lose our sense . . .": Robert Quinn, *Change the World*, Jossey-Bass, 2000, p. 136.

145 "As Herminia Ibarra says in her book . . .": Ibarra, *Working Identity*, p. 36.

145 "As Edward Hunter says . . .": Hunter, *Brain-Washing in Red China*, Vanguard Press, 1951, p. 16.

Seven It's Not About Time

PAGE

158 "As he took account . . .": *Chasing Daylight: How My Forthcoming Death Transformed My Life*, by Eugene O'Kelly, McGraw-Hill, 2005, p. 132.

170 "A study published in MIT's *Sloan Management Review* in 2003 . . .": Rob Cross, Wayne Baker, and Andrew Parker, "What Creates Energy in Organizations?," *M.I.T. Sloan Management Review*, Summer 2003, p. 52.

170 "The desire to work for or with energizers seems to account for our last finding about energy and performance . . .": ibid.

170 "People are energized in interactions, says the study . . .": ibid., p. 55.

Eight Do You Have the Resources to Live Your Best Story?

PAGE

172 "According to Charles Czeisler, a leading authority on sleep, 80,000 drivers . . .": "Sleep Deficit: The Performance Killer, A Conversation with Harvard Medical School Professor Charles A. Czeisler," *Harvard Business Review*, October 2006.

185 "A study published in the January 2006 issue . . .": *ACE Fitness Matters*, January/February 2006, p. 12.

185 "More proof, once again, that good health is good business—even though far fewer than half of all major U.S. companies actively encourage exercise among their workforce . . .": ibid.

189 "Interns who work 24-hour shifts increase the chance of stabbing themselves . . .": Czeisler, "Sleep Deficit."

189 "The risk of crashing a vehicle following a 24-hour shift increases . . .": ibid.

Nine Indoctrinate Yourself

PAGE

190 "According to two studies on brain function . . .": R. F. Baumeister and K. L. Sommer, "What Do Men Want? Gender Differences and Two Spheres of Belongingness," *Psychological Bulletin*, 122 (1997); John Bargh and Tanya Chartrand, "The Unbearable Automaticity of Being," *American Psychologist*, 54 (1999).

Eleven More Than Mere Words: Finishing the Story, Completing the Mission

PAGE

224 "We abdicate responsibility for our own lives . . .": Joost Merloo in Denise Winn, *The Manipulated Mind*, Malor Books, 2000, p. 93.

Bibliography

Armstrong, David 1992. *Managing By Storying Around: A New Method of Leadership*. Doubleday.

Baldwin, Christina 2005. *Storycatcher*. New World Library.

Bateson, Mary Catherine 1990. *Composing a Life*. Penguin Books.

Baumeister, Roy 1991. *Meanings of Life*. Guilford Press.

Brown, John et al. 2004. *Storytelling in Organizations*. Butterworth-Heinemann.

Callahan, David 2004. *The Cheating Culture*. Harcourt.

Callahan, David 2006. *The Moral Center*. Harcourt.

Cameron, Dulton, Quinn 2003. *Positive Organizational Scholarship*. Berrett-Koehler.

Clark, Evelyn 2004. *Around the Corporate Campfire*. Insight.

Covey, Stephen M.R. 2007. *The Speed of Trust*. Simon & Schuster.

Covey, Stephen R. 2004. *The Eighth Habit*. Simon & Schuster.

Covey, Stephen R. 1989. *The Seven Habits of Highly Effective People*. Simon & Schuster.

Denning, Stephen 2005. *The Leader's Guide to Storytelling*. John Wiley & Sons.

Denning, Stephen 2001. *The Springboard*. Butterworth-Heinemann.

Dutton, Jane 2003. *Energize Your Workplace*. Jossey-Bass.

Ealsin, Paul John 1999. *How Our Lives Become Stories*. Cornell University Press.

Freedman, Jill and Combs, Gene 1996. *Narrative Therapy*. W.W. Norton.

Gabriel, Yiannis 2000. *Storytelling in Organizations*. Oxford.

Galanter, Marc 1999. *Cults*. Oxford University Press.

Gardner, Howard 2004. *Changing Minds*. Harvard Business School Press.

Gilbert, Daniel 2006. *Stumbling on Happiness*. Alfred A. Knopf.

Gouré, Leon 1973. *The Military Indoctrination of Soviet Youth*. National Strategy Information Center.

Hindery, Roderick R. 2001. *Indoctrination and Self-Deception or Free and Critical Thought?* Edwin Mellen Press.

Howard, George 1989. *A Tale of Two Stories*. Academic Pub.

Hunter, Edward 1951. *Brain-Washing in Red China*. Vanguard Press.

Hyde, Margaret O. 1977. *Brainwashing*. McGraw-Hill.

Ibarra, Herminia 2002. *Working Identity*. Harvard Business School Press.

Keyes, Corey 2002. *Flourishing*. American Psychological Association.

Langone, Michael 1993. *Recovery from Cults*. W.W. Norton.

Layton, Deborah 1998. *Seductive Poison*. Anchor Books.

Leonard, George & Murphy, Michael 1995. *The Life We Are Given*. Tarcher/Putnam.

Loehr, Jim & Schwartz, Tony 2003. *The Power of Full Engagement*. Simon & Schuster.

Maguire, Jack 1998. *The Power of Personal Storytelling*. Penguin Putnam.

McAdams, Dan 1988. *Power, Intimacy and the Life Story*. Guilford Press.

McAdams, Dan 1993. *The Stories We Live By*. Guilford Press.

McKee, Robert 1997. *Story*. Regan Books.

Milgram, Stanley 1969. *Obedience to Authority*. HarperCollins.

Monk, G., Winslade, J., Crocket, K., and Epton, D. 1997. *Narrative Therapy in Practice*. Jossey-Bass.

Pattakos, Alex 2004. *Prisoners of Our Thoughts*. Berrett-Koehler.

Quinn, Robert 2000. *Change the World*. Jossey-Bass.

Quinn, Robert 1996. *Deep Change*. Jossey-Bass.

Ripman, Doug 1999. *Improving Your Storytelling*. August House.

Ruiz, Don Miguel 2004. *The Voice of Knowledge*. Amber-Allen.

Sarbin, Theodore 1986. *Narrative Psychology*. Praeger.

Sargant, William 1959. *The Battle for the Mind*. Pan Books.

Sawyer, Ron 1976. *The Way of the Storyteller*. Penguin Books.

Schein, Edgar 1999. *Process Consultation Revised*. Addison-Wesley.

Simmons, Annette 2001. *The Story Factor*. Basic Books.

Smith, Hyrum 2000. *What Matters Most*. Simon & Schuster.

Taylor, Shelley 1989. *Positive Illusions*. Basic Books.

Turner, Mark 1996. *The Literary Mind*. Oxford Press.

Verdies, Paul 1977. *Brainwashing and the Cults*. Wilshire Book Co.

Warren, Rick 2002. *The Purpose Driven Life*. Zondervan.

Weinstein, Arnold 2006. *Recovering Your Story*. Random House.

White, Michael 1995. *Re-Authoring Lives: Interviews and Essays*. Dulwich Centre.

Winn, Denise 2000. *The Manipulated Mind*. Malor Books.

Zimbardo, Philip & Ebbesen, Ebbe 1970. *Influencing Attitudes and Changing Behaviour*. Addison-Wesley.

Index

About the Author

DR. JIM LOEHR, Chairman, CEO and co-Founder of the Human Performance Institute, is a world-renowned performance psychologist, co-author of the bestseller *The Power of Full Engagement*, and pioneer in the growing field of Energy Management. He has worked with thousands of world-class performers from sport, business, medicine, and law enforcement, including Fortune 100 executives, FBI and Army Special Forces, and athletes such as Mark O'Meara, Michelle Wie, Jim Courier, Monica Seles, Eric Lindros, and Olympic gold medal speed skater Dan Jansen. Dr. Loehr's work has been chronicled in the *Harvard Business Review, Fortune, Newsweek, Time,* and *US News and World Report,* among other publications. He has a master's and a doctorate degree in psychology, and serves on numerous scientific boards.